Births and Deaths in Ireland Registrar General of Marriages

Registrar General of Marriages, Births and Deaths in Ireland

Supplement to twenty-seventh annual Report (Decennial Summaries, 1881-90)

Births and Deaths in Ireland Registrar General of Marriages

Registrar General of Marriages, Births and Deaths in Ireland
Supplement to twenty-seventh annual Report (Decennial Summaries, 1881-90)

ISBN/EAN: 9783741199837

Manufactured in Europe, USA, Canada, Australia, Japa

Cover: Foto ©Lupo / pixelio.de

Manufactured and distributed by brebook publishing software
(www.brebook.com)

Births and Deaths in Ireland Registrar General of Marriages

Registrar General of Marriages, Births and Deaths in Ireland

SUPPLEMENT

TO THE

TWENTY-SEVENTH REPORT

OF THE

REGISTRAR-GENERAL

OF

MARRIAGES, BIRTHS, AND DEATHS, IN IRELAND,

CONTAINING

DECENNIAL SUMMARIES

OF THE

RETURNS OF MARRIAGES, BIRTHS, DEATHS, AND CAUSES OF DEATH IN IRELAND,

FOR THE YEARS 1881-1890.

Presented to both Houses of Parliament by Command of Her Majesty.

DUBLIN:
PRINTED FOR HER MAJESTY'S STATIONERY OFFICE,
BY ALEXANDER THOM & CO. (LIMITED).

And to be purchased, either directly or through any Bookseller, from
Hodges, Figgis, and Co. (Limited), 104, Grafton-street, Dublin; or
Eyre and Spottiswoode, East Harding-street, Fleet-street, E.C.; or
John Menzies and Co., 12, Hanover-street, Edinburgh, and 90, West Nile-street, Glasgow.

1894.

Dublin Castle,

30th *January*, 1895.

Sir,

I have to acknowledge the receipt of your letter of the 29th instant, *forwarding*, for submission to His Excellency the Lord Lieutenant, the Supplement to your Twenty-seventh Report containing Decennial Summaries of the Returns of Marriages, Births, Deaths, and causes of Death in Ireland for the years 1881–1890.

I am,

Sir,

Your obedient Servant,

D. HARREL.

The Registrar-General,

Charlemont House,

Dublin.

CONTENTS.

A 2

SUPPLEMENT

TO THE

TWENTY-SEVENTH REPORT OF THE REGISTRAR-GENERAL

OF

MARRIAGES, BIRTHS, AND DEATHS IN IRELAND,

CONTAINING

DECENNIAL SUMMARIES

FOR THE YEARS 1881-1890.

TO

HIS EXCELLENCY, ROBERT OFFLEY ASHBURTON, BARON HOUGHTON,

&c., &c., &c.,

LORD LIEUTENANT-GENERAL AND GENERAL GOVERNOR OF IRELAND.

MAY IT PLEASE YOUR EXCELLENCY:

I have the honour to submit to Your Excellency a Report and Summary Tables relating to the Marriages, Births, and Deaths registered in Ireland during the ten years ended on the 31st December, 1890.

This is the second occasion on which a Report of this character has been prepared, the first decennial summary of the results of the Registration of Marriages, Births, and Deaths in Ireland having been submitted to Your Excellency's predecessor, Earl Spencer, in the year 1884. In that Report it was explained that the year 1880 completed the first decade ending sufficiently near a Census period to make comparisons between the number and nature of the population, and the statistics of Marriages, Births, and Deaths comprised in the Report with sufficient accuracy to obtain a correct indication of the movement of the population. A period has now been reached at which the second of two decades synchronous with two intercensal periods has been completed. Many improvements in registration have taken place in the interval, and twenty-seven years of registration of Marriages, Births, and Deaths have been completed in Ireland.

The systematic registration of Births and Deaths was instituted in Ireland in 1864; therefore, at the time of taking the Census of 1871, there was not a complete decade of registration records to deal with; so that, as already stated, in 1881 the first opportunity presented itself of making a summary of the kind here submitted.

The registration of Marriages, other than those celebrated by the Roman Catholic clergy, was provided for under the Act 7 & 8 Vic., cap. 81, which came into force on the 1st April, 1845, but Roman Catholic Marriages were not registered until the year 1864, when the Act 26 & 27 Vic., cap. 90, for the registration of those Marriages came into operation.

The following Acts amending the law relating to the registration of Births, Deaths, and Marriages, came into operation during the period from the 1st January, 1881, to 31st December, 1890.

Marriages—49 & 50 Vic., cap. 27 (1886)—Guardianship of Infants Act.—This enactment altered the requirements as to consent in cases of Marriages of minors.

Births and Deaths—43 & 44 Vic., cap. 13 (1880).—This statute amended the 26 Vic., cap. 11, and introduced alterations in the law of which the following are the principal:—

1. Change in the limit of time for registering Births and Deaths. 2. Change in the Legal Qualifications of Informants. 3. Provision for registering Births, within three months, when the Informant has left the District in which the Birth took place. 4. Change in the limit of time for adding Baptismal or other name; and provision for altering name. 5. Certificate of Registry of Birth to be given on payment of a fee of 3*d*. 6. Limit of time fixed within which the Certificate of "Finding of Jury" must be sent by the Coroner. 7. Certificate of Registry or Notification of Death to be given without fee to parties named in the 17th section. 8. Certificate of Cause of Death to be procured, and produced to the Registrar by the Informant, and not forwarded direct to the Registrar by the Medical Practitioner as heretofore. 9. Every "Deputy Superintendent Registrar" and "Deputy Registrar" to be, and be, styled "Assistant Superintendent Registrar" and "Assistant Registrar" respectively; and to act, when required so to do, by the Superintendent Registrar and Registrar. 10. Change as to Correction of Errors in Entries of Births and Deaths. These are divided into Clerical Errors and Errors of Fact or Substance—the latter to be corrected by the Registrar on "Statutory Declaration" before a Justice of the Peace, while the former (Clerical Errors) are divided into two classes, particulars as to which will be found in the Regulations. 11. Change as to Fees.

The Burial Clauses of this Statute also make provision for the transmission to the Registrar of Notice of Burial, in case neither an Order of the Coroner nor a Certificate from the Registrar was presented at the interment. Certain requirements are also laid down with respect to the burial of Still-born children, and of more than one body in the same coffin.

The following Acts of Parliament, which came into operation during the decade, have also more or less affected this Department:—

Veterinary Surgeons Act, 44 & 45 Vic., cap. 62 (1881).

Savings Banks Act, 50 & 51 Vic., cap. 40 (1887).

Friendly Societies Amendment Act, 50 & 51 Vic., cap. 56 (1887).

GENERAL SUMMARY.

Table I. gives a general summary of the numbers of Marriages, Births, and Deaths registered in Ireland from the commencement of the Registration Acts in 1864, to the close of the year 1890, and of the amount of emigration during the same period, with the yearly averages for the two decennial periods 1871–80 and 1881–90.

TABLE I.—Showing for each of the years 1864–90, the estimated POPULATION; the number of MARRIAGES, BIRTHS, and DEATHS registered, and the number of EMIGRANTS enumerated, with the rates per 1,000 of the Population represented thereby, and the averages for the ten years 1871–80 and the ten years 1881–90.

Years	*Estimated Population in the middle of each year	Numbers Registered			Number of Emigrants as enumerated by the Enumerators	Rate per 1,000 of Estimated Population			
		Marriages.	Births.	Deaths.		Marriages.	Births.	Deaths.	Emigrants.
[illegible]	[illegible]	[illegible]	[illegible]	[illegible]	[illegible]	[illegible]	[illegible]	[illegible]	[illegible]
[illegible]	[illegible]	[illegible]	[illegible]	[illegible]	[illegible]	[illegible]	[illegible]	[illegible]	[illegible]
[illegible]	[illegible]	[illegible]	[illegible]	[illegible]	[illegible]	[illegible]	[illegible]	[illegible]	[illegible]
[illegible]	[illegible]	[illegible]	[illegible]	[illegible]	[illegible]	[illegible]	[illegible]	[illegible]	[illegible]
[illegible]	[illegible]	[illegible]	[illegible]	[illegible]	[illegible]	[illegible]	[illegible]	[illegible]	[illegible]
[illegible]	[illegible]	[illegible]	[illegible]	[illegible]	[illegible]	[illegible]	[illegible]	[illegible]	[illegible]
[illegible]	[illegible]	[illegible]	[illegible]	[illegible]	[illegible]	[illegible]	[illegible]	[illegible]	[illegible]
1871,	[illegible]	[illegible]	[illegible]	[illegible]	[illegible]	[illegible]	[illegible]	[illegible]	[illegible]
[illegible]	[illegible]	[illegible]	[illegible]	[illegible]	[illegible]	[illegible]	[illegible]	[illegible]	[illegible]
[illegible]	[illegible]	[illegible]	[illegible]	[illegible]	[illegible]	[illegible]	[illegible]	[illegible]	[illegible]
[illegible]	[illegible]	[illegible]	[illegible]	[illegible]	[illegible]	[illegible]	[illegible]	[illegible]	[illegible]
[illegible]	[illegible]	[illegible]	[illegible]	[illegible]	[illegible]	[illegible]	[illegible]	[illegible]	[illegible]
[illegible]	[illegible]	[illegible]	[illegible]	[illegible]	[illegible]	[illegible]	[illegible]	[illegible]	[illegible]
[illegible]	[illegible]	[illegible]	[illegible]	[illegible]	[illegible]	[illegible]	[illegible]	[illegible]	[illegible]
[illegible]	[illegible]	[illegible]	[illegible]	[illegible]	[illegible]	[illegible]	[illegible]	[illegible]	[illegible]
[illegible]	[illegible]	[illegible]	[illegible]	[illegible]	[illegible]	[illegible]	[illegible]	[illegible]	[illegible]
[illegible]	[illegible]	[illegible]	[illegible]	[illegible]	[illegible]	[illegible]	[illegible]	[illegible]	[illegible]
Ten-yearly Average, 1871–80,	[illegible]	[illegible]	[illegible]	[illegible]	[illegible]	[illegible]	[illegible]	[illegible]	[illegible]
[illegible]	[illegible]	[illegible]	[illegible]	[illegible]	[illegible]	[illegible]	[illegible]	[illegible]	[illegible]
[illegible]	[illegible]	[illegible]	[illegible]	[illegible]	[illegible]	[illegible]	[illegible]	[illegible]	[illegible]
[illegible]	[illegible]	[illegible]	[illegible]	[illegible]	[illegible]	[illegible]	[illegible]	[illegible]	[illegible]
[illegible]	[illegible]	[illegible]	[illegible]	[illegible]	[illegible]	[illegible]	[illegible]	[illegible]	[illegible]
[illegible]	[illegible]	[illegible]	[illegible]	[illegible]	[illegible]	[illegible]	[illegible]	[illegible]	[illegible]
[illegible]	[illegible]	[illegible]	[illegible]	[illegible]	[illegible]	[illegible]	[illegible]	[illegible]	[illegible]
[illegible]	[illegible]	[illegible]	[illegible]	[illegible]	[illegible]	[illegible]	[illegible]	[illegible]	[illegible]
[illegible]	[illegible]	[illegible]	[illegible]	[illegible]	[illegible]	[illegible]	[illegible]	[illegible]	[illegible]
[illegible]	[illegible]	[illegible]	[illegible]	[illegible]	[illegible]	[illegible]	[illegible]	[illegible]	[illegible]
[illegible]	[illegible]	[illegible]	[illegible]	[illegible]	[illegible]	[illegible]	[illegible]	[illegible]	[illegible]
Ten-yearly Average, 1881–90,	[illegible]	[illegible]	[illegible]	[illegible]	[illegible]	[illegible]	[illegible]	[illegible]	[illegible]

* See Page [illegible]. † Mean of Census Populations 1871–81 and 1881–91.

those for the registration counties in the previous decade, the counties of Meath and Antrim are the only ones which show an increase, the former of from 3·5 to 3·6, and the latter from 6·2 to 6·6 per 1,000.

The five counties in which the Marriage rate was highest were, Dublin 6·9, Antrim 6·6, Down 4·9, Armagh 4·7, and Londonderry 4·7; and those in which it was lowest were, Galway 2·8, Clare 3·1, Cavan 3·1, Sligo 3·1, and Roscommon 3·2.

TABLE II.—MARRIAGES, BIRTHS, and DEATHS registered in each PROVINCE and COUNTY during the Ten Years [illegible], with the AVERAGE ANNUAL RATES per 1,000 of the MEAN POPULATION represented thereby; also the number of Births to one Marriage, and the proportion of the total Births which were Illegitimate.

Provinces and Counties.	Mean Population [illegible]	Marriages. Number Registered in the Ten Years.	Marriages. Average Annual Rate per 1,000 of Population.	Births (including Illegitimate Births). Number Registered in the Ten Years.	Births. Average Annual Rate per 1,000 of Population.	Births to one Marriage.	Illegitimate Births. Number Registered in the Ten Years.	Illegitimate Births. Per cent. of total Births.	Deaths. Number Registered in the Ten Years.	Deaths. Average Annual Rate per 1,000 of Population.
IRELAND,	[illegible]	[illegible]	[illegible]	[illegible]	[illegible]	[illegible]	[illegible]	[illegible]	[illegible]	[illegible]
PROVINCES.										
I. LEINSTER,	[illegible]	[illegible]	[illegible]	[illegible]	[illegible]	[illegible]	[illegible]	[illegible]	[illegible]	[illegible]
II. MUNSTER,	[illegible]	[illegible]	[illegible]	[illegible]	[illegible]	[illegible]	[illegible]	[illegible]	[illegible]	[illegible]
III. ULSTER,	[illegible]	[illegible]	[illegible]	[illegible]	[illegible]	[illegible]	[illegible]	[illegible]	[illegible]	[illegible]
IV. CONNAUGHT,	[illegible]	[illegible]	[illegible]	[illegible]	[illegible]	[illegible]	[illegible]	[illegible]	[illegible]	[illegible]
I. PROVINCE OF LEINSTER.										
Carlow,	[illegible]	[illegible]	[illegible]	[illegible]	[illegible]	[illegible]	[illegible]	[illegible]	[illegible]	[illegible]
Dublin,	[illegible]	[illegible]	[illegible]	[illegible]	[illegible]	[illegible]	[illegible]	[illegible]	[illegible]	[illegible]
Kildare,	[illegible]	[illegible]	[illegible]	[illegible]	[illegible]	[illegible]	[illegible]	[illegible]	[illegible]	[illegible]
Kilkenny,	[illegible]	[illegible]	[illegible]	[illegible]	[illegible]	[illegible]	[illegible]	[illegible]	[illegible]	[illegible]
King's,	[illegible]	[illegible]	[illegible]	[illegible]	[illegible]	[illegible]	[illegible]	[illegible]	[illegible]	[illegible]
Longford,	[illegible]	[illegible]	[illegible]	[illegible]	[illegible]	[illegible]	[illegible]	[illegible]	[illegible]	[illegible]
Louth,	[illegible]	[illegible]	[illegible]	[illegible]	[illegible]	[illegible]	[illegible]	[illegible]	[illegible]	[illegible]
Meath,	[illegible]	[illegible]	[illegible]	[illegible]	[illegible]	[illegible]	[illegible]	[illegible]	[illegible]	[illegible]
Queen's,	[illegible]	[illegible]	[illegible]	[illegible]	[illegible]	[illegible]	[illegible]	[illegible]	[illegible]	[illegible]
Westmeath,	[illegible]	[illegible]	[illegible]	[illegible]	[illegible]	[illegible]	[illegible]	[illegible]	[illegible]	[illegible]
Wexford,	[illegible]	[illegible]	[illegible]	[illegible]	[illegible]	[illegible]	[illegible]	[illegible]	[illegible]	[illegible]
Wicklow,	[illegible]	[illegible]	[illegible]	[illegible]	[illegible]	[illegible]	[illegible]	[illegible]	[illegible]	[illegible]
II. PROVINCE OF MUNSTER.										
Clare,	[illegible]	[illegible]	[illegible]	[illegible]	[illegible]	[illegible]	[illegible]	[illegible]	[illegible]	[illegible]
Cork,	[illegible]	[illegible]	[illegible]	[illegible]	[illegible]	[illegible]	[illegible]	[illegible]	[illegible]	[illegible]
Kerry,	[illegible]	[illegible]	[illegible]	[illegible]	[illegible]	[illegible]	[illegible]	[illegible]	[illegible]	[illegible]
Limerick,	[illegible]	[illegible]	[illegible]	[illegible]	[illegible]	[illegible]	[illegible]	[illegible]	[illegible]	[illegible]
Tipperary,	[illegible]	[illegible]	[illegible]	[illegible]	[illegible]	[illegible]	[illegible]	[illegible]	[illegible]	[illegible]
Waterford,	[illegible]	[illegible]	[illegible]	[illegible]	[illegible]	[illegible]	[illegible]	[illegible]	[illegible]	[illegible]
III. PROVINCE OF ULSTER.										
Antrim,	[illegible]	[illegible]	[illegible]	[illegible]	[illegible]	[illegible]	[illegible]	[illegible]	[illegible]	[illegible]
Armagh,	[illegible]	[illegible]	[illegible]	[illegible]	[illegible]	[illegible]	[illegible]	[illegible]	[illegible]	[illegible]

The total number of Marriages registered during the ten years 1881–90 was 213,095 as compared with 250,162 during the previous decade, showing a decrease of 37,067, or 14·8 per cent. The average marriage rates per 1,000 of the population were, for the two decades, 4·75 for the earlier and 4·31 for the later. The largest number of Marriages which took place in any one year was 22,585, or at the rate of 4·54 per 1,000 in the year 1884; the smallest was for the year 1886, when the number was 20,060, or at the rate of 4·18 per 1,000 of the population.

The total number of Births registered during the decade was 1,150,463, as compared with 1,402,277 for the previous ten years, being 251,814, or 18·0 per cent. less. The average birth-rate for the earlier period was 26·5, and for the later 23·3 per 1,000 living. The greatest number of births in any one year during the ten years 1881–90 took place in the year 1881, when there were 125,847, and the smallest number in 1890, namely, 105,254, or at the respective rates of 24·5 and 22·3 per 1,000 of the population.

The Deaths for the period under consideration numbered 883,156 as compared with 966,745 for the previous ten years, thus showing a decrease of 83,589 or 8·6 per cent., and a decrease of death-rate from 18·3 in the earlier to 17·9 per 1,000 living in the later period. This decreased death-rate is no doubt owing to an advance in sanitary measures by which the public health has been materially improved.

As the Births numbered 1,150,463 and the Deaths 883,156, the former exceeded the latter by 267,307, indicating a natural increase in the population of Ireland to this amount; while the estimated diminution has been 164,889, the natural increase having been more than counterbalanced by emigration.

The greatest number of Deaths during the decade occurred in the year 1883, when there were 96,229, and the smallest in 1889, when there were 82,908 only, the respective rates being 19·2 and 17·4 per 1,000 living.

During the decade 770,706 emigrants left Ireland as compared with 623,933 for the period 1871–80—the rates respectively being 15·6 and 11·8 per 1,000 of the mean population of the respective periods. A decrease therefore of 503,399 in the population would appear to have taken place during the decade, the real decrease up to the Census date (5th April, 1891), according to the Census Returns of 1891, being 470,086, showing a discrepancy of 33,313, or only 0·6 per cent. of the population.

I have already dealt with this question in detail in my report for the second quarter of 1891, and my detailed annual report for the same year.*

In selecting the areas for which the abstract tables were to be compiled, it was not considered necessary to compile statistics for areas smaller than Superintendent Registrars' districts which coincide with the districts of the Registrars of Marriages under 7 & 8 Vic., cap. 81, and with the Poor Law Unions. Of these there are 160, having in 1891 an average population of 29,405. The Registrars' districts, of which there are 799, with an average population of 5,888 in 1891, appear to be too small in area and population to warrant separate abstracts being made for each.

I shall now proceed to submit, for Your Excellency's consideration, remarks upon some of the more important features connected with the returns of Marriages, Births, and Deaths during the decade 1881–90. In discussing these statistics, I shall avoid detail as much as possible, and only touch upon those matters which may serve to indicate important social movements, or which may afford useful information to those whose duty it is to take measures for the preservation of the public health. Although many interesting professional points would naturally arise in considering the tables of causes of death, yet I do not consider it advisable to deal particularly with these, and I shall only treat of details where they bear upon great questions of public health or sanitation.

MARRIAGES.

The number of Marriages registered during the decade was 213,095, or at the average annual rate of 4·31 per 1,000 of the mean population. The greatest annual number registered was 22,585, or at the rate of 4·54 per 1,000 of the population, in the year 1884, and the smallest number was in 1886, when but 20,060 were recorded, being at the rate of 4·18 per 1,000 of the population.

* "Quarterly Return of Marriages, Births, and Deaths in Ireland," No. 70, pages 60 and 61; and "Eighteenth Detailed Annual Report of the Registrar-General of Marriages, Births, and Deaths in Ireland," [illegible]

Of the marriages registered during the decade, 146,159 were according to the rites and ceremonies of the Roman Catholic Church; 36,008 were celebrated according to the rites and ceremonies of the Church of Ireland; 22,441 were in Registered Presbyterian Meeting-houses; 3,715 in "Registered Buildings" belonging to various religious denominations; 4,645 by Civil Contract in District Registrars' Offices; 82 according to the usages of the Society of Friends; and 45 according to the Jewish rite. The relative average annual rates of these marriages, as deduced from the foregoing statement, to every 1,000 of the mean population of each of the principal religious denominations were, approximately, Roman Catholics, 3·90; Protestant Episcopalians, 5·81; Presbyterians, 4·90.

Comparing the foregoing statement with the corresponding figures for the previous decade, it appears that the number of marriages registered decreased by 37,067, or 14·1 per cent., and the marriage-rate per 1,000 of the population from 4·73 to 4·31.

The Roman Catholic marriages registered decreased from 176,248 to 146,159 to the extent of 30,089, or 17·1 per cent., the rate having declined from 4·35 to 3·90 per 1,000 persons. Those according to the rites of the Church of Ireland fell from 39,991 to 36,008, or to the extent of 3,983, or 9·96 per cent., the rate having changed from 6·19 to 5·81. Those in Presbyterian Meeting-houses (according to the Presbyterian form) fell from 25,011 to 22,441, being a decline of 2,570, or 10·28 per cent., the rate having altered from 5·17 to 4·90.

The marriages in Registered Buildings belonging to various religious denominations (under the Act 7 & 8 Vic., cap. 81) rose from 3,265 to 3,715, being an increase of 450, or 13·8 per cent. This increase is mainly due to marriages between members of the Methodist community, a body which increased in number between the Census periods of 1881 and 1891, while the numbers of all the other larger religious denominations materially decreased. Marriages by Civil Contract have decreased from 5,507 to 4,645, or to the extent of 862, or 15·65 per cent. The marriages among members of the Society of Friends fell from 117 to 82, being a decline of 35, or 29·91 per cent. Among the Jews marriages increased from 23 to 45, or nearly double, which accords with what might have been anticipated from the large proportional increase of the number of the Jewish community in Ireland shown by the Census of 1891.

TABLE III.—MARRIAGES registered in IRELAND in each of the ten years, 1881-90, according to the MODES of CELEBRATION; with the RATES per 1,000 of the POPULATION represented.

Years.	Marriages registered under 7 and 8 Vic., cap. 81							Roman Catholic Marriages.	Total Marriages Registered.	Rate per 1,000 of estimated corresponding Population represented by:		
	According to the Rites of the Church of Ireland.	In Registered Presbyterian Meeting-houses.	In Registered Buildings.	In the Registrars' Offices.	Society of Friends.	Jews.	Total.			Marriages under 7 and 8 Vic., cap. 81.	Roman Catholic Marriages.	Total Marriages.
[illegible]	[illegible]	[illegible]	[illegible]	[illegible]	[illegible]	–	[illegible]	[illegible]	[illegible]	[illegible]	[illegible]	[illegible]
[illegible]	[illegible]	[illegible]	[illegible]	[illegible]	[illegible]	[illegible]	[illegible]	[illegible]	[illegible]	[illegible]	[illegible]	[illegible]
[illegible]	[illegible]	[illegible]	[illegible]	[illegible]	[illegible]	[illegible]	[illegible]	[illegible]	[illegible]	[illegible]	[illegible]	[illegible]
[illegible]	[illegible]	[illegible]	[illegible]	[illegible]	[illegible]	[illegible]	[illegible]	[illegible]	[illegible]	[illegible]	[illegible]	[illegible]
[illegible]	[illegible]	[illegible]	[illegible]	[illegible]	[illegible]	[illegible]	[illegible]	[illegible]	[illegible]	[illegible]	[illegible]	[illegible]
[illegible]	[illegible]	[illegible]	[illegible]	[illegible]	[illegible]	[illegible]	[illegible]	[illegible]	[illegible]	[illegible]	[illegible]	[illegible]
[illegible]	[illegible]	[illegible]	[illegible]	[illegible]	[illegible]	[illegible]	[illegible]	[illegible]	[illegible]	[illegible]	[illegible]	[illegible]
[illegible]	[illegible]	[illegible]	[illegible]	[illegible]	[illegible]	[illegible]	[illegible]	[illegible]	[illegible]	[illegible]	[illegible]	[illegible]
[illegible]	[illegible]	[illegible]	[illegible]	[illegible]	[illegible]	–	[illegible]	[illegible]	[illegible]	[illegible]	[illegible]	[illegible]
[illegible]	[illegible]	[illegible]	[illegible]	[illegible]	[illegible]	[illegible]	[illegible]	[illegible]	[illegible]	[illegible]	[illegible]	[illegible]
Average, [illegible]	[illegible]	[illegible]	[illegible]	[illegible]	[illegible]	[illegible]	[illegible]	[illegible]	[illegible]	[illegible]	[illegible]	[illegible]

As in many parts of the country about one-half of the annual Roman Catholic Marriages take place between Christmas and Shrovetide, the number of marriages recorded in the first quarter of the year is much greater than that in any other, as shown in the following Table.

TABLE IV.—MARRIAGES registered during each QUARTER of the TEN YEARS, 1881–90.

Years.	March: Roman Catholic Marriages	March: Others	March: Total	June: Roman Catholic Marriages	June: Others	June: Total	September: Roman Catholic Marriages	September: Others	September: Total	December: Roman Catholic Marriages	December: Others	December: Total
[illegible]	[illegible]	[illegible]	[illegible]	[illegible]	[illegible]	[illegible]	[illegible]	[illegible]	[illegible]	[illegible]	[illegible]	[illegible]
[illegible]	[illegible]	[illegible]	[illegible]	[illegible]	[illegible]	[illegible]	[illegible]	[illegible]	[illegible]	[illegible]	[illegible]	[illegible]
[illegible]	[illegible]	[illegible]	[illegible]	[illegible]	[illegible]	[illegible]	[illegible]	[illegible]	[illegible]	[illegible]	[illegible]	[illegible]
[illegible]	[illegible]	[illegible]	[illegible]	[illegible]	[illegible]	[illegible]	[illegible]	[illegible]	[illegible]	[illegible]	[illegible]	[illegible]
[illegible]	[illegible]	[illegible]	[illegible]	[illegible]	[illegible]	[illegible]	[illegible]	[illegible]	[illegible]	[illegible]	[illegible]	[illegible]
[illegible]	[illegible]	[illegible]	[illegible]	[illegible]	[illegible]	[illegible]	[illegible]	[illegible]	[illegible]	[illegible]	[illegible]	[illegible]
[illegible]	[illegible]	[illegible]	[illegible]	[illegible]	[illegible]	[illegible]	[illegible]	[illegible]	[illegible]	[illegible]	[illegible]	[illegible]
[illegible]	[illegible]	[illegible]	[illegible]	[illegible]	[illegible]	[illegible]	[illegible]	[illegible]	[illegible]	[illegible]	[illegible]	[illegible]
[illegible]	[illegible]	[illegible]	[illegible]	[illegible]	[illegible]	[illegible]	[illegible]	[illegible]	[illegible]	[illegible]	[illegible]	[illegible]
[illegible]	[illegible]	[illegible]	[illegible]	[illegible]	[illegible]	[illegible]	[illegible]	[illegible]	[illegible]	[illegible]	[illegible]	[illegible]
Ten Years, [illegible]	[illegible]	[illegible]	[illegible]	[illegible]	[illegible]	[illegible]	[illegible]	[illegible]	[illegible]	[illegible]	[illegible]	[illegible]
Average Proportion per cent. of the yearly number of each class of Marriages, registered in each Quarter,	[illegible]	[illegible]	[illegible]	[illegible]	[illegible]	[illegible]	[illegible]	[illegible]	[illegible]	[illegible]	[illegible]	[illegible]

From this it appears that the average proportion per cent. of all the marriages in Ireland which took place in the first quarter of the year was 33·7, while in the other quarters the proportions were respectively 21·1, 21·5, and 23·4; in other words the proportion was nearly constant during each of the last three quarters of the year. The table shows that the average proportion of Roman Catholic marriages during the first quarter of the year was 38·3 per cent. of the total marriages according to the rites of that Church, and that during the other three quarters the proportion varied from 20·0 to 21·0 per cent. only. The marriages of persons of other denominations were slightly more numerous in the last than in any other quarter.

Table V. shows for the decade the number and proportion per cent. of persons who wrote their names in the Registers, of minors, of widowers, and widows who were married.

TABLE V.—Showing as regards MARRIAGES in Ireland and in each of the Four Provinces during the years 1881-90, the Proportion per cent. of Persons who SIGNED THEIR NAMES, of Persons NOT OF FULL AGE, and of RE-MARRIAGES. The figures for the years 1881-84 refer to Registration Provinces; those for 1885-90 to the Provinces Proper.

Provinces	Year	Signed their Names in Writing: Of 100 Men Married	Signed their Names in Writing: Of 100 Women Married	Persons not of Full Age: Of 100 Men Married	Persons not of Full Age: Of 100 Women Married	Re-marriages, Widowers: Of 100 Men Married	Re-marriages, Widows: Of 100 Women Married
IRELAND	[illegible]	[illegible]	[illegible]	[illegible]	[illegible]	[illegible]	[illegible]
	[illegible]	[illegible]	[illegible]	[illegible]	[illegible]	[illegible]	[illegible]
	[illegible]	[illegible]	[illegible]	[illegible]	[illegible]	[illegible]	[illegible]
	[illegible]	[illegible]	[illegible]	[illegible]	[illegible]	[illegible]	[illegible]
	[illegible]	[illegible]	[illegible]	[illegible]	[illegible]	[illegible]	[illegible]
	[illegible]	[illegible]	[illegible]	[illegible]	[illegible]	[illegible]	[illegible]
	[illegible]	[illegible]	[illegible]	[illegible]	[illegible]	[illegible]	[illegible]
	[illegible]	[illegible]	[illegible]	[illegible]	[illegible]	[illegible]	[illegible]
	[illegible]	[illegible]	[illegible]	[illegible]	[illegible]	[illegible]	[illegible]
	[illegible]	[illegible]	[illegible]	[illegible]	[illegible]	[illegible]	[illegible]
LEINSTER	[illegible]	[illegible]	[illegible]	[illegible]	[illegible]	[illegible]	[illegible]
	[illegible]	[illegible]	[illegible]	[illegible]	[illegible]	[illegible]	[illegible]
	[illegible]	[illegible]	[illegible]	[illegible]	[illegible]	[illegible]	[illegible]
	[illegible]	[illegible]	[illegible]	[illegible]	[illegible]	[illegible]	[illegible]
	[illegible]	[illegible]	[illegible]	[illegible]	[illegible]	[illegible]	[illegible]
	[illegible]	[illegible]	[illegible]	[illegible]	[illegible]	[illegible]	[illegible]
	[illegible]	[illegible]	[illegible]	[illegible]	[illegible]	[illegible]	[illegible]
	[illegible]	[illegible]	[illegible]	[illegible]	[illegible]	[illegible]	[illegible]
	[illegible]	[illegible]	[illegible]	[illegible]	[illegible]	[illegible]	[illegible]
	[illegible]	[illegible]	[illegible]	[illegible]	[illegible]	[illegible]	[illegible]
MUNSTER	[illegible]	[illegible]	[illegible]	[illegible]	[illegible]	[illegible]	[illegible]
	[illegible]	[illegible]	[illegible]	[illegible]	[illegible]	[illegible]	[illegible]
	[illegible]	[illegible]	[illegible]	[illegible]	[illegible]	[illegible]	[illegible]
	[illegible]	[illegible]	[illegible]	[illegible]	[illegible]	[illegible]	[illegible]
	[illegible]	[illegible]	[illegible]	[illegible]	[illegible]	[illegible]	[illegible]
MUNSTER—continued	[illegible]	[illegible]	[illegible]	[illegible]	[illegible]	[illegible]	[illegible]
	[illegible]	[illegible]	[illegible]	[illegible]	[illegible]	[illegible]	[illegible]
	[illegible]	[illegible]	[illegible]	[illegible]	[illegible]	[illegible]	[illegible]
	[illegible]	[illegible]	[illegible]	[illegible]	[illegible]	[illegible]	[illegible]
	[illegible]	[illegible]	[illegible]	[illegible]	[illegible]	[illegible]	[illegible]
ULSTER	[illegible]	[illegible]	[illegible]	[illegible]	[illegible]	[illegible]	[illegible]
	[illegible]	[illegible]	[illegible]	[illegible]	[illegible]	[illegible]	[illegible]
	[illegible]	[illegible]	[illegible]	[illegible]	[illegible]	[illegible]	[illegible]
	[illegible]	[illegible]	[illegible]	[illegible]	[illegible]	[illegible]	[illegible]
	[illegible]	[illegible]	[illegible]	[illegible]	[illegible]	[illegible]	[illegible]
	[illegible]	[illegible]	[illegible]	[illegible]	[illegible]	[illegible]	[illegible]
	[illegible]	[illegible]	[illegible]	[illegible]	[illegible]	[illegible]	[illegible]
	[illegible]	[illegible]	[illegible]	[illegible]	[illegible]	[illegible]	[illegible]
	[illegible]	[illegible]	[illegible]	[illegible]	[illegible]	[illegible]	[illegible]
	[illegible]	[illegible]	[illegible]	[illegible]	[illegible]	[illegible]	[illegible]
CONNAUGHT	[illegible]	[illegible]	[illegible]	[illegible]	[illegible]	[illegible]	[illegible]
	[illegible]	[illegible]	[illegible]	[illegible]	[illegible]	[illegible]	[illegible]
	[illegible]	[illegible]	[illegible]	[illegible]	[illegible]	[illegible]	[illegible]
	[illegible]	[illegible]	[illegible]	[illegible]	[illegible]	[illegible]	[illegible]
	[illegible]	[illegible]	[illegible]	[illegible]	[illegible]	[illegible]	[illegible]
	[illegible]	[illegible]	[illegible]	[illegible]	[illegible]	[illegible]	[illegible]
	[illegible]	[illegible]	[illegible]	[illegible]	[illegible]	[illegible]	[illegible]
	[illegible]	[illegible]	[illegible]	[illegible]	[illegible]	[illegible]	[illegible]
	[illegible]	[illegible]	[illegible]	[illegible]	[illegible]	[illegible]	[illegible]
	[illegible]	[illegible]	[illegible]	[illegible]	[illegible]	[illegible]	[illegible]

EDUCATION OF PERSONS MARRIED.

The proportion of persons who "signed their names in writing" as compared with those who signed "by mark" in the marriage registers and certificates affords an interesting indication of the degree of elementary education of persons married, and when these indications are compared from period to period they afford a useful test of the progress of education. Thus—

In 1864, 51·4 per cent. of the men and 49·7 per cent. of the women signed in writing; in 1871 the proportions were—men 62·5 per cent., women 54·8 per cent.; in 1880, men 73·8 per cent., women 69·1; in 1890, men 79·6, women 76·1. It is interesting to note that while there has been a steady increase in both sexes in the proportion signing by writing, the proportion among women, which was much below that for men in 1864, became almost equal to the rate for men in 1890. Table V shows that this test of education for 1890 would arrange the Provinces in the following order of merit—Leinster, Munster, Ulster, Connaught, for both sexes. It is curious to note that while in Leinster, Munster, and Connaught the married women seem to be better educated than the men, in Ulster the reverse is the case. This, however, is not the place to go into further details in connexion with the question of education which is fully dealt with in the Report of the Census Commissioners for 1891.

EARLY MARRIAGES.

During the last thirty years there has been a well marked decrease in early marriages in Ireland. In the year 1864 of the males married 3·47 per cent. were under full age, in 1880 the proportion was 3·64 per cent., and in 1890 it was but 2·02 per cent.; and at no time during the interval between 1880 and 1890 was the percentage of 2·64 reached. Among females the decrease of early marriages is more marked; in 1864 the proportion of minors was 15·16 per cent. of all the women married; in 1880 it was only 11·72 per cent. or less than two-thirds of the proportion in the former year; and in 1890 it fell to 8·75 per cent., or less than one-half of the percentage for 1864. The highest proportion of minors married in 1890 was in Ulster, and the lowest in Munster. In the former province the husbands who were not of age formed 2·71 per cent. of the males married, and the wives under age constituted 9·23 per cent. of the total; and in Munster the corresponding percentages were 1·27 for the males and 7·32 for the females married. As may be observed from Table V, the diminution of early marriages since 1881 is more marked in the West than in any other portion of Ireland. In 1864 the proportions of males and females not of full age who were married in the Western Registration Division (which nearly coincides with the province of Connaught) were respectively 2·81 per cent. and 24·09 per cent.; in 1880 they were 3·74 per cent. and 17·37 per cent., showing a slight increase of the number of very young men married, but a material decrease of very young women married. During the decade 1881-90 the proportion of marriages of minors in Connaught decreased among males from 2·51 per cent. in 1881 to 1·50 per cent. in 1890, and among females from 13·03 per cent. to 5·42 for the same period. It would thus appear that since 1864 through Ireland generally, and especially in the West, very early marriages have become less frequent. This decrease of early marriages among women accounts to a great extent for the diminution in the average size of families in Ireland, and also explains in part the diminished birth-rate. Further information on this important point will be found in the General Reports of the Census Commissioners for 1881 and 1891.*

BIRTHS.

The number of Births registered in Ireland during the decade was 1,150,463, being an annual average of 115,046, or at the rate of 23·4 per 1,000 of the mean population. The largest number of births occurred in the year 1881, viz., 122,847, or at the rate of 24·5 of the population, and the smallest number in 1890, when there were 105,254 registered, or at the rate of only 22·3 per 1,000 of the population.

As regards the distribution of the Births in Ireland, the following statement shows the four provinces arranged according to the average annual rate per 1,000 of the mean population represented by the births registered during the ten years, 1881-90:—

Provinces.	Birth-rate per 1,000.	Provinces.	Birth-rate per 1,000.
Leinster,	23·7	Munster,	23·0
Ulster,	23·6	Connaught,	22·4

* See "Census of Ireland, 1881; Part II.; General Report," pp. 17–19; and "Census of Ireland, 1891; Part II.; General Report," pp. 20–22.

Illegitimacy

Of the 1,150,462 births registered in Ireland during the decade, 31,162 or 2·7 per cent. were illegitimate. In the preceding decennium the corresponding percentage was 2·4.

In the following Table the proportion of illegitimate births is set out by Provinces.

Table VI.—Per-centage of Illegitimate to Total Births in Ireland and each of the Provinces during the Ten Years, [illegible].

Provinces.	Per-centage of [illegible]										
	Year										The Years, [illegible]
	[illegible]	[illegible]	[illegible]	[illegible]	[illegible]	[illegible]	[illegible]	[illegible]	[illegible]	[illegible]	
IRELAND, . . .	[illegible]	[illegible]	[illegible]	[illegible]	[illegible]	[illegible]	[illegible]	[illegible]	[illegible]	[illegible]	[illegible]
LEINSTER, . .	[illegible]	[illegible]	[illegible]	[illegible]	[illegible]	[illegible]	[illegible]	[illegible]	[illegible]	[illegible]	[illegible]
MUNSTER, . . .	[illegible]	[illegible]	[illegible]	[illegible]	[illegible]	[illegible]	[illegible]	[illegible]	[illegible]	[illegible]	[illegible]
ULSTER, ...	[illegible]	[illegible]	[illegible]	4·1	[illegible]	[illegible]	[illegible]	[illegible]	[illegible]	[illegible]	[illegible]
CONNAUGHT, . .	[illegible]	[illegible]	[illegible]	[illegible]	[illegible]	[illegible]	[illegible]	[illegible]	[illegible]	[illegible]	[illegible]

From the foregoing (Table VI.) it will be observed that the proportion of illegitimate births to the total births registered was greatest in the province of Ulster, where it reached 4·3 per cent., and least in the province of Connaught, where the percentage was only 0·8. In Table VIII. it will also be noticed that illegitimate births were proportionally more numerous in some of the districts comprising manufacturing towns. It is also observed that in the rural districts of Ulster, in which are situated many small towns and "mill villages," the proportion of illegitimate births is slightly (0·1 per cent. of all births in those localities) higher than in the civic districts taken collectively. A similar state of things is also found regarding the province of Leinster, but the reverse is found in the other two provinces, where the rural population bears a greater proportion to the town population than in either Leinster or Ulster. Further attention will be called to this subject when discussing the relation between the number of marriages and the number of births registered.

The number and relative proportion of births in each quarter are shown in Table VII., from which it appears that the birth-rate is higher in the first two than in the last two quarters of the year, the births, as might be anticipated, corresponding closely with the larger number of marriages which take place in the first quarter of the year as already pointed out (page 10).

TABLE VIII.—Showing, for each of those UNIONS or SUPERINTENDENT REGISTRARS' DISTRICTS containing TOWNS which, in 1881 or in 1891, had a population of 10,000 or upwards:—the number of MARRIAGES, BIRTHS, and DEATHS registered in the TEN YEARS, 1881-90, and the respective AVERAGE ANNUAL RATES per 1,000 of the Mean Population, also the Ratio of BIRTHS to MARRIAGES, the number of ILLEGITIMATE BIRTHS, and the proportion of ILLEGITIMATE BIRTHS in every 100 BIRTHS; with a Summary thereof for each PROVINCE, and corresponding details for the remaining portion of each Province.

Table VIII. is constructed mainly with the view of showing the relations between the number of marriages registered and the number of births registered in Ireland, and in the more important groups of districts, distinguishing town districts from country districts.

Taking the whole of Ireland it will be observed that the annual average rate throughout the decade 1881–90 per 1,000 of the mean population was—for marriages 4·3 and for births 23·3, and that the average number of births to each marriage was 5·4. For the previous decade 1871–80 the respective numbers were 4·7, 26·5, and 5·6, showing a decrease under each head in the last as compared with the former decade.

These figures cannot be taken as an exact measure of the fecundity of marriages in Ireland, but nevertheless they show a tendency to decrease in the average number of children to each marriage; and, taking the twenty years for which we have now complete records, and even making some allowance for illegitimate births, it may be fairly assumed that the average fecundity of Irish marriages is about 5·5 children per marriage. It is, however, always to be noted that many young married people emigrate shortly after marriage, and that therefore, although their marriages appear in the Irish registers, the births of their children do not. The figures in Table VIII. afford a ready method of comparing the fecundity of marriages in town with those in the country, which give respectively 4·4 and 6·1 children per marriage. It is to be noted that the aggregate population of towns of 10,000 inhabitants and upwards in Ireland increased from 824,935 to 844,549 between the Census periods of 1881 and 1891, while the rural population diminished: thus we have a partial explanation of the general diminution in the fecundity of Irish marriages when the past two decades are compared with one another, inasmuch as the less prolific portion of the population have increased and the more prolific diminished. The fact that a considerable number of people go into the larger towns to get married is a disturbing element which cannot be estimated, but which nevertheless should not be overlooked when comparing town and country marriage rates and their relative fecundity. It will be observed that the greater tendency to fecundity of marriages in country than in town districts prevails in each of the four provinces the respective rates—being 4·3 and 5·5 for Leinster, 4·4 and 6·7 for Munster, 4·4 and 5·4 for Ulster, and 5·6 and 7·4 for Connaught.

The four provinces are related to one another in regard to fecundity of marriages as follows—Leinster, 4·8; Munster, 6·0; Ulster, 5·0; and Connaught, 7·2, as compare with 5·4 for the whole of Ireland. Thus the provinces of Leinster and Ulster, with their large town population, are under the average of Ireland, while Munster and Connaught, with their large rural population, are over the average. It will be observed that the group with the highest rate is that comprising the rural districts of Connaught, where the ratio is 7·4, and the lowest is the civic group of Leinster where it is but 4·3.

If the relation between the number of births to marriages, and the death-rate of the population be compared, it will be found that where the death-rates are highest the proportion of births to marriages is lowest, and vice versâ. A comparison between columns 8 and 10 of Table VIII. shows that this rule is almost invariable, and that it is most strongly marked in the contrast between town and country groups of districts, thus pointing to the conclusion that the lower state of vitality of town populations tends to diminish the birth-rate, although the marriage-rate is high.

It must not be inferred from the increase of illegitimate in proportion to legitimate births that an increase of immorality has occurred. The legitimate births have fallen from 1,335,288 for the decade 1871–80 to 1,119,301 for the decade 1881–90, being a decrease of 215,987, or 16·2 per cent., while during the same period the number of marriages fell from 250,162 to 213,095, being a decrease of 37,067, or 14·8 per cent.—the decreased fecundity accounting for the difference in ratio between the decrease of marriages and the decrease of births. The illegitimate births fell from 34,059 for the former to 31,182 in the latter decade, being a decrease of 2,877, or 8·5 per cent., which is somewhat greater than the percentage of decline in the mean population of the respective decades, thus tending to show that immorality had decreased.

DEATHS

The deaths registered in Ireland during the decade 1881–90 amounted to 885,156. The mean population estimated for the same period was 4,989,792, which would on calculation afford an average annual death-rate of 17·68 per 1,000 of the population for the whole of Ireland; but, as will be seen further on, the variations in death-rate were very great in different parts of the country. The death-rate also varied considerably during different years of the decade; thus in 1883 it was 19·2, but in 1882 only 17·3 per 1,000.

TABLE IX.—The number of DEATHS registered in Ireland during each QUARTER of the Ten Years 1881-90, with the Average Quarterly Numbers for that period, and the Annual Rates per 1,000 of the Mean Population represented thereby.

[illegible]	[illegible]	[illegible]	[illegible]	[illegible]	[illegible]	[illegible]	[illegible]	[illegible]	[illegible]	[illegible]	[illegible]	[illegible]	[illegible]
[illegible]	[illegible]	[illegible]	[illegible]	[illegible]	[illegible]	[illegible]	[illegible]	[illegible]	[illegible]	[illegible]	[illegible]	[illegible]	[illegible]
[illegible]	[illegible]	[illegible]	[illegible]	[illegible]	[illegible]	[illegible]	[illegible]	[illegible]	[illegible]	[illegible]	[illegible]	[illegible]	[illegible]
[illegible]	[illegible]	[illegible]	[illegible]	[illegible]	[illegible]	[illegible]	[illegible]	[illegible]	[illegible]	[illegible]	[illegible]	[illegible]	[illegible]
[illegible]	[illegible]	[illegible]	[illegible]	[illegible]	[illegible]	[illegible]	[illegible]	[illegible]	[illegible]	[illegible]	[illegible]	[illegible]	[illegible]
Year,	[illegible]	[illegible]	[illegible]	[illegible]	[illegible]	[illegible]	[illegible]	[illegible]	[illegible]	[illegible]	[illegible]	[illegible]	[illegible]

The above Table shows the number of deaths registered in each quarter during the decade, with the average rates for the ten years, and the average percentage of deaths registered during each of the four quarters. The average percentage of the annual number of deaths registered in the first quarter was 30·2, and the rate 21·7 per 1,000 of the mean population; for the second, 26·5 per cent., with a rate of 19·1 per 1,000; for the third, 20·4 per cent., with a rate of 14·7 per 1,000; and in the fourth quarter, 22·8 per cent., with a rate of 16·4 per 1,000, the highest rate being in the first quarter, when the cold weather and the continued privations of the winter months have the greatest effect on the health of the people, as will be pointed out further on when discussing the causes of death.

DISTRIBUTION OF DEATHS IN IRELAND.

On the passing of the Act for the Registration of Births and Deaths in Ireland, the country was divided into eight registration divisions, and until the year 1881 the statistics of deaths were arranged according to these divisions. For reasons explained in the Annual Report for 1881,* these artificial divisions have been abandoned as cumbersome and inconvenient, but the Tables were compiled according to "Registration" Provinces, Counties, and Superintendent Registrars' Districts to the close of the year 1884. Since that date the ordinary geographical boundaries have been followed, and in the Abstracts in this Report the number of deaths will be found recorded for the entire decade in accordance with this latter arrangement.

Arranging the provinces from the lowest death-rate to the highest, it appears that the average annual rates per 1,000 living were as follow:—

Connaught,	13·9	Ulster,	18·9
Munster,	17·3	Leinster,	20·4

In the following statement the counties are arranged in order according to their death-rates from the lowest to the highest:—

IRELAND.

Deaths Registered, 1881–90.

Counties and Provinces arranged according to Death-rates.

Counties.

Counties.	Death-rate per 1,000.	Counties.	Death-rate per 1,000.
1. Mayo,	13·6	18. Tipperary,	17·6
2. Sligo,	13·6	19. Cork,	17·6
3. Roscommon,	13·6	20. Meath,	17·9
4. Galway,	14·1	21. Wicklow,	18·1
5. Kerry,	14·2	22. Louth (excl. Co. of the Town of Drogheda),	18·2
6. Cavan,	14·6	23. Westmeath,	18·5
7. Donegal,	14·6	24. Carlow,	18·6
8. Leitrim,	14·7	25. Limerick,	19·0
9. Clare,	15·1	26. Down,	19·1
10. Fermanagh,	15·3	27. Armagh,	19·1
11. Longford,	15·5	28. Kilkenny,	19·3
12. Tyrone,	16·4	29. Wexford,	19·7
13. Monaghan,	16·7	30. Waterford,	19·8
14. Queen's,	16·8	31. Antrim,	21·0
15. King's,	16·9	32. Dublin,	26·3
16. Kildare,	17·1		
17. Londonderry,	17·4		

Provinces.

1. Connaught,	13·9	3. Ulster,	18·6
2. Munster,	17·5	4. Leinster,	20·6

Ireland, 17·9.

It will be here again observed that **the counties containing large towns occupy** unfavourable positions on the list.

This is especially noticeable when Mayo and Dublin, which occupy the extremes of the list, are contrasted with one another; the rate of mortality in the former being only about half of that in the latter.

In Tables X. and XI., pages 19 and 20, the Superintendent Registrars' districts have been classified into those containing towns with over 10,000 inhabitants, and those which do not contain any large towns. The former may for convenience be called "Civic," the latter "Rural" Unions.

If the death-rates in these two groups of districts be contrasted, it will be observed that the average death-rate for the "Civic" group is 229·2 per 10,000 inhabitants per annum; whereas in the "Rural" group it is but 160·4, or 68·8 less. In round numbers, therefore, the deaths among a million of inhabitants of such an urban population would exceed those of a rural population of the same amount by about 6,000 per annum. If the rural population of Ireland died at the same rate as the urban there would be an average increase of about 22,000 deaths in Ireland per annum.

In considering the causes of death and their distribution throughout Ireland, a further and more detailed reference will be made to these remarkable contrasts between civic and rural death-rates.

TABLE X. TOTAL DEATHS and DEATHS from several causes registered during the TEN YEARS 1881–90 in those UNIONS or SUPERINTENDENT REGISTRARS' DISTRICTS containing TOWNS which in 1881 or in 1891 had a population of 10,000 or upwards; with a SUMMARY thereof for each PROVINCE.

Poor Law Union or Superintendent Registrars' Districts	Towns of 10,000 or upwards (in 1881 or in 1891) situated in the respective Unions	Population	TOTAL DEATHS	1	2	3	4	5	6	7	8	9	10	11	12	13	14	15	16	17
PROVINCE OF LEINSTER.																				
Drogheda	Drogheda	[illegible]	[illegible]	[illegible]	[illegible]	[illegible]	[illegible]	[illegible]	[illegible]	[illegible]	[illegible]	[illegible]	[illegible]	[illegible]	[illegible]	[illegible]	[illegible]	[illegible]	[illegible]	[illegible]
Dublin, North	Dublin, Rathmines and Pembroke	[illegible]	[illegible]	[illegible]	[illegible]	[illegible]	[illegible]	[illegible]	[illegible]	[illegible]	[illegible]	[illegible]	[illegible]	[illegible]	[illegible]	[illegible]	[illegible]	[illegible]	[illegible]	[illegible]
Dublin, South		[illegible]	[illegible]	[illegible]	[illegible]	[illegible]	[illegible]	[illegible]	[illegible]	[illegible]	[illegible]	[illegible]	[illegible]	[illegible]	[illegible]	[illegible]	[illegible]	[illegible]	[illegible]	[illegible]
Dundalk	Dundalk	[illegible]	[illegible]	[illegible]	[illegible]	[illegible]	[illegible]	[illegible]	[illegible]	[illegible]	[illegible]	[illegible]	[illegible]	[illegible]	[illegible]	[illegible]	[illegible]	[illegible]	[illegible]	[illegible]
Kilkenny	Kilkenny	[illegible]	[illegible]	[illegible]	[illegible]	[illegible]	[illegible]	[illegible]	[illegible]	[illegible]	[illegible]	[illegible]	[illegible]	[illegible]	[illegible]	[illegible]	[illegible]	[illegible]	[illegible]	[illegible]
Rathdown	Kingstown	[illegible]	[illegible]	[illegible]	[illegible]	[illegible]	[illegible]	[illegible]	[illegible]	[illegible]	[illegible]	[illegible]	[illegible]	[illegible]	[illegible]	[illegible]	[illegible]	[illegible]	[illegible]	[illegible]
Wexford	Wexford	[illegible]	[illegible]	[illegible]	[illegible]	[illegible]	[illegible]	[illegible]	[illegible]	[illegible]	[illegible]	[illegible]	[illegible]	[illegible]	[illegible]	[illegible]	[illegible]	[illegible]	[illegible]	[illegible]
Total Civic Unions,*		[illegible]	[illegible]	[illegible]	[illegible]	[illegible]	[illegible]	[illegible]	[illegible]	[illegible]	[illegible]	[illegible]	[illegible]	[illegible]	[illegible]	[illegible]	[illegible]	[illegible]	[illegible]	[illegible]
PROVINCE OF MUNSTER.																				
Cork	Cork & Queenstown	[illegible]	[illegible]	[illegible]	[illegible]	[illegible]	[illegible]	[illegible]	[illegible]	[illegible]	[illegible]	[illegible]	[illegible]	[illegible]	[illegible]	[illegible]	[illegible]	[illegible]	[illegible]	[illegible]
Limerick	Limerick	[illegible]	[illegible]	[illegible]	[illegible]	[illegible]	[illegible]	[illegible]	[illegible]	[illegible]	[illegible]	[illegible]	[illegible]	[illegible]	[illegible]	[illegible]	[illegible]	[illegible]	[illegible]	[illegible]
Waterford	Waterford	[illegible]	[illegible]	[illegible]	[illegible]	[illegible]	[illegible]	[illegible]	[illegible]	[illegible]	[illegible]	[illegible]	[illegible]	[illegible]	[illegible]	[illegible]	[illegible]	[illegible]	[illegible]	[illegible]
Total Civic Unions,*		[illegible]	[illegible]	[illegible]	[illegible]	[illegible]	[illegible]	[illegible]	[illegible]	[illegible]	[illegible]	[illegible]	[illegible]	[illegible]	[illegible]	[illegible]	[illegible]	[illegible]	[illegible]	[illegible]
PROVINCE OF ULSTER.																				
Armagh	Armagh	[illegible]	[illegible]	[illegible]	[illegible]	[illegible]	[illegible]	[illegible]	[illegible]	[illegible]	[illegible]	[illegible]	[illegible]	[illegible]	[illegible]	[illegible]	[illegible]	[illegible]	[illegible]	[illegible]
Belfast	Belfast	[illegible]	[illegible]	[illegible]	[illegible]	[illegible]	[illegible]	[illegible]	[illegible]	[illegible]	[illegible]	[illegible]	[illegible]	[illegible]	[illegible]	[illegible]	[illegible]	[illegible]	[illegible]	[illegible]
Lisburn	Lisburn	[illegible]	[illegible]	[illegible]	[illegible]	[illegible]	[illegible]	[illegible]	[illegible]	[illegible]	[illegible]	[illegible]	[illegible]	[illegible]	[illegible]	[illegible]	[illegible]	[illegible]	[illegible]	[illegible]
Londonderry	Londonderry	[illegible]	[illegible]	[illegible]	[illegible]	[illegible]	[illegible]	[illegible]	[illegible]	[illegible]	[illegible]	[illegible]	[illegible]	[illegible]	[illegible]	[illegible]	[illegible]	[illegible]	[illegible]	[illegible]
Lurgan	Lurgan	[illegible]	[illegible]	[illegible]	[illegible]	[illegible]	[illegible]	[illegible]	[illegible]	[illegible]	[illegible]	[illegible]	[illegible]	[illegible]	[illegible]	[illegible]	[illegible]	[illegible]	[illegible]	[illegible]
Newry	Newry	[illegible]	[illegible]	[illegible]	[illegible]	[illegible]	[illegible]	[illegible]	[illegible]	[illegible]	[illegible]	[illegible]	[illegible]	[illegible]	[illegible]	[illegible]	[illegible]	[illegible]	[illegible]	[illegible]
Total Civic Unions,*		[illegible]	[illegible]	[illegible]	[illegible]	[illegible]	[illegible]	[illegible]	[illegible]	[illegible]	[illegible]	[illegible]	[illegible]	[illegible]	[illegible]	[illegible]	[illegible]	[illegible]	[illegible]	[illegible]
PROVINCE OF CONNAUGHT.																				
Galway	Galway	[illegible]	[illegible]	[illegible]	[illegible]	[illegible]	[illegible]	[illegible]	[illegible]	[illegible]	[illegible]	[illegible]	[illegible]	[illegible]	[illegible]	[illegible]	[illegible]	[illegible]	[illegible]	[illegible]
Sligo	Sligo	[illegible]	[illegible]	[illegible]	[illegible]	[illegible]	[illegible]	[illegible]	[illegible]	[illegible]	[illegible]	[illegible]	[illegible]	[illegible]	[illegible]	[illegible]	[illegible]	[illegible]	[illegible]	[illegible]
Total Civic Unions,*		[illegible]	[illegible]	[illegible]	[illegible]	[illegible]	[illegible]	[illegible]	[illegible]	[illegible]	[illegible]	[illegible]	[illegible]	[illegible]	[illegible]	[illegible]	[illegible]	[illegible]	[illegible]	[illegible]
IRELAND.																				
Civic Unions,*		[illegible]	[illegible]	[illegible]	[illegible]	[illegible]	[illegible]	[illegible]	[illegible]	[illegible]	[illegible]	[illegible]	[illegible]	[illegible]	[illegible]	[illegible]	[illegible]	[illegible]	[illegible]	[illegible]
Rural Unions,†		[illegible]	[illegible]	[illegible]	[illegible]	[illegible]	[illegible]	[illegible]	[illegible]	[illegible]	[illegible]	[illegible]	[illegible]	[illegible]	[illegible]	[illegible]	[illegible]	[illegible]	[illegible]	[illegible]
Total		[illegible]	[illegible]	[illegible]	[illegible]	[illegible]	[illegible]	[illegible]	[illegible]	[illegible]	[illegible]	[illegible]	[illegible]	[illegible]	[illegible]	[illegible]	[illegible]	[illegible]	[illegible]	[illegible]

* Unions or Superintendent Registrars' Districts containing Towns which in 1881 or 1891 had a population of 10,000 or upwards.

† All Unions other than those specified at Note (*).

TABLE XI.—AVERAGE ANNUAL RATES per 10,000 of the MEAN POPULATION (1881-91) represented by the Deaths from Several Causes registered during the Ten Years 1881-90, in (1) the Unions or Superintendent Registrars' Districts containing Towns which in 1881 or in 1891 had a population of 10,000 or upwards; (2) the Group of such Unions in each Province; (3) all such Unions; and (4) all other Unions in Ireland.

Poor Law Unions or Superintendent Registrars' Districts.	Towns of 10,000 or upwards (in 1881 or in 1891) situated in the respective Unions.	Mean Population	All Causes	1	2	3	4	5	6	7	8	9	10	11	12	13	14	15	16	17
PROVINCE OF LEINSTER.																				
Drogheda	Drogheda	[illegible]	[illegible]	[illegible]	[illegible]	[illegible]	[illegible]	[illegible]	[illegible]	[illegible]	[illegible]	[illegible]	[illegible]	[illegible]	[illegible]	[illegible]	[illegible]	[illegible]	[illegible]	[illegible]
Dublin North	[illegible]	[illegible]	[illegible]	[illegible]	[illegible]	[illegible]	[illegible]	[illegible]	[illegible]	[illegible]	[illegible]	[illegible]	[illegible]	[illegible]	[illegible]	[illegible]	[illegible]	[illegible]	[illegible]	[illegible]
Dublin South	[illegible]	[illegible]	[illegible]	[illegible]	[illegible]	[illegible]	[illegible]	[illegible]	[illegible]	[illegible]	[illegible]	[illegible]	[illegible]	[illegible]	[illegible]	[illegible]	[illegible]	[illegible]	[illegible]	[illegible]
Dundalk	Dundalk	[illegible]	[illegible]	[illegible]	[illegible]	[illegible]	[illegible]	[illegible]	[illegible]	[illegible]	[illegible]	[illegible]	[illegible]	[illegible]	[illegible]	[illegible]	[illegible]	[illegible]	[illegible]	[illegible]
Kilkenny	Kilkenny	[illegible]	[illegible]	[illegible]	[illegible]	[illegible]	[illegible]	[illegible]	[illegible]	[illegible]	[illegible]	[illegible]	[illegible]	[illegible]	[illegible]	[illegible]	[illegible]	[illegible]	[illegible]	[illegible]
Rathdown	Kingstown	[illegible]	[illegible]	[illegible]	[illegible]	[illegible]	[illegible]	[illegible]	[illegible]	[illegible]	[illegible]	[illegible]	[illegible]	[illegible]	[illegible]	[illegible]	[illegible]	[illegible]	[illegible]	[illegible]
Wexford	Wexford	[illegible]	[illegible]	[illegible]	[illegible]	[illegible]	[illegible]	[illegible]	[illegible]	[illegible]	[illegible]	[illegible]	[illegible]	[illegible]	[illegible]	[illegible]	[illegible]	[illegible]	[illegible]	[illegible]
Total, Civic Unions,*		[illegible]	[illegible]	[illegible]	[illegible]	[illegible]	[illegible]	[illegible]	[illegible]	[illegible]	[illegible]	[illegible]	[illegible]	[illegible]	[illegible]	[illegible]	[illegible]	[illegible]	[illegible]	[illegible]
PROVINCE OF MUNSTER.																				
Cork	Cork and Queenstown	[illegible]	[illegible]	[illegible]	[illegible]	[illegible]	[illegible]	[illegible]	[illegible]	[illegible]	[illegible]	[illegible]	[illegible]	[illegible]	[illegible]	[illegible]	[illegible]	[illegible]	[illegible]	[illegible]
Limerick	Limerick	[illegible]	[illegible]	[illegible]	[illegible]	[illegible]	[illegible]	[illegible]	[illegible]	[illegible]	[illegible]	[illegible]	[illegible]	[illegible]	[illegible]	[illegible]	[illegible]	[illegible]	[illegible]	[illegible]
Waterford	Waterford	[illegible]	[illegible]	[illegible]	[illegible]	[illegible]	[illegible]	[illegible]	[illegible]	[illegible]	[illegible]	[illegible]	[illegible]	[illegible]	[illegible]	[illegible]	[illegible]	[illegible]	[illegible]	[illegible]
Total, Civic Unions,*		[illegible]	[illegible]	[illegible]	[illegible]	[illegible]	[illegible]	[illegible]	[illegible]	[illegible]	[illegible]	[illegible]	[illegible]	[illegible]	[illegible]	[illegible]	[illegible]	[illegible]	[illegible]	[illegible]
PROVINCE OF ULSTER.																				
Armagh	Armagh	[illegible]	[illegible]	[illegible]	[illegible]	[illegible]	[illegible]	[illegible]	[illegible]	[illegible]	[illegible]	[illegible]	[illegible]	[illegible]	[illegible]	[illegible]	[illegible]	[illegible]	[illegible]	[illegible]
Belfast	Belfast	[illegible]	[illegible]	[illegible]	[illegible]	[illegible]	[illegible]	[illegible]	[illegible]	[illegible]	[illegible]	[illegible]	[illegible]	[illegible]	[illegible]	[illegible]	[illegible]	[illegible]	[illegible]	[illegible]
Lisburn	Lisburn	[illegible]	[illegible]	[illegible]	[illegible]	[illegible]	[illegible]	[illegible]	[illegible]	[illegible]	[illegible]	[illegible]	[illegible]	[illegible]	[illegible]	[illegible]	[illegible]	[illegible]	[illegible]	[illegible]
Londonderry	Londonderry	[illegible]	[illegible]	[illegible]	[illegible]	[illegible]	[illegible]	[illegible]	[illegible]	[illegible]	[illegible]	[illegible]	[illegible]	[illegible]	[illegible]	[illegible]	[illegible]	[illegible]	[illegible]	[illegible]
Lurgan	Lurgan	[illegible]	[illegible]	[illegible]	[illegible]	[illegible]	[illegible]	[illegible]	[illegible]	[illegible]	[illegible]	[illegible]	[illegible]	[illegible]	[illegible]	[illegible]	[illegible]	[illegible]	[illegible]	[illegible]
Newry	Newry	[illegible]	[illegible]	[illegible]	[illegible]	[illegible]	[illegible]	[illegible]	[illegible]	[illegible]	[illegible]	[illegible]	[illegible]	[illegible]	[illegible]	[illegible]	[illegible]	[illegible]	[illegible]	[illegible]
Total, Civic Unions,*		[illegible]	[illegible]	[illegible]	[illegible]	[illegible]	[illegible]	[illegible]	[illegible]	[illegible]	[illegible]	[illegible]	[illegible]	[illegible]	[illegible]	[illegible]	[illegible]	[illegible]	[illegible]	[illegible]
PROVINCE OF CONNAUGHT.																				
Galway	Galway	[illegible]	[illegible]	[illegible]	[illegible]	[illegible]	[illegible]	[illegible]	[illegible]	[illegible]	[illegible]	[illegible]	[illegible]	[illegible]	[illegible]	[illegible]	[illegible]	[illegible]	[illegible]	[illegible]
Sligo	Sligo	[illegible]	[illegible]	[illegible]	[illegible]	[illegible]	[illegible]	[illegible]	[illegible]	[illegible]	[illegible]	[illegible]	[illegible]	[illegible]	[illegible]	[illegible]	[illegible]	[illegible]	[illegible]	[illegible]
Total, Civic Unions,*		[illegible]	[illegible]	[illegible]	[illegible]	[illegible]	[illegible]	[illegible]	[illegible]	[illegible]	[illegible]	[illegible]	[illegible]	[illegible]	[illegible]	[illegible]	[illegible]	[illegible]	[illegible]	[illegible]
IRELAND.																				
Civic Unions*		[illegible]	[illegible]	[illegible]	[illegible]	[illegible]	[illegible]	[illegible]	[illegible]	[illegible]	[illegible]	[illegible]	[illegible]	[illegible]	[illegible]	[illegible]	[illegible]	[illegible]	[illegible]	[illegible]
Rural Unions†		[illegible]	[illegible]	[illegible]	[illegible]	[illegible]	[illegible]	[illegible]	[illegible]	[illegible]	[illegible]	[illegible]	[illegible]	[illegible]	[illegible]	[illegible]	[illegible]	[illegible]	[illegible]	[illegible]
Total		[illegible]	[illegible]	[illegible]	[illegible]	[illegible]	[illegible]	[illegible]	[illegible]	[illegible]	[illegible]	[illegible]	[illegible]	[illegible]	[illegible]	[illegible]	[illegible]	[illegible]	[illegible]	[illegible]

* Unions or Superintendent Registrars' Districts containing Towns which in 1881 or in 1891 had a population of 10,000 or upwards.
† All Unions other than those specified in Note (*).

Urban Sanitary Districts.

Separate statistics for the Urban Sanitary Districts, compiled from Weekly and Quarterly Returns furnished by the various Registrars, are given in Table XII.

The average annual death-rate per 1,000 of the mean population (1881–91) in these districts, which comprise a population of nearly one-fourth of the total of the country, was [illegible], and the birth-rate 27·0; in the remainder of the country the death-rate was 15·1, and the birth-rate 22·9 per 1,000.

The average annual rate represented by the deaths from the Principal Zymotic Diseases† in the Urban Sanitary districts during the ten years was 2·7 per 1,000 of the mean population; in the remainder of the country the rate was 1·1 per 1,000.

Table XII.—Births and Deaths registered during the Ten Years 1881–90, in the Dublin Registration District, and in each of the Principal Urban Sanitary Districts in Ireland [illegible] with the number of Deaths from each of the Principal Zymotic Diseases.†

[illegible]

[illegible]	[illegible]	[illegible]	[illegible]	[illegible]	[illegible]	[illegible]	[illegible]	[illegible]	[illegible]	[illegible]	[illegible]	[illegible]	[illegible]	[illegible]	[illegible]	[illegible]	[illegible]	[illegible]	[illegible]	[illegible]	[illegible]
[illegible]	[illegible]	[illegible]	[illegible]	[illegible]	[illegible]	[illegible]	[illegible]	[illegible]	[illegible]	[illegible]	[illegible]	[illegible]	[illegible]	[illegible]	[illegible]	[illegible]	[illegible]	[illegible]	[illegible]	[illegible]	[illegible]
[illegible]	[illegible]	[illegible]	[illegible]	[illegible]	[illegible]	[illegible]	[illegible]	[illegible]	[illegible]	[illegible]	[illegible]	[illegible]	[illegible]	[illegible]	[illegible]	[illegible]	[illegible]	[illegible]	[illegible]	[illegible]	[illegible]
[illegible]																					
I. Leinster.																					
[illegible]	[illegible]	[illegible]	[illegible]	[illegible]	[illegible]	[illegible]	[illegible]	[illegible]	[illegible]	[illegible]	[illegible]	[illegible]	[illegible]	[illegible]	[illegible]	[illegible]	[illegible]	[illegible]	[illegible]	[illegible]	[illegible]
[illegible]	[illegible]	[illegible]	[illegible]	[illegible]	[illegible]	[illegible]	[illegible]	[illegible]	[illegible]	[illegible]	[illegible]	[illegible]	[illegible]	[illegible]	[illegible]	[illegible]	[illegible]	[illegible]	[illegible]	[illegible]	[illegible]
[illegible]	[illegible]	[illegible]	[illegible]	[illegible]	[illegible]	[illegible]	[illegible]	[illegible]	[illegible]	[illegible]	[illegible]	[illegible]	[illegible]	[illegible]	[illegible]	[illegible]	[illegible]	[illegible]	[illegible]	[illegible]	[illegible]
[illegible]	[illegible]	[illegible]	[illegible]	[illegible]	[illegible]	[illegible]	[illegible]	[illegible]	[illegible]	[illegible]	[illegible]	[illegible]	[illegible]	[illegible]	[illegible]	[illegible]	[illegible]	[illegible]	[illegible]	[illegible]	[illegible]
[illegible]	[illegible]	[illegible]	[illegible]	[illegible]	[illegible]	[illegible]	[illegible]	[illegible]	[illegible]	[illegible]	[illegible]	[illegible]	[illegible]	[illegible]	[illegible]	[illegible]	[illegible]	[illegible]	[illegible]	[illegible]	[illegible]
[illegible]	[illegible]	[illegible]	[illegible]	[illegible]	[illegible]	[illegible]	[illegible]	[illegible]	[illegible]	[illegible]	[illegible]	[illegible]	[illegible]	[illegible]	[illegible]	[illegible]	[illegible]	[illegible]	[illegible]	[illegible]	[illegible]
[illegible]	[illegible]	[illegible]	[illegible]	[illegible]	[illegible]	[illegible]	[illegible]	[illegible]	[illegible]	[illegible]	[illegible]	[illegible]	[illegible]	[illegible]	[illegible]	[illegible]	[illegible]	[illegible]	[illegible]	[illegible]	[illegible]
[illegible]	[illegible]	[illegible]	[illegible]	[illegible]	[illegible]	[illegible]	[illegible]	[illegible]	[illegible]	[illegible]	[illegible]	[illegible]	[illegible]	[illegible]	[illegible]	[illegible]	[illegible]	[illegible]	[illegible]	[illegible]	[illegible]
[illegible]	[illegible]	[illegible]	[illegible]	[illegible]	[illegible]	[illegible]	[illegible]	[illegible]	[illegible]	[illegible]	[illegible]	[illegible]	[illegible]	[illegible]	[illegible]	[illegible]	[illegible]	[illegible]	[illegible]	[illegible]	[illegible]
[illegible]	[illegible]	[illegible]	[illegible]	[illegible]	[illegible]	[illegible]	[illegible]	[illegible]	[illegible]	[illegible]	[illegible]	[illegible]	[illegible]	[illegible]	[illegible]	[illegible]	[illegible]	[illegible]	[illegible]	[illegible]	[illegible]
[illegible]	[illegible]	[illegible]	[illegible]	[illegible]	[illegible]	[illegible]	[illegible]	[illegible]	[illegible]	[illegible]	[illegible]	[illegible]	[illegible]	[illegible]	[illegible]	[illegible]	[illegible]	[illegible]	[illegible]	[illegible]	[illegible]
[illegible]	[illegible]	[illegible]	[illegible]	[illegible]	[illegible]	[illegible]	[illegible]	[illegible]	[illegible]	[illegible]	[illegible]	[illegible]	[illegible]	[illegible]	[illegible]	[illegible]	[illegible]	[illegible]	[illegible]	[illegible]	[illegible]
[illegible]	[illegible]	[illegible]	[illegible]	[illegible]	[illegible]	[illegible]	[illegible]	[illegible]	[illegible]	[illegible]	[illegible]	[illegible]	[illegible]	[illegible]	[illegible]	[illegible]	[illegible]	[illegible]	[illegible]	[illegible]	[illegible]
[illegible]	[illegible]	[illegible]	[illegible]	[illegible]	[illegible]	[illegible]	[illegible]	[illegible]	[illegible]	[illegible]	[illegible]	[illegible]	[illegible]	[illegible]	[illegible]	[illegible]	[illegible]	[illegible]	[illegible]	[illegible]	[illegible]
[illegible]	[illegible]	[illegible]	[illegible]	[illegible]	[illegible]	[illegible]	[illegible]	[illegible]	[illegible]	[illegible]	[illegible]	[illegible]	[illegible]	[illegible]	[illegible]	[illegible]	[illegible]	[illegible]	[illegible]	[illegible]	[illegible]
[illegible]	[illegible]	[illegible]	[illegible]	[illegible]	[illegible]	[illegible]	[illegible]	[illegible]	[illegible]	[illegible]	[illegible]	[illegible]	[illegible]	[illegible]	[illegible]	[illegible]	[illegible]	[illegible]	[illegible]	[illegible]	[illegible]
[illegible]	[illegible]	[illegible]	[illegible]	[illegible]	[illegible]	[illegible]	[illegible]	[illegible]	[illegible]	[illegible]	[illegible]	[illegible]	[illegible]	[illegible]	[illegible]	[illegible]	[illegible]	[illegible]	[illegible]	[illegible]	[illegible]
[illegible]	[illegible]	[illegible]	[illegible]	[illegible]	[illegible]	[illegible]	[illegible]	[illegible]	[illegible]	[illegible]	[illegible]	[illegible]	[illegible]	[illegible]	[illegible]	[illegible]	[illegible]	[illegible]	[illegible]	[illegible]	[illegible]
II. Munster.																					
[illegible]	[illegible]	[illegible]	[illegible]	[illegible]	[illegible]	[illegible]	[illegible]	[illegible]	[illegible]	[illegible]	[illegible]	[illegible]	[illegible]	[illegible]	[illegible]	[illegible]	[illegible]	[illegible]	[illegible]	[illegible]	[illegible]
[illegible]	[illegible]	[illegible]	[illegible]	[illegible]	[illegible]	[illegible]	[illegible]	[illegible]	[illegible]	[illegible]	[illegible]	[illegible]	[illegible]	[illegible]	[illegible]	[illegible]	[illegible]	[illegible]	[illegible]	[illegible]	[illegible]
[illegible]	[illegible]	[illegible]	[illegible]	[illegible]	[illegible]	[illegible]	[illegible]	[illegible]	[illegible]	[illegible]	[illegible]	[illegible]	[illegible]	[illegible]	[illegible]	[illegible]	[illegible]	[illegible]	[illegible]	[illegible]	[illegible]
[illegible]	[illegible]	[illegible]	[illegible]	[illegible]	[illegible]	[illegible]	[illegible]	[illegible]	[illegible]	[illegible]	[illegible]	[illegible]	[illegible]	[illegible]	[illegible]	[illegible]	[illegible]	[illegible]	[illegible]	[illegible]	[illegible]
[illegible]	[illegible]	[illegible]	[illegible]	[illegible]	[illegible]	[illegible]	[illegible]	[illegible]	[illegible]	[illegible]	[illegible]	[illegible]	[illegible]	[illegible]	[illegible]	[illegible]	[illegible]	[illegible]	[illegible]	[illegible]	[illegible]

Urban Sanitary Districts—continued.

Table XII.—Births and Deaths registered during the Ten Years 1881-90, in the Dublin Registration District, and in each of the Provincial Urban Sanitary Districts in Ireland (exclusive of Deaths in Public Institutions of Persons admitted from other localities), with the number of Deaths from each of the Principal Zymotic Diseases—continued.

Provinces and Urban Sanitary Districts	Census Population, 1891	[illegible]	Births	Annual Rate per 1,000 [illegible]	[illegible]	Births	Deaths	[illegible]	[illegible]	Caused by Principal Zymotic Diseases
II. Munster—con.										
[illegible]	[illegible]	[illegible]	[illegible]	[illegible]	[illegible]	[illegible]	[illegible]	[illegible]	[illegible]	[illegible]
III. Ulster.										
[illegible]	[illegible]	[illegible]	[illegible]	[illegible]	[illegible]	[illegible]	[illegible]	[illegible]	[illegible]	[illegible]
IV. Connaught.										
[illegible]	[illegible]	[illegible]	[illegible]	[illegible]	[illegible]	[illegible]	[illegible]	[illegible]	[illegible]	[illegible]

[illegible]

CAUSES OF DEATH.

I.—ZYMOTIC DISEASES.

The principal Zymotic diseases, namely, small-pox, measles, scarlet fever, diphtheria, whooping-cough, fever (including typhus, enteric, and simple continued fever), diarrhœa (including dysentery), and simple cholera caused 70,717 deaths during the decade, or at the average annual rate of 14·8 per 10,000 of the mean population. Of these, 33,272, or 47·0 per cent., equivalent to a rate of 27·9 per 10,000, occurred in the civic Unions (already described), and 37,445 or 53·0 per cent., equivalent to a rate of 10·7 per 10,000, occurred in the rural Unions. The general mortality of the civic districts as compared with rural is as 1·4 to 1, while in the case of the principal zymotics the ratio between civic and rural districts is 2·1 to 1, showing a very considerable excess for the civic districts beyond the rural death-rate. This difference is easily accounted for by the manner in which these zymotic diseases are promoted. With the exception of some of the forms of diarrhœa all the principal zymotics are infective diseases, and their main promoting cause is infection from person to person either directly or indirectly. Hence density of population is probably the most important factor in favouring the spread of the principal zymotic diseases, and therefore the denser the population the greater, more minute, and more constant must be all the precautions taken against the spread of infective disease. The high death-rate from certain forms of zymotic disease in towns as compared with country districts, and the rates in the several districts in the former group compared one with another, will be again referred to when discussing separately the mortality from these diseases.

Small-pox.

vaccination was noticed. This defect has now been to a great extent remedied, and regular quarterly records of vaccination are collected and published in the quarterly reports of the Registrar-General. This system, which was commenced in the year 1882, has been continued up to the present, and shows that during the nine years, 1882–90, 893,787 primary vaccinations, and 57,705 deaths of unvaccinated children under 3 months old were recorded as compared with 1,024,616 births registered. It should be added that in the same period only 169 deaths were registered from small-pox. A Table showing the number of successful primary vaccinations by Unions will be found at page 75.

Measles.

Measles caused 9,429 deaths during the decade: Table XVI. (pages 38–9) shows that the mortality from this disease varied much in different years during the period. In 1886 there were only 284 deaths from measles registered, while in 1888, when there was a very general epidemic of this disease throughout Ireland, there were 1,935.

As to the distribution of the disease between town and country districts, the usual law followed by infective disease is observed, the mortality according to Tables X. and XI. being 3·8 per 1,000 for town and 1·1 for rural Unions. The disease was most destructive in the Dublin, Belfast, and Cork districts, in which there were 4,315 deaths, or nearly one half of all the deaths from measles in Ireland. Table XII. shows the number of deaths from measles in the Urban Sanitary Districts.

As might be expected, the disease was most destructive during the early periods of life. Of the 9,429 deaths, no less than 7,547 (3,895 males, and 3,652 females) or 80·0 per cent. occurred under the age of five years; 1,609 (910 males, and 699 females), were under one year; and 2,990 (1,569 males, and 1,431 females), between one and two years. Taking the last two years together, it may be said that about one-half (4,599 or 48·8 per cent.), of all the deaths from measles occurred in infants under two years of age, or at the average annual rate of 24·1 per 10,000 of children living at that age.

Scarlatina.

DIPHTHERIA.

Diphtheria caused 3,465 deaths during the decade, or an average of 347 per annum, being at the rate of 0·7 per 10,000 of the population. In the preceding decade the number of deaths was 3,403. The mortality from this disease was lowest in 1885 when 239 deaths occurred, and highest in 1888 when there were 447 deaths.

In the following Unions—Clifden, Glenties, Kenmare, Killadysert, Longford, Newcastle, and Portumna—there were not any deaths from diphtheria registered during the whole decade. Most of these Unions are rather out of the way, or in remote districts. Tables X. and XI. show that diphtheria follows the usual rule of infective diseases, and prevails to a greater extent in town than in country districts, but this is not so marked as in the other forms of zymotic disease which have been already considered.

A comparison between the town districts shows that the mortality from diphtheria has been equal to an average rate of 1·3 per 10,000 of the mean population in Ulster; 0·7 in Leinster and Munster respectively; and 0·5 in Connaught. The rate for Armagh is 1·5, Belfast 1·4, Lurgan 1·4, and Lisburn 1·3. More than half of the total number of deaths in the Civic Unions of Ireland occurred in Ulster. Of the 949 deaths from this disease in the Urban Districts, 316 were in Belfast, and 267 in the Dublin Registration District.

Diphtheria, like scarlatina, is especially fatal to children. Of the 3,465 deaths, 1,673, or 48 per cent., were in children under 5 years of age, or at the average annual rate of 3·9 per 10,000 living at that age-period. Of these 1,673 there were 198 under the age of one year; 372 between 1 and 2 years; 371 from 2 to 3 years; 388 from 3 to 4 years; and 344 from 4 to 5 years. Above 5 years of age, there were 1,074 deaths between 5 and 10 years, and 324 between 10 and 15 years—making together 1,398, which with those under 5 years, gives 3,071, or 88·6 per cent., of the whole for the years of childhood.

WHOOPING-COUGH.

Whooping-cough caused 14,639 deaths during the decade, or at the average annual rate of 2·9 per 10,000 of the population. A general relation has been noticed by many observers between the prevalence of whooping-cough and measles, and there is no doubt that in many localities an epidemic of measles is frequently accompanied or followed by a prevalence of whooping-cough. A comparison of the figures in Table XVI., which represent the mortality from these two diseases, does not point to any very close relationship. Whooping-cough was a much more fatal disease in Ireland during the decade than measles, but it is more than probable that measles was equally prevalent.

Table XVI., however, does not show that an increase of measles was contemporaneous with an increase of whooping-cough. In the years 1882, 1885, and 1888, when measles increased, whooping-cough diminished, and in the years 1883 and 1889, when whooping-cough exhibited an increased mortality, measles was less fatal. It must, however, be admitted, in justice to the opinion of those who consider there is a necessary relation between one disease and the other, that the periods being calendar years, are too long and too arbitrary for exact comparison. It might naturally be expected that there would be a close relationship between the deaths from whooping-cough and those from diseases of the respiratory system. A reference to Table XVI. serves to show that there is some such relationship.

The distribution of the mortality from whooping-cough was tolerably even over the whole of Ireland. There is not any Union in Ireland whose population escaped, and in many Unions a large number of deaths took place during the decade.

Tables X. and XI. show that, like other infective diseases, whooping-cough is more fatal in town (Dublin and Belfast contributing 22·7 per cent. of the mortality from this disease) than in country districts, but the difference is not so well marked as in the and four years; and 646 between the ages of four and five years; on passing the age of five there were 1,176 between five and ten years; and only 149 between the ages of ten and fifteen years, with the insignificant number of 28 above the age of fifteen. Excepting, perhaps, the case of croup, this is the most remarkable instance of a disease the mortality from which is almost exclusively confined to early childhood.

Fevers.

In former times several diseases were collectively described under the term "Fever," and in the earlier reports of this department four forms of disease, namely, typhus, enteric, relapsing, and simple continued fevers are dealt with under the single head "fever"; however, during the two decades 1871-80 and 1881-90, these diseases (except relapsing fever in the first decade) have been dealt with separately and tabulated under their respective heads in the annual reports. "Typhus" is promoted if not caused by overcrowding of human beings. "Enteric or typhoid fever," the promoting cause of which is usually recognised as attributable to defective drainage and sewerage, has for the last twenty-five years been more common in Ireland than typhus, although apparently it was not so formerly. "Relapsing fever," which arises in connexion with scarcity of food, and which is hence called "Famine fever," has at certain times prevailed in Ireland, but has not been classified as a cause of death in the Reports for the years 1871–80, and probably did not occur at all, or only in a very few isolated cases during that period, but twenty-two deaths were registered as occurring from it in the decade 1881-90. "Simple continued" fever, no doubt, comprises imperfectly developed forms of the three first mentioned specific fevers, and many high authorities decline to recognise simple continued fever as a specific form of disease, nevertheless, during the decade, very many deaths were attributed to this cause.

Table XIII., contains a summary by ages of the deaths from the three forms of continued fever dealt with in the Abstracts.

TABLE XIII.—DEATHS at each of ELEVEN AGE-PERIODS from the several forms of Continued Fever registered in Ireland during the Ten Years 1881-90, with the Ratio of the average annual number of these Deaths to every 100,000 of the living at the same age.

	No. of Deaths registered.	Average annual number of Deaths to 100,000 of the living at each age.

rates of 3·12 and 2·24. This remarkable difference may be fairly accounted for by advances in diagnosis, by which many cases of disease, which formerly would have been classified as simple fever, were more correctly defined in the death certificates. It is, however, very gratifying to note that the death rates from all forms of continued fever, whether taken separately or collectively, have materially diminished during the later as compared with the earlier decade.

An investigation into the relative number of deaths at different ages in typhus and enteric fever is very interesting. Table XIII. sets out these deaths by 11 age-periods. Under five years the proportion of deaths from typhus is smaller than at any other period of life—indeed it is almost insignificant—while in enteric fever it is very large; after this period of life the death-rate from typhus increases materially, and remains high as life advances, while in the case of enteric fever the highest rate of mortality is reached at the age-periods 15–20 and 20–25, and then it materially diminishes. In the case of simple fever the rate of mortality steadily increases as age advances, reaching its maximum in advanced life. Many of the deaths attributed to this disease in advanced life are so designated, owing to the fact that in many cases death from senile decay is accompanied by a form of fever sometimes described as "febris senilis."

The distribution of the various forms of fever throughout Ireland is shown in the Abstracts at p. 96–103. The more remarkable features are shown in Table X., from which it will be seen that the greater number of deaths from the different forms of continued fever are to be found in towns. Thus of 18,067 deaths from fever, 7,364 occurred in large town districts—the rate of mortality for continued fever being, for the whole of Ireland, 3·7; for districts containing large towns, 5·0; and for rural districts, 3·1 per 10,000 inhabitants, as compared with 5·7, 7·2, and 5·1 respectively for the preceding decade.

When the distribution of the different forms of continued fever between town and country is considered, it will be seen that the town exceeds the country death-rate in the cases of typhus and enteric fever; but in the case of simple and ill-defined fever the country rate exceeds the town rate. In the case of enteric fever the town rate is more than double that for the rural districts, and the typhus town rate is nearly double the rural rate.

If the Unions comprising the great towns of Dublin, Belfast, and Cork be treated as a group, it will be found that of the 5,457 deaths from typhus, 1,432, or 26·2 per cent., occurred in these districts taken collectively; and in the case of enteric fever, of the 7,995 deaths, 3,082, or 38·5 per cent., took place in these great town districts. These town districts have a population of 808,047, or 16·4 per cent., of the total inhabitants of Ireland. If the various town districts be compared with one another, it will be found that in those of Leinster, whether taken individually or collectively, the death-rate from enteric fever exceeds the death-rate from typhus. The same is true of Ulster; but in the case of the town districts of Munster and Connaught it is the reverse, as in every case in the western and southern provinces, the death-rate from typhus exceeds that from enteric fever. The highest death-rate from typhus fever is found in Waterford Union, where it reached 3·5 per 10,000 of the mean population, Cork coming next with a rate of 3·0. The highest death-rate from enteric fever was in the North Dublin Union, where the rate reached was 4·7, the Belfast and South Dublin Unions standing next in order with death-rates of 4·5 and 3·9 respectively. The combined enteric fever deaths for the three Dublin Unions, including the whole town district of Dublin, represent a rate of 4·0 per 10,000, being about the same as Belfast. Thus the two greatest towns in Ireland appear to be the chief foci of enteric fever, while the chief foci of typhus are found in less important places; and, as shown in the Abstract, this disease has caused many deaths in rural districts.

Erysipelas

Erysipelas caused 2,421 deaths during the decade, being an average of 242 per annum, or at the annual rate of 0·5 per 10,000 of the mean population.

The number and proportion of males who died of erysipelas are greater than those of females, although females preponderate in the population of Ireland. 1,345 males and 1,076 females died of erysipelas, being at the respective average annual rates of 0·6 per 10,000 of the male population, and 0·4 per 10,000 of the female population. The deaths of males amounted to 55·6 per cent., and those of females to 44·4 per cent. of the total deaths.

The greater proportion of deaths from erysipelas among males than females may be accounted for—firstly, by the fact that many deaths from erysipelas are probably due to that disease supervening on injuries (often of a slight nature) to which men, from the nature of their occupations, are more liable than females; secondly, intemperate persons are more prone to die of erysipelas than sober people, and as there are more intemperate men than intemperate women this condition also accounts for the excessive male death-rate. Of the 2,431 deaths from erysipelas—342 were among infants under one year of age, or equal to a rate of 2·5 per 10,000 of children born, and forming 14·0 per cent. of the total deaths from the disease; the number in each succeeding year of early life is small, the total under five years being 436, or at the average annual rate of 0·8 per 10,000 living at that age, and equal to 17·9 per cent. of the total. There were in all 541 deaths from erysipelas under ten years of age, or 22·3 per cent. of the total. After the age of twenty-five years the rate of mortality is found to rise very considerably, and by far the larger proportion of deaths occurs after this period, especially when middle life is passed. The deaths between twenty and forty-five years amount to 412, or 17·0 per cent. of the total deaths from this cause, being at the rate of 0·8 per 10,000 of the mean population at those ages. The number between the ages of forty-five and sixty-five is 603, or at the rate of 0·9 per 10,000, and from sixty-five to eighty-five 804, or at the annual rate of 2·1 per 10,000 of the mean population, thus showing a steady increase of mortality towards advanced life.

Puerperal Fever and Childbirth.

It is difficult completely to separate the statistics of deaths from puerperal fever and from childbirth, as they may be all put down to a common cause, namely, parturition, and no doubt a considerable number of deaths from puerperal fever, especially in the country, are returned simply as deaths from "childbirth."

The total number of deaths under these two heads was 8,226, or at the annual rate of 15·0 per 10,000 of married women within the child-bearing ages (namely, 15 to 45). The deaths from puerperal fever numbered 3,351, or at the rate of 6·0 per 10,000 of married women of the child-bearing ages, and the other deaths from childbirth numbered 4,875, or at the rate of 9·0 per 10,000 at the same age-periods. The deaths from puerperal fever were at the rate of 2·8 per 1,000, and those from childbirth at the rate of 4·3 per 1,000 of the births registered, the two combined being equal to one in 142, or at the rate of 7·1 per 1,000 of the births registered.

The Abstract (pages 98–103) shows that in every Union in Ireland, except Ballyvaughan, deaths from puerperal fever were recorded; and that deaths from other forms of the affections of childbirth were recorded in all Unions. Tables X. and XI. show the relative distribution of deaths from this group of diseases between town and country. A result is shown by this comparison which differs remarkably from the results obtained when the town and country death-rates are compared for any of the other diseases or groups of diseases dealt with in those Tables. The average annual death-rates to the population from puerperal fever and childbirth combined are almost the same in town and country, namely, 1·8 and 1·6 per 10,000 respectively; taken separately, the death-rate from puerperal fever, which is an infective disease, is slightly higher in town than in country, and in other forms of death from childbirth the mortality is also greater in town than in the country.

If the number of these deaths be compared with the number of births registered we have the result as set out in the following statement:—

Ten Years 1881–90.

"Puerperal Fever" and "Childbirth" in "Civic" and "Rural" Unions.

In Civic Unions	Deaths from Puerperal Fever	1 in 321 or 3·1	per 1,000 Births registered.
" Rural "	" "	" 376 or 2·7	" " "
" Civic "	" Childbirth	" 251 or 4·0	" " "
" Rural "	" "	" 229 or 4·4	" " "
" Civic "	" Puerperal Fever and Childbirth combined	" 141 or 7·1	" " "
" Rural "	" " "	" 143 or 7·1	" " "
Total Deaths from Puerperal Fever		" 354 or 2·8	" " "
" " "Childbirth"		" 234 or 4·3	" " "
" " Puer. Fever and Childbirth combined		" 142 or 7·1	" " "

From this it appears that the relation of deaths from puerperal fever and childbirth combined to births registered is, for the whole of Ireland, at the rate of 1 in 142, or 7·1 per 1,000; for puerperal fever alone, it is 1 in 934 or 2·8 per 1,000; and for childbirth 1 in 236, or at the rate of 4·3 per 1,000 births. If, however, town and country are compared, it appears that the mortality from puerperal fever in town districts is at the rate of 1 in 821, or 3·1 per 1,000 births, while in country districts it is 1 in 373, or 2·7 per 1,000, being somewhat less. On the other hand, the deaths from "childbirth" are proportionately less in town than in country; in the civic districts the rate is 1 in 250, or at the rate of 4·0 per 1,000, while in country districts it is 1 in 229, or 4·4 per 1,000 births. If the two be taken together the result is, that deaths from parturition are at the rate of 7·1 per 1,000 births both in town and country districts.

The ages at which deaths in child-bed occur must be considered on different principles from those followed in considering deaths by ages with reference to other forms of disease. Taking the widest range, it may be said that all child-bearing women are comprised between the ages of 15 and 55 years, though the number must be very small towards the latter period. In order to set out the relative liability to death from childbirth at various periods of life, the following statement has been drawn up:—

TABLE XIV.—DEATHS from PUERPERAL FEVER and "CHILDBIRTH," 1881–90.

		15–20	20–25	25–35	35–45	45–55	Total 15 to 55 years
Married Women, Census of 1881,		[illegible]	[illegible]	[illegible]	[illegible]	[illegible]	[illegible]
" " 1891,		[illegible]	[illegible]	[illegible]	[illegible]	[illegible]	[illegible]
Mean,		[illegible]	[illegible]	[illegible]	[illegible]	[illegible]	[illegible]
Deaths from Puerperal Fever,	Total Number in Ten Years, 1881–90,	[illegible]	[illegible]	[illegible]	[illegible]	[illegible]	[illegible]
	Average Annual Rate per 10,000 Married Women of same age,	[illegible]	[illegible]	[illegible]	[illegible]	[illegible]	[illegible]
Deaths from "Childbirth,"	Total Number in Ten Years, 1881–90,	[illegible]	[illegible]	[illegible]	[illegible]	[illegible]	[illegible]
	Average Annual Rate per 10,000 Married Women of same age,	[illegible]	[illegible]	[illegible]	[illegible]	[illegible]	[illegible]
Total Deaths from Puerperal Fever and "Childbirth,"	Total Number in Ten Years, 1881–90,	[illegible]	[illegible]	[illegible]	[illegible]	[illegible]	[illegible]
	Average Annual Rate per 10,000 Married Women of same age,	[illegible]	[illegible]	[illegible]	[illegible]	[illegible]	[illegible]

The above comprise all the registered deaths from puerperal fever, and, with two exceptions, those from the accidents of childbirth. The two deaths from the accidents of childbirth were of persons aged "55 years or upwards."

From this statement it appears that between the ages of 15 and 20 years the average annual death-rate from puerperal fever and childbirth combined during the decade was at the rate of 53·6 per 10,000 of the mean number of married women living at those ages; between the ages of 20 and 25 the rate was 24·5; from 25 to 35 years it was 22·6; from 35 to 45 years it was 16·2; and from 45 to 55, when child-bearing has nearly ceased, the rate was only 1·5. Thus the risks of child-bed appear to diminish as the period of married life increases, and are materially greater among very young wives. This tendency is more marked in the case of puerperal fever than in other forms of death in child-bed. In puerperal fever the death-rates are, from 15 to 20 years, 29·3; from 20 to 25 years, 15·9; from 25 to 35 years, 10·1; from 35 to 45 years, 5·0; and from 45 to 55, 0·4; the average rate being 6·0. In other forms of death in childbed the rates are—from 15 to 20 years, 24·3; from 20 to 25 years, 11·6; from 25 to 35 years, 12·5; from 35 to 45 years, 11·2; and from 45 to 55 years, 1·1; the average rate being 9·0. Thus the risks of death from puerperal fever and childbirth are very much greater among young wives, and steadily diminish as life advances.

During the previous decade the total deaths from puerperal fever and childbirth combined represented a rate of 15·3 per 10,000 of the mean number of married women living at child-bearing ages; thus the death-rate from these forms of disease, taken collectively, has slightly decreased, the fall of rate being 0·3 per 10,000. The death-rate from puerperal fever, however, rose from 5·8 in the previous to 6·0 in the later decade, while in other forms of deaths in childbed the rate fell from 9·5 to 9·0. When the numbers for 1871–80 are analysed and compared with those for 1881–90, and each with the number of births registered, it will be found that, whether in town or country, whether from puerperal fever or from the accidents of childbirth, there has been a general increase all round.

Influenza.

The deaths from Influenza amounted, during the decade, to 2,096 (1,067 males and 1,029 females), or at the average annual rate of 0·4 per 10,000 of the mean population.

During the preceding decade the number of deaths from this disease was comparativly insignificant, amounting to but 973, being an average annual mortality at the rate of only 0·2 per 10,000: during the whole period from the commencement of death registration in Ireland up to the year 1890, the average number of deaths was only 103 per annum. During the whole of that period there was not any epidemic noticeable, but in the year 1890, which concluded the decade now under consideration, the disease assumed a serious form and prevailed as an epidemic causing no less than 1,719 deaths, or at the rate of 3·6 per 10,000 of the estimated population. Since that period up to the date of this report, the disease has prevailed in a more or less epidemic form, but the statistics with reference to its prevalence and mortality, after the termination of the year 1890, do not come within the scope of this report. A reference to pp. 14 and 15 of the Annual Report of Marriages, Births, and Deaths for the year 1893, will give the fullest available information on this subject.

Bowel Affections.

from this disease falls rapidly till middle life is reached, but it shows a considerable tendency to increase in fatality when middle life is passed. There were 6,989 deaths from diarrhoea in children under five years of age, being 45·3 per cent., or nearly one half of the total mortality from this disease, or at the average annual rate of 13·4 per 10,000 living at that age-period. These 6,989 deaths mainly occurred among the children of the large town populations, as has already been pointed out when considering the distribution of the disease between town and country districts.

The general result of a comparison of the deaths from these diseases during the decades 1871–80 and 1881–90 is that a material diminution in the rate has taken place almost everywhere—the general rate for Ireland having fallen from 4·0 per 10,000 persons to 3·0.

Parasitic Diseases.

In this class thrush caused 259, and worms and other parasitic diseases 700 deaths, nearly all among children.

Alcoholism.

The number of deaths caused by the abuse of alcoholic drinks cannot be accurately stated, owing to the fact that there are many diseases which are promoted by and sometimes owe their origin to the excessive consumption of alcohol, and the deaths from which are returned under the heads of the special organs affected. Thus alcohol is no doubt accountable for many deaths from kidney, liver, and brain diseases, but there is no reason to suppose that the larger proportion of diseases of these organs are so caused. In filling death certificates for deaths from such causes, the certifying medical practitioner in the majority of cases does not attach any qualifying word to the cause of death implying that the origin of the disease was alcoholic. Thus, in dealing with the statistics of death from alcoholic causes, we have only two heads under which they can be grouped—these heads are "Delirium Tremens" and "Intemperance," the latter term being rather indefinite. In Table XV. the number of deaths from these two specified causes are dealt with.

TABLE XV.—DEATHS FROM ALCOHOLISM.

Year.	Delirium Tremens.			Intemperance.			Total, Delirium Tremens and Intemperance.		
	M.	F.	Total.	M.	F.	Total.	M.	F.	Total.
1881, . . .	36	—	36	99	15	114	135	15	150
1882, . . .	48	1	44	92	16	108	136	17	153
1883, . . .	42	6	47	100	23	123	142	28	170
1884, . . .	54	9	63	79	23	102	133	32	165
1885, . . .	47	6	53	84	18	102	131	23	154
1886, . . .	47	9	56	80	23	107	127	34	161
1887, . . .	35	9	44	81	10	91	116	19	135
1888, . . .	34	4	38	77	23	100	111	27	138
1889, . . .	33	1	34	89	25	114	123	26	148
1890, . . .	33	2	35	91	17	108	124	19	143
Total, . .	359	68	427	877	192	1,069	1,236	260	1,496

From this statement it would appear that during the decade under consideration there were 427 deaths from "delirium tremens," and 1,069 from conditions directly caused by alcoholic excess, making a total of 1,496 deaths directly due to alcohol. Comparing the numbers specified from year to year, it would appear there is but little variation. If the numbers are compared with those for the previous decade 1871–80, they do not present any appreciable variations as to their relation to the population, the average annual ratio per million of the mean population being 30·4 in the first and 30·3 in the last decade. So far as the figures go, while they do not point to any advance in temperance, they do not show that intemperance has increased. Compared with the previous decade it would appear that "delirium tremens" as a cause of death among men has considerably diminished, while among women it has very slightly increased. In the case of other forms of deaths directly resulting from intemperance the mortality among men has slightly increased, while among women it has diminished.

CAUSES OF

The following TABLE (XVI.) shows (1) the Number of Deaths from All Causes and from
and (2) the respective Rates per 100,000 of the

YEARS	Total Number of Deaths.	CAUSES OF DEATH. [illegible]	[illegible]	[illegible]	[illegible]	[illegible]	[illegible]	[illegible]	[illegible]	[illegible]	[illegible]	[illegible]	[illegible]
(1.) NUMBER													
[illegible]	[illegible]	—	[illegible]	[illegible]	[illegible]	[illegible]	[illegible]	[illegible]	[illegible]	[illegible]	[illegible]	[illegible]	[illegible]
[illegible]	[illegible]	—	[illegible]	[illegible]	[illegible]	[illegible]	[illegible]	[illegible]	[illegible]	[illegible]	[illegible]	[illegible]	[illegible]
[illegible]	[illegible]	3	[illegible]	[illegible]	[illegible]	[illegible]	[illegible]	[illegible]	[illegible]	[illegible]	[illegible]	[illegible]	[illegible]
[illegible]	[illegible]	[illegible]	[illegible]	[illegible]	[illegible]	[illegible]	[illegible]	[illegible]	[illegible]	[illegible]	[illegible]	[illegible]	[illegible]
[illegible]	[illegible]	[illegible]	[illegible]	[illegible]	[illegible]	[illegible]	[illegible]	[illegible]	[illegible]	[illegible]	[illegible]	[illegible]	[illegible]
[illegible]	[illegible]	[illegible]	[illegible]	[illegible]	[illegible]	[illegible]	[illegible]	[illegible]	[illegible]	[illegible]	[illegible]	[illegible]	[illegible]
[illegible]	[illegible]	[illegible]	[illegible]	1,077	[illegible]	[illegible]	[illegible]	[illegible]	[illegible]	[illegible]	[illegible]	[illegible]	[illegible]
[illegible]	[illegible]	[illegible]	[illegible]	[illegible]	[illegible]	[illegible]	[illegible]	[illegible]	[illegible]	[illegible]	[illegible]	[illegible]	[illegible]
[illegible]	[illegible]	[illegible]	[illegible]	[illegible]	[illegible]	[illegible]	[illegible]	[illegible]	[illegible]	[illegible]	[illegible]	[illegible]	[illegible]
[illegible]	[illegible]	[illegible]	[illegible]	[illegible]	[illegible]	[illegible]	[illegible]	[illegible]	[illegible]	[illegible]	[illegible]	[illegible]	[illegible]
(2.) RATES PER 100,000 OF													
[illegible]	[illegible]	—	[illegible]	[illegible]	[illegible]	[illegible]	[illegible]	[illegible]	[illegible]	[illegible]	[illegible]	[illegible]	[illegible]
[illegible]	[illegible]	—	[illegible]	[illegible]	[illegible]	[illegible]	[illegible]	[illegible]	[illegible]	[illegible]	[illegible]	[illegible]	[illegible]
[illegible]	[illegible]	[illegible]	[illegible]	[illegible]	[illegible]	[illegible]	[illegible]	[illegible]	[illegible]	[illegible]	[illegible]	[illegible]	[illegible]
[illegible]	[illegible]	[illegible]	[illegible]	[illegible]	[illegible]	[illegible]	[illegible]	[illegible]	[illegible]	[illegible]	[illegible]	[illegible]	[illegible]
[illegible]	[illegible]	—	[illegible]	[illegible]	[illegible]	[illegible]	[illegible]	[illegible]	[illegible]	[illegible]	[illegible]	[illegible]	[illegible]
[illegible]	[illegible]	[illegible]	[illegible]	[illegible]	[illegible]	[illegible]	[illegible]	[illegible]	[illegible]	[illegible]	[illegible]	[illegible]	[illegible]
[illegible]	[illegible]	—	[illegible]	[illegible]	[illegible]	[illegible]	[illegible]	[illegible]	[illegible]	[illegible]	[illegible]	[illegible]	[illegible]
[illegible]	[illegible]	[illegible]	[illegible]	[illegible]	[illegible]	[illegible]	[illegible]	[illegible]	[illegible]	[illegible]	[illegible]	[illegible]	[illegible]
[illegible]	[illegible]	[illegible]	[illegible]	[illegible]	[illegible]	[illegible]	[illegible]	[illegible]	[illegible]	[illegible]	[illegible]	[illegible]	[illegible]
[illegible]	[illegible]	[illegible]	[illegible]	[illegible]	[illegible]	[illegible]	[illegible]	[illegible]	[illegible]	[illegible]	[illegible]	[illegible]	[illegible]

II.—CONSTITUTIONAL DISEASES.

This class of diseases is not now, as formerly, divided into orders, but constitutes a group without regular sub-classification of the various specific forms of disease which it includes—viz., rheumatism, rheumatic fever, and rheumatic carditis, gout, rickets, cancer, tabes mesenterica, tubercular diseases (which may be taken to include tubercular meningitis or acute hydrocephalus), phthisis or pulmonary consumption with other forms of tuberculosis and scrofula, purpura and hæmorrhagic diathesis, anæmia, chlorosis and leucocythæmia, diabetes mellitus, and some other constitutional diseases. Dropsy was formerly specified under this class; but dropsy, being a consequence of other forms of disease, has now been omitted, and would take its place, according to circumstances, under the head of the disease which caused it, such as disease of the heart, liver, or kidney.

Cancer caused 20,036 deaths (8,964 males and 11,072 females) during the decade, being 2·28 per cent. of the total deaths, and equal to an average annual rate of 4·1 per 10,000 of the mean population for the period. During the previous decade

DEATH.

each of the Principal Causes registered in Ireland during each of the ten years 1881–90, estimated Population represented by these numbers.

Constitutional Diseases: Cancer	Tabes mesenterica	Tubercular Meningitis	Phthisis	Other Constitutional Diseases	Local Diseases: Nervous System	Circulatory System	Respiratory System	Digestive System	Urinary System	Parturition	Other Local Diseases	Violence: Accidental	Homicidal	Suicidal	Execution	[illegible] causes
OF DEATHS																
[illegible]	[illegible]	[illegible]	[illegible]	[illegible]	[illegible]	[illegible]	[illegible]	[illegible]	[illegible]	[illegible]	[illegible]	[illegible]	[illegible]	[illegible]	—	[illegible]
[illegible]	[illegible]	[illegible]	[illegible]	[illegible]	[illegible]	[illegible]	[illegible]	[illegible]	[illegible]	[illegible]	[illegible]	[illegible]	[illegible]	[illegible]	[illegible]	[illegible]
[illegible]	[illegible]	[illegible]	[illegible]	[illegible]	[illegible]	[illegible]	[illegible]	[illegible]	[illegible]	[illegible]	[illegible]	[illegible]	[illegible]	[illegible]	[illegible]	[illegible]
[illegible]	[illegible]	[illegible]	[illegible]	[illegible]	[illegible]	[illegible]	[illegible]	[illegible]	[illegible]	[illegible]	[illegible]	[illegible]	[illegible]	[illegible]	—	[illegible]
[illegible]	[illegible]	[illegible]	[illegible]	[illegible]	[illegible]	[illegible]	[illegible]	[illegible]	[illegible]	[illegible]	[illegible]	[illegible]	[illegible]	[illegible]	[illegible]	[illegible]
[illegible]	[illegible]	[illegible]	[illegible]	[illegible]	[illegible]	[illegible]	[illegible]	[illegible]	[illegible]	[illegible]	[illegible]	[illegible]	[illegible]	[illegible]	[illegible]	[illegible]
[illegible]	[illegible]	[illegible]	[illegible]	[illegible]	[illegible]	[illegible]	[illegible]	[illegible]	[illegible]	[illegible]	[illegible]	[illegible]	[illegible]	[illegible]	[illegible]	[illegible]
[illegible]	[illegible]	[illegible]	[illegible]	[illegible]	[illegible]	[illegible]	[illegible]	[illegible]	[illegible]	[illegible]	[illegible]	[illegible]	[illegible]	[illegible]	[illegible]	[illegible]
[illegible]	[illegible]	[illegible]	[illegible]	[illegible]	[illegible]	[illegible]	[illegible]	[illegible]	[illegible]	[illegible]	[illegible]	[illegible]	[illegible]	[illegible]	[illegible]	[illegible]
[illegible]	[illegible]	[illegible]	[illegible]	[illegible]	[illegible]	[illegible]	[illegible]	[illegible]	[illegible]	[illegible]	[illegible]	[illegible]	[illegible]	[illegible]	—	[illegible]
THE ESTIMATED POPULATION																
[illegible]	[illegible]	[illegible]	[illegible]	[illegible]	[illegible]	[illegible]	[illegible]	[illegible]	[illegible]	[illegible]	[illegible]	[illegible]	[illegible]	[illegible]	—	[illegible]
[illegible]	[illegible]	[illegible]	[illegible]	[illegible]	[illegible]	[illegible]	[illegible]	[illegible]	[illegible]	[illegible]	[illegible]	[illegible]	[illegible]	[illegible]	[illegible]	[illegible]
[illegible]	[illegible]	[illegible]	[illegible]	[illegible]	[illegible]	[illegible]	[illegible]	[illegible]	[illegible]	[illegible]	[illegible]	[illegible]	[illegible]	[illegible]	[illegible]	[illegible]
[illegible]	[illegible]	[illegible]	[illegible]	[illegible]	[illegible]	[illegible]	[illegible]	[illegible]	[illegible]	[illegible]	[illegible]	[illegible]	[illegible]	[illegible]	—	[illegible]
[illegible]	[illegible]	[illegible]	[illegible]	[illegible]	[illegible]	[illegible]	[illegible]	[illegible]	[illegible]	[illegible]	[illegible]	[illegible]	[illegible]	[illegible]	—	[illegible]
[illegible]	[illegible]	[illegible]	[illegible]	[illegible]	[illegible]	[illegible]	[illegible]	[illegible]	[illegible]	[illegible]	[illegible]	[illegible]	[illegible]	[illegible]	—	[illegible]
[illegible]	[illegible]	[illegible]	[illegible]	[illegible]	[illegible]	[illegible]	[illegible]	[illegible]	[illegible]	[illegible]	[illegible]	[illegible]	[illegible]	[illegible]	—	[illegible]
[illegible]	[illegible]	[illegible]	[illegible]	[illegible]	[illegible]	[illegible]	[illegible]	[illegible]	[illegible]	[illegible]	[illegible]	[illegible]	[illegible]	[illegible]	[illegible]	[illegible]
[illegible]	[illegible]	[illegible]	[illegible]	[illegible]	[illegible]	[illegible]	[illegible]	[illegible]	[illegible]	[illegible]	[illegible]	[illegible]	[illegible]	[illegible]	[illegible]	[illegible]
[illegible]	[illegible]	[illegible]	[illegible]	[illegible]	[illegible]	[illegible]	[illegible]	[illegible]	[illegible]	[illegible]	[illegible]	[illegible]	[illegible]	[illegible]	—	[illegible]

the corresponding statistics were:—total number of deaths, 17,190 (7,739 males and 10,05[illegible] females); percentage of total deaths, 1·84, and the death-rate per 10,000 3·4. The increasing death-rate from cancer has been noticed for many years, and has been steadily progressive, not only in Ireland, but also in the other divisions of the United Kingdom. The numbers given above shew that although the population declined the deaths from cancer increased by 2,246 in the later as compared with the earlier decade, or at the rate of 12·6 per cent. The deaths among males increased by 1,175, or at the rate of 15·1 per cent., and among females to the extent of 1,071, or at the rate of 10·7 per cent. Thus the greater portion of the increase was among men, or in the sex which hitherto has been considered to be the less liable to cancer. Still the number of deaths from cancer among females is greater than among men. The greater preponderance of deaths among females seems due to the special liability of the uterus and breasts to be attacked by malignant disease.

Malignant disease is extremely rare among the young; thus there were only 37 deaths from cancer recorded among children under 5 years of age, 18 being males and 19 females. The Abstracts show that in middle life deaths from malignant disease are found to constitute a large proportion of the deaths from all causes.

PHTHISIS.

Phthisis or pulmonary consumption, or as it is popularly termed "consumption" or "decline," is the cause of more deaths in Ireland than any other single disease, and therefore should be of more interest to the physician and sanitarian than any other malady. The disease is well known to have hereditary tendencies, and is also generally, though not universally, admitted to be infective. There are considerable difficulties encountered in dealing accurately with the statistics of deaths from phthisis as many persons affected by phthisis have their lives terminated by other forms of disease, especially of pulmonary disease. Thus phthisical people, whose lungs may not at the time be extensively injured by tubercular disease, are frequently attacked by acute lung affections, such as bronchitis or pneumonia, which, acting on already unhealthy lungs, prove rapidly fatal. Such cases have the cause of death frequently certified as due to the acute disease only, although had the more chronic tuberculosis been absent the patient might have recovered. Such cases are no doubt numerous, but they tend to increase, not to diminish, the importance of tuberculosis of the lungs as a cause of death. It is clear from the foregoing considerations that phthisis and other forms of disease of the respiratory organs are so intimately mingled in the statistics of the cause of death, that it is desirable to treat them collectively when discussing this subject.

The deaths from diseases of the respiratory organs numbered 153,279 (79,591 males and 73,688 females) during the decade. Phthisis caused 103,314 (47,850 males and 55,464 females); taken collectively 256,593 deaths were attributed to these diseases, or 29·1 per cent. of the total deaths recorded in Ireland, and at the average annual rate of 51·9 per 10,000 of the mean population. Owing to an alteration in the classification, croup which was formerly included in the "miasmatic" order of diseases is now classed among the diseases of the respiratory system, and as the deaths from croup in the decade 1871–80 numbered 14,256, the deaths from diseases of the respiratory system as given in the Report for that period must, for purposes of comparison, be increased by that number, making a total of 260,775. These figures show that there was an absolute decrease of deaths from phthisis and diseases of the respiratory system combined in 1881–90, as compared with the previous decade to the extent of 4,182, but the average annual rate in proportion to the mean population rose from 49·3 per 10,000 to 51·9, and the percentage, as compared with deaths from all causes, from 27·0 to 29·1. If, however, the details are looked into it will be found that the deaths from phthisis diminished by a very little—namely, from 103,528 to 103,314. It is remarkable that this decrease occurred altogether among the male sex, in which the number decreased from 49,438 to 47,850, while the deaths among females actually increased from 54,090 to 55,464. In the deaths from diseases of the respiratory organs, exclusive of phthisis, the decrease among males was double that among females. It is very unsatisfactory to find that the death-rate from phthisis has risen from 19·6 to 20·9 per 10,000 of the mean population, and that in other diseases of the respiratory organs the rate has risen from 29·7 to 31·0.

TABLE XVII.—MORTALITY from PHTHISIS and from DISEASES of the RESPIRATORY SYSTEM in the Northern, Eastern, Southern, and Western LITTORAL POOR LAW UNIONS or SUPERINTENDENT REGISTRARS' DISTRICTS of IRELAND during the Ten Years 1881-90, distinguishing the Mortality in those Unions containing TOWNS which, in 1881 or in 1891, had 10,000 inhabitants, with like details for all INLAND UNIONS and for all LITTORAL UNIONS and INLAND UNIONS combined.

Poor Law Unions or Superintendent Registrars' Districts.		Mean Population [illegible]	Mortality from Phthisis.		Mortality from Diseases of the Respiratory System.		Total Mortality from Phthisis and Diseases of the Respiratory System.	
			No. of Deaths in the 10 years 1881-90.	Average Annual Rate per 10,000 Living.	No. of Deaths in the 10 years 1881-90.	Average Annual Rate per 10,000 Living.	No. of Deaths in the 10 years 1881-90.	Average Annual Rate per 10,000 Living.
Littoral Unions with Towns of 10,000 Inhabitants.	Northern Group,	[illegible]	[illegible]	[illegible]	[illegible]	[illegible]	[illegible]	[illegible]
	Eastern "	[illegible]	[illegible]	[illegible]	[illegible]	[illegible]	[illegible]	[illegible]
	Southern "	[illegible]	[illegible]	[illegible]	[illegible]	[illegible]	[illegible]	[illegible]
	Western "	[illegible]	[illegible]	[illegible]	[illegible]	[illegible]	[illegible]	[illegible]
	Total,	[illegible]	[illegible]	[illegible]	[illegible]	[illegible]	[illegible]	[illegible]
Other Littoral Unions.	Northern Group,	[illegible]	[illegible]	[illegible]	[illegible]	[illegible]	[illegible]	[illegible]
	Eastern "	[illegible]	[illegible]	[illegible]	[illegible]	[illegible]	[illegible]	[illegible]
	Southern "	[illegible]	[illegible]	[illegible]	[illegible]	[illegible]	[illegible]	[illegible]
	Western "	[illegible]	[illegible]	[illegible]	[illegible]	[illegible]	[illegible]	[illegible]
	Total,	[illegible]	[illegible]	[illegible]	[illegible]	[illegible]	[illegible]	[illegible]
All Littoral Unions.	Northern Group,	[illegible]	[illegible]	[illegible]	[illegible]	[illegible]	[illegible]	[illegible]
	Eastern "	[illegible]	[illegible]	[illegible]	[illegible]	[illegible]	[illegible]	[illegible]
	Southern "	[illegible]	[illegible]	[illegible]	[illegible]	[illegible]	[illegible]	[illegible]
	Western "	[illegible]	[illegible]	[illegible]	[illegible]	[illegible]	[illegible]	[illegible]
	Total,	[illegible]	[illegible]	[illegible]	[illegible]	[illegible]	[illegible]	[illegible]
SUMMARY for IRELAND—LITTORAL UNIONS and INLAND UNIONS								
Unions with Towns of 10,000 Inhabitants.	Littoral Unions,	[illegible]	[illegible]	[illegible]	[illegible]	[illegible]	[illegible]	[illegible]
	Inland Unions,	[illegible]	[illegible]	[illegible]	[illegible]	[illegible]	[illegible]	[illegible]
	Total,	[illegible]	[illegible]	[illegible]	[illegible]	[illegible]	[illegible]	[illegible]
Other Unions,	Littoral Unions,	[illegible]	[illegible]	[illegible]	[illegible]	[illegible]	[illegible]	[illegible]
	Inland Unions,	[illegible]	[illegible]	[illegible]	[illegible]	[illegible]	[illegible]	[illegible]
	Total,	[illegible]	[illegible]	[illegible]	[illegible]	[illegible]	[illegible]	[illegible]
Total,	Littoral Unions,	[illegible]	[illegible]	[illegible]	[illegible]	[illegible]	[illegible]	[illegible]
	Inland Unions,	[illegible]	[illegible]	[illegible]	[illegible]	[illegible]	[illegible]	[illegible]
	All Ireland,	[illegible]	[illegible]	[illegible]	[illegible]	[illegible]	[illegible]	[illegible]

Following the plan adopted in dealing with the geographical distribution of disease in Ireland, the Superintendent Registrars' districts have been classified into rural and civic—see Tables X. and XI. From these Tables it will be seen that the rate of mortality per 10,000 from phthisis in the civic Unions is 29·5, while in rural districts it is but 17·4. Comparing them with the corresponding rates for the previous decade, it will be found that the rates have increased almost equally in both country and town districts. It would also appear from an examination of these Tables, as also from the Abstract, that the increase of phthisis has been nearly equally distributed throughout the country, as have also the diseases of the respiratory organs other than phthisis.

Supplement to the Twenty-seventh Report of the Registrar-General disease or rather tubercular disease affecting three portions of the body caused 128,388 deaths or 14·0 per cent. of the total mortality of Ireland for the decade. By far the most destructive of the three was phthisis or pulmonary consumption, the deaths from which constitute 11·7 per cent. of the mortality for the decade.

Of the 10,096 cases of tabes mesenterica 8,236 (4,135 males and 4,101 females), or about four-fifths, were in young children under five years of age, hence the popular name "Infantile decay."

Of the 9,536 deaths from Tubercular Meningitis 5,598, or more than one-half were also in children under five years of age; it is remarkable that deaths among young boys (under five) numbered 3,244, while among girls the mortality only amounted to 2,354, or about one-third less. We have here two forms of tubercular disease among the most destructive diseases of childhood.

III.—LOCAL DISEASES.

LOCAL DISEASES caused 362,255 deaths during the decade, being 41·0 per cent., or more than two-fifths of the total deaths, as compared with 331,744 in the previous decade. These diseases are divided into ten orders, which caused deaths as follows:—Diseases of the nervous system, 83,514; of the organs of special sense, 494; of the organs of circulation, 50,800; of the respiratory organs, 150,279; of the digestive organs, 36,770; of the lymphatic system and ductless glands, 458; of the urinary organs, 13,158; of the reproductive system (organs of generation, 1,713; of child-birth, 4,877); of the organs of locomotion, 3,684; and of the integumentary system, 2,565.

Diseases of the Nervous System caused 83,514 deaths during the decade. Of these 44,772, or 53·6 per cent., were males, and 38,742, or 46·4 per cent., females, showing a great preponderance of the former over the latter. During the previous decade the numbers were males, 47,308; females, 36,190; total 83,498; the proportion being 57 males to 43 females. A reference to the Abstract (pp. 90–1), shows that the order entitled diseases of the nervous system includes several affections which are altogether diseases of the brain, such as cephalitis, apoplexy, and insanity, and several others, which are *generally* owing to diseases of the brain, such as paralysis, and, again, others which may be secondary affections resulting from other diseases or irritations, such as convulsions in children, chorea, and epilepsy. As the deaths ascribed to convulsions constitute the great bulk of this group, a fair idea of the prevalence of brain disease may be obtained by deducting convulsions from the total and leaving the balance to represent the proportion of deaths from brain disease.

The following statement has been drawn up upon this principle, and represents generally the number of deaths from brain disease and convulsions for each year during the decade 1881–90.

TABLE XVIII.—DEATHS from "CONVULSIONS," and Total Number of DEATHS from all "DISEASES of the NERVOUS SYSTEM," in Ireland in each of the Ten Years, 1881–90.

YEAR.	Deaths from Convulsions.			Deaths from all "Diseases of the Nervous System."			"Diseases of the Nervous System," exclusive of Convulsions.		
	Males.	Females.	Total.	Males.	Females.	Total.	Males.	Females.	Total.
	1.	2.	3.	4.	5.	6.	7.	8.	9.
1881, . .	1,784	1,460	3,244	4,684	3,819	8,503	2,900	2,359	5,259
1882, . .	1,768	1,479	3,247	4,412	3,898	8,310	2,644	2,419	5,063
1883, . .	1,823	1,417	3,240	4,654	3,955	8,609	2,831	2,538	5,369
1884, . .	1,691	1,286	2,977	4,490	3,721	8,211	2,799	2,435	5,234
1885, . .	1,692	1,417	3,109	4,614	4,039	8,653	2,922	2,622	5,544
1886, . .	1,775	1,416	3,191	4,690	4,036	8,726	2,915	2,620	5,535
1887, . .	1,737	1,420	3,157	4,601	3,969	8,570	2,864	2,549	5,413
1888, . .	1,623	1,283	2,906	4,416	3,860	8,276	2,793	2,578	5,368
1889, . .	1,654	1,370	2,838	4,306	3,813	8,018	2,660	2,512	5,192
1890, . .	1,615	1,166	2,781	4,007	3,621	7,628	2,392	2,455	5,047
	16,846	13,644	30,490	44,772	38,742	83,514	27,926	25,098	53,024

In columns 1, 2, and 3 of the Table the number of deaths from convulsions is given, by which it is seen that deaths ascribed to this cause have shown a decided

is still
The t
or an

were males and 24,899 females. If these cases are analysed it is found that 6,391 were ascribed to endocarditis (valvular disease) 470 to pericarditis (or inflammation of the heart's covering), 459 to angina pectoris, 1,779 to syncope, 804 to aneurism, 1,236 to senile gangrene, and 38,647, or at the annual rate of 8·0 per 10,000, to other forms of heart disease. A reference to the Abstract (pages 90 and 91), will show that but few of these deaths occurred in childhood or early adult life, and that the liability to death from heart disease steadily increases as life advances. Many of those cases which occur in middle life have had their origin in the cardiac complications of acute rheumatism or rheumatic fever. At the more advanced ages diseases of the heart arise as secondary complications of diseases of the respiratory organs, and also in consequence of the natural decay which the heart shares in common with the other organs of the body. The deaths from aneurism, were 804, of which 588 or 73·1 per cent. were males and 216 or 26·9 per cent. females, the proportion of male to female deaths being much greater in this (the only fatal disease of arteries) than in diseases of the heart. This difference is attributable to several causes, which, however, it would be out of place here to discuss.

Diseases of the Respiratory Organs caused 153,379 (79,531 males and 73,848 females) deaths during the decade or at the annual rate of 31·0 per 10,000 of the mean population as compared with 142,981, exclusive of those from croup which numbered 14,256 (74,534 males and 68,447 females), or at the rate of 27·0 per 10,000 for the previous decade. The relations between diseases of the respiratory organs and consumption have already been discussed under the head of consumption and in the same place the distribution of these deaths among town and country districts and the aspect of the localities in which they occurred have been dealt with.

In the Abstracts the diseases of the respiratory organs have been grouped under eight heads to which are ascribed the number of deaths stated after each, namely, laryngitis, 1,189; croup, 8,635 (formerly classified under zymotic (symotic) diseases); other diseases of the larynx and trachea, 30; bronchitis, 101,811; pleurisy, 2,364; pneumonia, 27,570; asthma, 2,281, lung disease unspecified, &c., 7,353.

Table XVI. shows that the rate of mortality from diseases of the respiratory organs was much greater in some years than in others.

As has already been pointed out the deaths from croup were included under the head zymotic diseases for the decade 1871–80, and are now classified with diseases of the respiratory organs. If the 14,256 deaths from croup registered during the decade 1871–80 were added to the other deaths then classified as diseases of the respiratory organs, the total would be 157,237, which exceeds the total for the later decade by 3,858 deaths from this group of causes, thus showing a decrease instead of an increase in deaths from diseases of the respiratory organs in the later as compared with the earlier decade, but still leaving the rate for the former at 29·7 per 10,000, as compared with 31·0 for the latter. The increase in mortality from pneumonia or inflammation of the lungs appears to be the most remarkable feature in this group of statistics: inflammation of the lungs caused 27,570 deaths as compared with 19,712, or an increase of 7,858, which alone would account for the whole increase in the death rate from diseases of the respiratory organs. There has been a decided decrease in the number of deaths from asthma and bronchitis, and, as already shown, a decrease in croup; the number of deaths from other forms of disease of the respiratory organs remains much the same. As diseases of the respiratory organs (and phthisis) constitute a large proportion of the total deaths, it frequently arises that a high death-rate for a particular year is also accompanied by a high rate of mortality from this group of diseases. Thus the year 1883 had the highest death-rate of the decade, 19·9 (Table XIX.), and we find in that year the deaths from diseases of the respiratory organs were the second highest of the decade, and numbered 16,467. Again in 1886 the second highest death-rate, 18·4, was reached, and in it we find the third highest number of deaths from diseases of the respiratory organs, namely, 16,003; however, in 1881, when the annual death-rate was only 17·9 the deaths from diseases of the respiratory organs numbered 16,936, being the highest during the ten years. And, again, the lowest death-rate but one during the period was in the year 1884 when the rate was 17·6 (the lowest being 17·3 in 1888), and in this year the deaths from diseases of the respiratory organs numbered only 13,545.

The average number of deaths per annum from these causes during the decade was 15,338. In 1881 the number reached 16,936, being 1,598 or 10·4 per cent. above the average, while in 1889 the number only reached 13,545, which is 1,793 below the average, the variation between the highest and lowest being 3,391, or 25 per cent. of the latter. Table XIX. shows the maximum, minimum, and mean temperature of the air, and the yearly rainfall in Dublin, compared with the total death-rate in Ireland, for each of the several years during the decade, and in Table XX. is shown the mean temperature for each month during the decade, for reference in connexion with the same subject.

It will be observed by reference to Table XVI. that in 1881 the deaths from diseases of the respiratory organs registered were more numerous than in any of the other years of the decade. Column 3, of Table XIX., shows that the minimum temperature of the air was lower in that than in any other year during the decade except the following year, 1882, and also that the mean temperature of the year was below the average.

It is well known that a sudden fall of temperature or a long continued low temperature is especially productive of diseases of the respiratory organs, and causes these affections to be particularly fatal to the very young and the very old.

TABLE XIX.—EXTREME TEMPERATURE of the AIR, and MEAN TEMPERATURE deduced from them, and Rainfall in the City of DUBLIN for the Ten years 1881–90, with the DEATH-RATE in IRELAND for each of those years.

YEAR.	THERMOMETER.			TOTAL RAINFALL.	DEATH-RATE per 1,000.
	Maximum.	Minimum.	Mean.		
(1)	° (2)	° (3)	° (4)	Inches. (5)	(6)
1881,	78·6	15·3	48·4	27·038	17·9
1882,	77·1	[illegible]	48·4	31·184	17·2
1883,	71·6	25·4	47·8	29·901	17·8
1884,	75·4	27·3	50·9	20·467	17·6
1885,	77·0	21·3	48·0	28·614	18·6
1886,	72·7	20·0	46·4	33·996	17·4
1887,	79·8	23·1	49·0	16·201	18·2
1888,	72·4	24·0	49·3	28·679	17·9
1889,	77·8	21·7	49·3	27·373	17·4
1890,	74·7	24·4	49·6	31·641	18·1
AVERAGE OF TEN YEARS,	° 75·4	° 23·1	° 48·8	Inches. 28·473	17·9

TABLE XX.—MEAN TEMPERATURE of the AIR in DUBLIN, deduced from the readings of the MAXIMUM and MINIMUM THERMOMETERS in the Years 1881–90, and Average for the Ten Years.

tory system—pure and simple—but also in the case of respiratory complications of other forms of disease, especially zymotic diseases, that this severe effect of cold weather is demonstrated. As already pointed out, bronchitis, is by far the most destructive of the diseases of the respiratory system, and it, too, is the most common form of pulmonary complication of other acute diseases, and it is the one above all others, promoted by sudden depression of temperature, or by long-continued cold weather.

Diseases of the Digestive Organs caused 46,776 deaths (24,404 males and 22,372 females), being equal to an annual rate of 9·5 per 10,000 of the mean population. This group includes a large number of diseases, but, unfortunately for statistical purposes, the returns are not of as definite a character as could be desired. Many cases are uncertified, and in many others the medical certificates are, from several reasons, necessarily of an indefinite character. Many of the diseases are of a sub-acute or chronic nature and the medical attendant finds a history difficult to obtain. In other cases the exact nature of the affection is so obscure that without a *post-mortem* examination the medical attendant finds it impossible to certify in more than general terms. It therefore follows that comparatively little advantage would be obtained by a lengthy analysis of the causes of death in this group. Of the 46,776 deaths from diseases of the digestive organs, 3,052 were ascribed to dentition, 7,729 to diseases of stomach, 4,616 to enteritis or inflammation of the bowels, 3,819 to peritonitis, or inflammation of the membrane covering the bowels and other abdominal organs, 1,380 to ascites or dropsy of the abdomen (belly), 2,350 to ulceration of the intestines (bowels), 1,175 to hernia or "rupture," 4,086 to ileus, 509 to intussusception, 510 to stricture of the intestines, 96 to fistula, 2,918 to cirrhosis of liver, and 10,099 to various other forms of disease of the liver. It is right here to point out that several of these diseases are closely associated with one another. Thus, there are deaths ascribed to enteritis, ulceration of the intestines, and peritonitis, making in all 10,785 deaths; generally speaking, ulceration of the intestines is preceded by enteritis, and in a great number of cases peritonitis is the result of ulceration of the intestines, so that we have enteritis followed by ulceration, followed by peritonitis, and the enteritis itself in many cases was owing to enteric fever, or some closely allied cause, in which medical advice had not been obtained in sufficient time to enable the case to be properly dealt with by the physician. It is highly probable that a large number of these 10,785 deaths were the result of neglected enteric fever. Again, there are 1,380 deaths ascribed to ascites or dropsy of the abdomen, which form of dropsy is generally caused by disease of the liver. The various forms of liver disease contribute 13,770 deaths or 29·4 per cent. of all deaths from diseases of the organs connected with the promotion of digestion. Again, there are 7,729 deaths ascribed to diseases of stomach, which is equal to 16·5 per cent. of the total deaths in this order of disease. The other deaths from diseases of the digestive organs do not appear to call for particular comment. Many of the deaths in this order are, no doubt, owing to local development of constitutional disease, such as scrofula, tuberculosis, or cancer, and many, especially among those from "diseases of stomach," and some forms of liver disease, are no doubt due to chronic alcoholism.

Diseases of the Urinary Organs caused 15,156 deaths; of these 10,769 or 71·1 per cent. were males and 4,387 females. These deaths comprise 1,472 from nephritis or inflammation of the kidneys, 5,310 from Bright's disease, which may be considered as chronic forms of kidney disease; 164 from calculus or stone in the bladder. There are also 4,320 deaths from diseases of bladder and of prostate, and 3,796 from "other diseases of the urinary system"; the great bulk of the latter are due to various forms of Bright's disease, of which there are many.

When these various forms of disease are considered with reference to sexes: we find that the number of deaths of males exceeds that of females in every case, and that this preponderance is in a measure due to intemperance as a fruitful cause of kidney disease, and, therefore, this disease is more likely to affect men than women. Owing to the alteration in the classification of deaths the various forms of diseases of this class cannot be compared with the preceding decade to any considerable extent. The Abstract (pages 92 and 93), shows that all forms of disease of the urinary organs are comparatively rare in early life and increase considerably after the age of 20.

Diseases of the Organs of Generation caused 1,712 deaths, of which 1,654 were females and only 58 males: these deaths are nearly all attributable to diseases of the uterus and ovaries of females in advanced life and do not call for special remarks.

Diseases of the Organs of Locomotion caused 2,884 deaths during the decade: many of them were due either to diseases established as the result of accidents or to local

Diseases of the Integumentary System are seldom fatal and when so are of a rare and unusual character, and scarcely call for any remark in this place; 2,505 deaths were ascribed to these diseases.

IV.—DEVELOPMENTAL DISEASES.

This class caused 181,498 deaths (82,466 males and 98,952 females), or 20·5 per cent. of the entire number of deaths.

In the preceding decade, deaths from teething and childbirth were included in this class; the former is now known as dentition, and belongs to the digestive order, and childbirth to the reproductive system, the latter having been already sufficiently discussed in connection with the subject of puerperal fever. But in both decades we can contrast the deaths from premature birth and old age. In the ten years, 1871-80 there resulted 2,802 fatal cases from premature birth, and in 1881–90 the number was 3,801, or 999 of an increase. To what cause this increase is due it is impossible to say, but probably, and this applies to both decades, many cases of premature birth might have been avoided if the mothers had been living under healthy circumstances, or had been free from disease or accident.

To the natural decay of old age, there were attributed 177,225 deaths (80,185 males and 97,040 females); in the earlier decade, the males and females together amounted to 206,349. Many of the deaths assigned to old age might, no doubt, have been more accurately described, but at such advanced ages as the great bulk of these persons were at the time of death, illnesses which at earlier ages would be insignificant, readily prove fatal. Atrophy and debility formed an order of developmental disease in the previous decade, and caused 50,738 deaths, but are now included in the class of "ill-defined and not specified causes," and described as "debility," "atrophy," "inanition." The deaths from them amount to 53,988 (26,251 males and 27,737 females), a large proportion (56·2 per cent.) being of children under one year old.

V.—DEATHS FROM VIOLENCE.

Deaths from violence do not form an important class in a country like Ireland, where manufacturing industry constitutes but a small portion of the occupation of the people, and where mining operations are carried on to but a limited extent.

The deaths from violence numbered 18,883 during the decade, or at the average annual rate of 3·9 per 10,000 of the mean population. As might be anticipated, the death-rate from violence is higher, namely, 5·2 per 10,000, in town than it is in country districts, where it reaches a rate of 3·3 only. It is, however, a remarkable fact that the deaths from violence do not bear as high a proportion to the population in the great manufacturing town of Belfast, where the rate is 5·0, as in the Dublin districts, where the rates are 7·2 and 6·2 for north and south respectively, or in Cork, where the rate is 5·3. In the smaller towns the numbers are not sufficiently large to enable us to draw conclusions, for in these any single catastrophe causing the loss of several lives might seriously raise the death-rate from violence. The general distribution of violent deaths throughout Ireland does not call for any special remark.

The following statement shows the distribution of the various order of deaths from violence between the sexes:—

	Males.	Females.	Total.
Accident or Negligence,	11,543	5,133	16,676
Homicide,	729	431	1,160
Suicide,	832	294	1,126
Execution,	32	—	32
Total,	13,136	5,846	18,883

From this it appears that the deaths from violence among males were more than double the number among females, the former being equal to 69·2 per cent., and the latter equal to 30·8 per cent. of the total deaths from violence. This excess of male over female deaths exists throughout all the four orders of this class. If, however, the deaths in each sex are compared at different ages, as shown in the Abstract (pages 94 and 95), it will be observed that among children the excess of male over female deaths from violence is not great, whereas at the more active periods of life it is much greater than the proportion shown in the above statement. Thus, in children under one year of age, there were among the males 686 deaths from accident or negligence, and among the females 511. Under five years there were from the same cause 2,112 deaths among males, and 1,609 among females, making a total of 3,721 deaths from accident or negligence among young children. It may be pretty confidently stated that nearly all these deaths may be more correctly ascribed to negligence than to accident, as will be pointed out further on, with special reference to the question of burns and scalds. During the more active periods of life, when exposure to accident is greatest, the number of deaths in males is 8,179, and in females only 1,847 or about one-fourth. If the modes of death by violence are more closely analysed it will be found that the three principal causes were fractures and contusions, burns or scalds, and drowning.

Fractures and contusions caused 6,755 deaths, of which 5,055 were males and 1,700 females. The great bulk of these occurred in middle or advanced life, comparatively few being among young children. It is remarkable the increasing mortality from this cause at such advanced ages. This is not that old persons are more liable to accidents, but that when accidents do occur to old people they are much more likely to be followed by fatal results.

The very large number of deaths from burns (including scalds) is remarkable: these constitute 3,709 (1,729 males and 1,980 females), or 19·5 per cent. of all the deaths from violence. The most prominent feature in this large mortality from burning is that of these 3,709 deaths, no less than 2,016 or 54 per cent. were in children under five years of age, and must, therefore, have been owing to the carelessness or neglect of the parents or other guardians of these helpless little ones. The suffering indicated by these figures must have been of a very terrible character. In addition to these deaths among very small children there were 443 (189 males and 254 females) of children from five to ten years of age. Among young adults and the middle aged—namely, from ten to forty-five years of age, the deaths were only 385 (149 males and 236 females). In advanced life from forty-five upwards the deaths were 865 (294 males and 571 females); in persons who were upwards of seventy-five years of age, and had to a great extent become helpless from age, in fact who had reached their second childhood, the number was no less than 295 (105 males and 190 females). With reference to sex it will be observed that of the whole 3,709 deaths from burning, 1,729 were males and 1,980 females, or 46·6 and 53·4 per cent. respectively, the number of female deaths being in excess of the males. This is almost certainly owing to the fact that a large number of these deaths are caused by the clothes accidentally taking fire, and this view is supported by the fact that the number of deaths from burning among males under five years of age is greater than the number of females—namely, 1,057 males and 959 females. At this period of life there is but little difference in the method of clothing the two sexes; at the ages of five to ten when the female garments become of a more inflammable description the deaths were 189 for males and 254 for females, showing a larger number for females, and this proportion is found to prevail pretty constantly through all the remaining age periods. In fact, adult females, owing to the nature of their clothing, have about double the chance of being burnt to death that males have.

Drowning caused 4,524 deaths, of which 3,883 were males and 640 females. As shown in the Abstract (pages 34 and 35) the greater number of these deaths occurred in males at the active periods of life.

The other causes of deaths by accident or negligence do not call for any specific notice.

Homicidal deaths numbered 1,150, of which 729 were males and 421 females: of these 525 (252 males and 273 females) were infants under one year and may be classed as infanticides, the balance, 625, of the total may be classed as murder or manslaughter. In connexion with this branch of the subject it may be mentioned that there were 32 persons (all males) executed in Ireland during the 10 years.

Deaths from suicide numbered 1,128—834 males and 294 females: nearly all were in persons over 20 years of age. The modes of death by suicide do not seem to call for any special remarks.

In the preceding decade 18,373 deaths were ascribed to accident or negligence, 905 to homicide, 958 to suicide, and 15 (all males) were executed.

AGES.

The deaths of infants under one year of age numbered 108,855, being at the rate of

The average annual number of deaths of persons aged sixty-five years and upwards is equivalent to 9·7 per cent. of the mean number of the living at that age.

Amongst the 833,136 deaths registered during the ten years are 6,463 of persons stated to have been aged ninety-five years and upwards—2,927 males and 3,535 females.

The following statement gives a summary of the death-rates of the population of Ireland at each age period :—

TABLE XXI.—AVERAGE ANNUAL Number of DEATHS of Males and of Females in IRELAND at each of TWELVE AGE PERIODS to every 10,000 LIVING at the same Ages.

Sex.	All Ages.	Under 5 years.	5-	10-	15-	20-	25-	35-	45-	55-	65-	75-	85 and upwards.
Males, . . .	[illegible]	878·2	49·3	32·0	52·1	77·6	90·3	108·3	154·9	287·9	640·4	1,349·6	2,824·6
Females, . .	[illegible]	840·9	53·7	41·0	61·9	72·4	90·9	102·9	142·8	284·7	649·5	1,339·0	2,697·6
Total, .	[illegible]	[illegible]	[illegible]	[illegible]	[illegible]	[illegible]	[illegible]	[illegible]	[illegible]	[illegible]	[illegible]	[illegible]	[illegible]

From this it appears that among male children under five years of age the average annual death-rate was 878·2 per 10,000, while the corresponding rate for female children was but 840·9 per 10,000; for each of the next three quinquennial age periods the female death-rate exceeded the male rate thus:—the rate among boys aged five and under ten was 49·3 per 10,000, and that for the girls 53·7 per 10,000; among boys aged ten years and under fifteen the rate was 32·0, and among girls it was 41·0, and the deaths of males aged fifteen and under twenty were equal to 52·1 per 10,000, while those of females of that age equalled 61·9 per 10,000. In each of the remaining age periods (except 25–35 and 65–75) the male death-rate was in excess of the female; for the period twenty and under twenty-five the respective rates were 77·6 (males), and 72·4 (females); for the period twenty five and under thirty-five, they were 90·3 and 90·9; for thirty five and under forty-five they were 108·3 and 102·9; for the next decennial period, 154·9 and 142·8; for fifty-five and under sixty-five they were 287·9 and 284·7; for sixty-five and under seventy-five 640·4 and 649·5; for the next ten-year period 1,349·6 and 1,339·0; and amongst persons aged eighty-five years and upwards 2,824·6 and 2,697·6.

The following is a supplement to the foregoing summary of deaths by ages, showing the per-centage of the total deaths which occurred during each age period :—

TABLE XXII.—PROPORTION PER CENT. of the DEATHS at ALL AGES in the Ten Years 1881–90, which occurred at EACH OF TWELVE AGE PERIODS.

Sex.	All Ages.	Under 5 years.	5-	10-	15-	20-	25-	35-	45-	55-	65-	75-	85 and upwards.
Males, . .	[illegible]	23·0	[illegible]	[illegible]	[illegible]	[illegible]	[illegible]	[illegible]	[illegible]	[illegible]	[illegible]	[illegible]	[illegible]
Females, . .	[illegible]	19·7	[illegible]	[illegible]	[illegible]	[illegible]	[illegible]	[illegible]	[illegible]	[illegible]	[illegible]	[illegible]	[illegible]
Total, .	[illegible]	[illegible]	[illegible]	[illegible]	[illegible]	[illegible]	[illegible]	[illegible]	[illegible]	[illegible]	[illegible]	[illegible]	[illegible]

From this it appears that 23·0 per cent. of the deaths of males and 19·7 per cent. of those of females occurred amongst children under five years of age. The deaths of males aged five and under twenty-five years formed 13·7 per cent. of the total number of deaths of males, and those of females of that age 13·8 per cent of the total female mortality; 11·8 per cent. of the deaths of males and 13·0 per cent. of those of females occurred among persons aged twenty-five and under forty-five; 18·6 per cent. of the male mortality was amongst men aged forty-five and under sixty-five, and 19·1 per cent. of the female mortality amongst women of those ages; and 33·9 per cent. of the deaths of males and 34·4 per cent. of those of females occurred among persons aged sixty-five years and upwards.

EMIGRATION.

According to the Returns obtained by the Royal Irish Constabulary and the Metropolitan Police, who acted as enumerators at the several Irish seaports, the number of emigrants who left Ireland during the ten years 1881-90 amounted to 770,706; of these 395,298 were males and 375,408 were females. In the previous decade 623,933 persons emigrated. Of the whole number in the late decade, 138,662 were from Leinster; 251,539 from Munster; 218,645 from Ulster; and 161,860 from Connaught.

Of the total emigrants from Ireland in the ten years, 13·7 per cent. were under fifteen years of age at the time of their departure; 75·9 per cent. were between fifteen and thirty-five years old; and 10·4 per cent. were thirty-five or upwards.

PRICES OF PROVISIONS, AND PAUPERISM.

The subjoined Table shows for each of the ten years, 1881-90, the average prices of provisions in Dublin, and the average number of persons in Ireland receiving indoor or out-door relief on Saturdays.

The mean price of oatmeal (1st quality) for the ten years was 15s. 7d., the yearly average prices ranging from 13s. 7d. in 1889 to 17s. 6d. in 1884 and 1885; the mean prices of potatoes were from 2s. 6d. to 3s. 7d., the lowest average prices for any year being from 2s. 2d. to 2s. 9d. in 1888, and the highest 3s. 9d. to 4s. 10d. in 1883; beef was lowest in 1887, the average prices being from 44s. to 53s. 6d., and highest in 1883, the average prices being from 66s. 6d. to 77s.; the mean prices for the ten years were from 54s. 6d. to 65s. 6d.

The mean number of workhouse inmates in Ireland on Saturdays during the ten years (derived from returns furnished by the Local Government Board) was 47,592, and the mean number of persons receiving out-door relief was 62,860. The lowest average number of workhouse inmates for any one year was 43,009 in 1890, and the highest 53,028 in 1881, and the average numbers on out-door relief ranged from 57,969 in 1884 to 77,456 in 1886.

TABLE XXIII.—AVERAGE PRICES in DUBLIN of BREAD, OATMEAL, POTATOES, and BEEF, during the years 1881-90, and the AVERAGE NUMBER of PERSONS in IRELAND receiving IN-DOOR and OUT-DOOR RELIEF on Saturdays in those years.

Years.	Average Prices of Provisions.				Pauperism.	
	Bread [illegible]*	Oatmeal [illegible]	Potatoes [illegible] per Cwt.	Beef [illegible] per Cwt.	Average Numbers [illegible]	
					In-door.	Out-door.
[illegible]	[illegible]	[illegible]	[illegible]	[illegible]	[illegible]	[illegible]
[illegible]	[illegible]	[illegible]	[illegible]	[illegible]	[illegible]	[illegible]
[illegible]	[illegible]	[illegible]	[illegible]	[illegible]	[illegible]	[illegible]
[illegible]	[illegible]	[illegible]	[illegible]	[illegible]	[illegible]	[illegible]
[illegible]	[illegible]	[illegible]	[illegible]	[illegible]	[illegible]	[illegible]
[illegible]	[illegible]	[illegible]	[illegible]	[illegible]	[illegible]	[illegible]
[illegible]	[illegible]	[illegible]	[illegible]	[illegible]	[illegible]	[illegible]
[illegible]	[illegible]	[illegible]	[illegible]	[illegible]	[illegible]	[illegible]
[illegible]	[illegible]	[illegible]	[illegible]	[illegible]	[illegible]	[illegible]
[illegible]	[illegible]	[illegible]	[illegible]	[illegible]	[illegible]	[illegible]
Mean [illegible]	[illegible]	[illegible]	[illegible]	[illegible]	[illegible]	[illegible]

* [illegible]

† [illegible]

of the thermometer in the shade by an empirical Formula, viz., min. + (max. − min. × C) = *Mean Temperature*. The co-efficient C is a variable quantity from month to month which has been determined by a careful comparison of the arithmetical means of the maximum and minimum thermometer readings with the results yielded by the tracings taken by the thermograph at self-recording observatories of the First Order. The co-efficients for the different months are—January and December, ·520; February and November, ·500; March and October, ·485; April and September, ·476; May and August, ·470; June and July, ·465. The Tension of Aqueous Vapour (expressed in terms of inches of mercury), Relative Humidity, and Amount of Cloud, are the result of observations taken daily at 9 A.M. and 9 P.M. The Rainfall is that measured at 9 A.M. each day and entered to the preceding day. A *Rainy Day* is one on which at least five-thousandths (·005) of an inch of rain falls within the twenty-four hours from 9 A.M. to 9 P.M. The number of days of rain, snow, hail, thunderstorms, clear sky, over-cast sky, and gales are calculated from observations at 9 A.M. and 9 P.M., and the same applies to the results obtained as to the Direction of the Wind.

The *Average Mean Height of the Barometer* during the ten years 1881-90, was 29·929 inches. The annual mean varied from 29·841 inches in 1883 to 30·015 in 18, a difference of somewhat more than an eighth of an inch (·134 inch.)

The monthly average ranged from 29·839 inches in November to 30·010 inches in June. The extreme monthly means were—highest, 30·236 inches in February, 1887; lowest, 29·543 in February, 1885. The absolute extreme readings of the Barometer were—maximum, 30·935 inches at 10·30 P.M., of January 18, 1882; minimum, 27·758 inches, at 3·30 P.M., of December 8, 1886.

The extreme range of atmospherical pressure was, therefore, 3·177 inches.

The *Average Mean Temperature* deduced from observations at 9 A.M. and 9 P.M. was 48·0°, the average at 9 A.M. being 49·3°, and that at 9 P.M. 46·5°. The annual mean varied from 46·2° in 1885 to 50·2° in 1881—a range of 9°. The monthly average varied from 41·2° in January to 59·4° in July—an annual range of 18·2°. The extreme monthly means were—highest, 63·4° in July, 1887; lowest, 37·3° in January, 1881—a range of 30·6°. The absolute extremes of temperature were—highest, 78·9° on August 8, 1887; lowest, 13·3° on December 14 and 15, 1882. These values give a range of 64·6° in the screen. The average temperature for the ten years deduced from the observed daily extremes was 49·3.

Rain fell on 1,961 days, including snow or sleet on 223 days, and hail on 313 days. The average annual number of rainy days was therefore 196·1, of snowy days 22·3, and of days of hail 31·3. The total rainfall measured 267·759 inches. The smallest annual fall was 18·601 on 190 days in 1887; the largest fall was 32·968 inches on 220 days in 1886. The average annual fall appears as 26·773 inches. The ten years' monthly fall varied from 16·336 inches on 144 days in June to 29·283 inches on 190 days in November.

The maximal rainfall in twenty-four hours was 1·943 inches, on August 19, 1889, a downpour which was nearly approached on October 15, 1886, when 1·800 inches were measured. June and July were the only months in the year in which no rainfall of one inch in twenty-four hours took place; the heaviest downpour in these months was ·951 inch on June 27, 1888, and ·824 inch July 22, 1882. The distribution of rain was as follows:—for the first quarter, 63·348 inches; for the second, 58·204; total for the first half year, 121·552 inches. In the third quarter 69·391 inches, and in the fourth quarter 76·586 inches fell. Total for the second half year, 146·177 inches, or only about one-fifth as much again as the rainfall of the first six months. The numbers representing rainy days for the first, third, and fourth quarters are 499, 485 and 527 respectively. In the second quarter the rainy days were much fewer, namely 450. From these figures we conclude that the second quarter is the driest, though the rain is heavier than in the first and fourth quarters. The heaviest rain occurs in the third quarter. If 127 will represent the heaviness of the rain in the first quarter, 129 will represent that in the second, 143 that in the third, and 120 that in the fourth. The rainfall in the fourth quarter, though not heavy, is distributed over a greater number of days.

Of the 229 snowy days, 134 were found in the first quarter, 21 in the second, none in the third, and 48 in the fourth. Of the 313 days on which hail was observed, 191 fell in the first quarter, 63 in the second, 17 in the third, and 72 in the fourth.

As regards the *Direction of the Wind*, 7,309 observations were made, with this result:—N., 470; N.E., 499; E., 680; S.E., 600; S., 714; S.W., 1,067; W., 1,948; N.W., 878; calm, 422. The preponderance of westerly (S.W. to N.W.) over easterly (N.E. to S.E.) winds is very striking—the figures are 3,007 and 1,779 respectively, more than 2 to 1 in favour of westerly winds. But the great excess of W. winds is still more remarkable. They number 1,948, or nearly double the number of S.W. winds, 1,067. Partial deflection of S.W. winds by a range of mountains—with summits of 2,000 feet and upwards—to the southward of the city in some measure accounts for this, and a further explanation is to be found in the frequent occurrence of light westerly land breezes during calm cold weather in winter, spring, and autumn. Correlated to this class of westerly winds are

The following are more detailed remarks upon the weather in the different months:—

JANUARY.—The average height of the barometer was 29·931 inches. It varied from 30·243 inches in 1882 to 29·673 inches in 1886—a range of not less than ·580 inch. The mean pressure, 30·244 inches, observed in 1882, is the highest monthly mean recorded during the ten years, with the exception of February, 1887, when it was 30·356 inches. The average mean temperature was 41·2°. In 1884 the mean dry bulb temperature was 45·2, in 1881 it was 39·6°. The absolute extreme temperatures were—highest 58·0°, on the 9th, in 1888; lowest, 15·2°, on the 15th, in 1887. The average rainfall was 2·093 inches on 16·0 days: the extremes of rainfall were—maximum, 3·244 inches on 20 days, in 1885; minimum, 1·347 inch, on 9 days, in 1888. The absolute maximal fall in 24 hours was 1·231 inches, on the 11th, in 1889. Snow or sleet fell on 54 and hail on 41 days during the ten years. There were 41 gales. The most prevalent wind was W., which was recorded 206 times out of a total of 620 observations. Next came S. W., with 122 observations. The N.E. and N. winds were the least frequent, with 22 and 17 observations respectively. The average amount of cloud was 64 per cent., 66 at 9 A.M. and 62 at 9 P.M.

FEBRUARY.—The average atmospheric pressure was 29·978 inches, the mean value varying from 30·356 inches in 1887 to 29·543 inches in 1883. The average mean dry bulb temperature was 41·5. It ranged from 45·0 in 1889 to 38·0 in 1888. The absolute extremes of temperature were—highest, 58·4, on the 26th, in 1883, lowest 21·7°, on the 11th, in 1889. The average rainfall was 2·169 inches on 13·7 days; the extremes of rainfall were—maximum, 3·753 inches, on 17 days, in 1883; minimum, 0·341 inch, on 11 days, in 1887. In 1890 there were only 7 rainy days, but in 1881 and also in 1889 there were 20 days. The absolute greatest fall in twenty-four hours was 1·007 inches, on the 1st, in 1883. Snow or sleet fell on 40 and hail on 36 days within the ten years. There were two thunderstorms. There were 60 gales. The wind blew most frequently from W.—on 146 occasions—least so from N. and N.E.: from each of these points on 26 and 40 occasions respectively. The average amount of cloud was 65 per cent.—71 at 9 A.M. and 63 at 9 P.M.

MARCH.—Average height of the barometer—29·913 inches, the mean ranging from 30·101 inches in 1887 to 29·641 inches in 1888. Average mean dry bulb temperature=41·1°, varying from 43·5° in 1882 to 38·1° in 1883. The absolute extremes of temperature were—highest, 60·6°, on the 7th, in 1882; lowest, 23·0°, on the 4th, in 1886. The average rainfall was 2·054 inches on 16·2 days; the extremes of rainfall were—largest, 3·753 inches on 18 days in 1883; smallest, 1·056 inch on 12 days in 1883. In 1886 there were 19 rainy days. The absolute maximal fall in twenty-four hours was 1·012 inches, on the 11th, in 1883. Snow or sleet fell on 60 days and hail on 64 days during the ten years. There were 2 thunderstorms and 53 gales. The most prevalent wind was once more W., observed on 177 occasions. The least prevalent winds were N.E. (33 observations) and S. (46 observations). The average amount of cloud was 62 per cent.—66 at 9 A.M. and 57 at 9 P.M.

APRIL.—Average height of the barometer—29·963 inches. The mean ranged from 30·051 inches, in 1887, to 29·744 inches in 1882, or only through ·307 inch, being only slightly over half the mean range observed in January (·589 inch). Average mean dry bulb temperature—44·9°, varying from 49·9°, in 1883, and also in 1883, to 44·8°, in 1887. The absolute extremes of temperature were—68·1°, on the 16th, in 1885, and 28·6°, on the 9th, in 1888. The average rainfall was 2·097 inches on 14·7 days; the extremes being—greatest, 3·580 inches, on 20 days, in 1882; least, 1·323 inch, on 12 days, in 1881. In 1880 there were 21 rainy days, producing 2·007 inches of rain, while for 10 days in 1883, the rainfall measured 2·207 inches. The absolute maximal fall in twenty-four hours was 1·289 inches on the 6th in 1882. Snow or sleet fell on 15 days, hail on 41 days in the ten years. There were 6 thunderstorms and also 11 gales. The E. wind was the most prevalent, being observed on 118 occasions. A S. wind was noted on only 49 occasions. There is a marked increase in the prevalence of easterly and north-easterly (85 observations) winds in this month. The average amount of cloud was 58 per cent.—66 at 9 A.M. and 51 at 9 P.M.

MAY.—The average pressure was 29·938 inches, the mean ranging from 30·092 inches in 1887 to 29·779 inches in 1883. Average mean dry bulb temperature=52·1°, ranging from 54·1° in 1889 to 45·7° in 1885. The absolute extremes of temperature were—highest, 72·5° on the 31st in 1889; lowest, 32·7° on the 7th in 1885. The average rainfall was 2·088 inches on 15·9 days. In 1886 no less than 5·472 inches of rain fell on 21 days; in 1887, on the contrary, the fall amounted to only 0·832 inch on 10 days. In 1886 there were 23 rainy days. The absolute maximal fall in twenty-four hours was 1·387 inches, on the 5th, in 1883. Snow or sleet fell on 6 days, hail on 34 days in the ten years. There were 7 thunderstorms, and 14 gales. W. winds were most frequent, being 117 in number, but were nearly equalled by E. winds which numbered 112. S. winds occurred on 45 occasions; while N., N.E. and N.W. together made up 163 out of 620 observations. The average amount of cloud was 55 per cent., 60 at 9 A.M. and 50 at 9 P.M. The comparative clearness of the sky at 9 P.M. is a striking feature of the meteorology of May.

JUNE.—Average pressure=30·010 inches, the mean varying from 30·218 inches in 1887, to 29·673 inches in 1882. Average mean dry bulb temperature=57·3°, the range being from 62·8° in 1887, to 55·6° in 1882. The absolute extreme temperatures were—maximum, 79·4°, on the 17th, in 1887, minimum, 38·6°, on the 8th, in 1881. The average rainfall was 1·630 inches, on 14·4 days. The monthly fall was 3·043 inches on 18 days in 1888, and only 0·100 inch on 6 days in 1889. In 1882 there were 25 rainy days, and the total fall was 1·734 inches. The absolute maximal fall in twenty-four hours was 0·951 inch on the 27th in 1888. There was no snow or sleet, but hail was noted on 8 days. There were three gales. Thunderstorms occurred on 12 occasions. The wind blew from W. on 129 occasions; from N. on 50. The average amount of cloud was 58 per cent.—64 at 9 A.M., the essentially rainy character of this month is demonstrated. The heaviest rainfall was 3·891 inches on 22 days in 1886; the slightest was 1·154 inch on 10 days in 1885. The maximal fall in twenty-four hours was 0·824 inches on the 22nd, in 1889. There were as many as 22 rainy days in each of the years 1882 and 1884 (in 1882, 3·722 inches fell). Neither snow nor sleet occurred. Hail fell on 6 days. There were 10 thunderstorms and 6 gales. The most prevalent wind was W., observed 174 out of 610 times. The least frequent wind was N.E. (26 observations). Average amount of cloud = 64 per cent.—[illegible] at 9 A.M. and 59 at 9 P.M.

August.—Average atmospheric pressure—29·929 inches, the mean ranging from 29·[illegible] inches in 1882 to 30·012 inches in 1881. Average mean dry bulb temperature, 58·1°—in 1884, 61·2°; in 1880, 56·9°. The extremes of temperature were—maximum, 77·0° on the 5th in 1887; minimum, 41·2° on the [illegible] in 1886. The average rainfall was 2·985 inches on 17·6 days, showing this month to be like July, a rainy one. The maximal rainfall was 5·747 inches on 22 days in 1886; the minimal fall was 0·777 inches on 8 days in 1884. Rain was measured on 21 days in 1882, but on only 11 days in 1884. The heaviest rainfall within twenty-four hours was 1·942 inches on the 19th in 1880. This downpour was quite exceptional for Dublin, and was never exceeded in the ten years. There was no snow or sleet. Hail fell on only 7 days. There were 11 thunderstorms and 3 gales. The most frequent wind was W. (168 observations); the least so was S.E. (29 observations). The average percentage of cloud was 59—that at 9 A.M. was 62, that at 9 P.M. 57.

September.—The average height of the barometer was 29·968 inches, the mean ranging from 30·176 inches in 1886 to 29·811 inches in 1883. The average mean dry bulb temperature was 54·[illegible]; in 1880 it was 58·[illegible]; in 1882 it fell to 52·7°. The absolute extremes of temperature were—highest, 73·7° on the 9th in 1884; lowest, 34·4° on the 27th in 1885. The average rainfall was 2·012 inches on 14·6 days. In 1883 the fall amounted to 3·037 inches on only 14 days, but in 1889 it was only 0·729 inches on 10 days. The maximal fall in twenty-four hours was 1·310 inches on the 1st in 1883. There was neither snow nor sleet, and hail fell on only 6 days. There were 6 thunderstorms and 20 gales. The W. wind as usual chiefly prevailed, being noted on 173 occasions. The least frequent wind was S. (37 observations). The average cloudiness was 57 per cent.—52 at 9 A.M. and 61 at 9 P.M.

October.—The average barometrical height was 29·[illegible] inches; the annual mean pressure ranging from 30·144 inches in 1887 to 29·673 inches in 1881. The average mean dry bulb temperature was 48·6°; in 1886 it was 51·4°; in 1885 it fell to 44·8°. The absolute extremes of temperature were—highest, 66·6° on the 27th, in 1888; lowest, 30·[illegible] on the 18th, in 1881. The average rainfall was 2·702 inches on 17·4 days. In 1886 the rainfall amounted to as much as 5·109 inches on 24 days; in 1880 also 4·[illegible] inches fell on 22 days. The least rainfall in this month was 0·[illegible] inches on 11 days in 1890. The maximal fall in twenty-four hours was 1·360 inches on the 18th, in 1886. Snow or sleet fell on 2 days—once in 1887 and once in 1890. Hail occurred on 19 days, of which 7 were in 1886. There were 5 thunderstorms and 28 gales. The wind blew most frequently from W. (on 175 occasions); least so from N.E. (on only 32 occasions). The average amount of cloud was 60 per cent.—at 9 A.M., 62, and at 9 P.M., 58.

November.—Average height of barometer—29·[illegible] inches, the mean ranging from 30·[illegible] in 1889 to 29·[illegible] inches in 1882. The average mean dry bulb temperature was 45·1°. It rose to 50·0 in 1881, and fell to 42·[illegible] in 1887. The absolute extremes of temperature were—highest, 60·[illegible] on the 10th in 1880; lowest, 26·3° on the 20th in 1890. The average rainfall was 2·[illegible] inches on 19·0 days. The fall ranged from 0·[illegible] inches on [illegible] days in 1885 to 6·[illegible] inches on [illegible] days in 1886. In 1880 there were 22 rainy days with 4·272 inches. The fall of 6·[illegible] inches exceeded that of any other month in the ten years, the nearest approach to this downpour being 5·[illegible] inches in October, 1886, and 5·747 inches in August, 1886. The maximal fall in twenty-four hours was 1·[illegible] inches on the 20th, in 1886. Snow or sleet fell on 15 days in the 10 years, and hail on 37 days. There were 3 thunderstorms and 39 gales. The W. wind was, as usual, most prevalent (158 observations out of 600); the N.E. wind was least prevalent (20 observations). The average cloudiness was 62 per cent.; at 9 A.M. 63, and at 9 P.M. 62.

December.—The average height of the barometer was 29·[illegible] inches, the mean varying from 30·184 inches in 1885 to 29·[illegible] inches in 1882. This range of the mean pressure, amounting to ·[illegible] inch, exceeds that observed in January, namely, ·[illegible] inch. The average mean temperature was 40·[illegible], lower by [illegible] than that of January, the next coldest month on the average of the 10 years. The anomaly of December being colder than January is explained by the intense cold of December in the years 1882, 1886, and 1890, when their mean temperatures were 37·7°, 37·2°, and 33·[illegible] respectively. In 1888, on the other hand, the mean temperature rose to 42·[illegible]. The absolute extremes of temperature were—maximum, 58·6° on the 3rd and 5th, in 1888; minimum, 18·3° on the 14th and 15th, in 1882. The average rain fall was 2·[illegible] inches on 18·3 days. It varied from 3·[illegible] inches on 21 days in 1882, to 0·[illegible] inch on only 10 days in 1885. The absolute heaviest fall in twenty-four hours was 0·[illegible] inch on the 14th in 1885. Snow or sleet fell on [illegible] days; hail on 28. One thunderstorm occurred. There were 30 gales. A vast preponderance of W. and S.W. winds was noted—237 observations of W. and 97 of S.W., together giving 334 out of a total of 620 observations, that is considerably more than one-half. In marked contrast, the N.E. wind was observed on only 18 occasions; the N. on only 21. The average quantity of cloud was 61 per cent.—[illegible] at 9 A.M. and 63 at 9 P.M.

I have the honour to be
Your Excellency's faithful servant,
Thos. W. Grimshaw,
Registrar-General.

General Register Office,
Charlemont House, Dublin.

POPULATION OF IRELAND (including Army, Navy, and Merchant Seamen on shore or in port) estimated to the middle of each of the seventy-five Years 1816 to 1890, inclusive:—

Middle of the Year.	Estimated Population. Persons.	Males.	Females.	Middle of the Year.	Estimated Population. Persons.	Males.	Females.	Middle of the Year.	Estimated Population. Persons.	Males.	Females.
[illegible]	[illegible]	[illegible]	[illegible]	[illegible]	[illegible]	[illegible]	[illegible]	[illegible]	[illegible]	[illegible]	[illegible]
[illegible]	[illegible]	[illegible]	[illegible]	[illegible]	[illegible]	[illegible]	[illegible]	[illegible]	[illegible]	[illegible]	[illegible]
[illegible]	[illegible]	[illegible]	[illegible]	[illegible]	[illegible]	[illegible]	[illegible]	[illegible]	[illegible]	[illegible]	[illegible]
[illegible]	[illegible]	[illegible]	[illegible]	[illegible]	[illegible]	[illegible]	[illegible]	[illegible]	[illegible]	[illegible]	[illegible]
[illegible]	[illegible]	[illegible]	[illegible]	[illegible]	[illegible]	[illegible]	[illegible]	[illegible]	[illegible]	[illegible]	[illegible]
[illegible]	[illegible]	[illegible]	[illegible]	[illegible]	[illegible]	[illegible]	[illegible]	[illegible]	[illegible]	[illegible]	[illegible]
[illegible]	[illegible]	[illegible]	[illegible]	[illegible]	[illegible]	[illegible]	[illegible]	[illegible]	[illegible]	[illegible]	[illegible]
[illegible]	[illegible]	[illegible]	[illegible]	[illegible]	[illegible]	[illegible]	[illegible]	[illegible]	[illegible]	[illegible]	[illegible]
[illegible]	[illegible]	[illegible]	[illegible]	[illegible]	[illegible]	[illegible]	[illegible]	[illegible]	[illegible]	[illegible]	[illegible]
[illegible]	[illegible]	[illegible]	[illegible]	[illegible]	[illegible]	[illegible]	[illegible]	[illegible]	[illegible]	[illegible]	[illegible]
[illegible]	[illegible]	[illegible]	[illegible]	[illegible]	[illegible]	[illegible]	[illegible]	[illegible]	[illegible]	[illegible]	[illegible]
[illegible]	[illegible]	[illegible]	[illegible]	[illegible]	[illegible]	[illegible]	[illegible]	[illegible]	[illegible]	[illegible]	[illegible]
[illegible]	[illegible]	[illegible]	[illegible]	[illegible]	[illegible]	[illegible]	[illegible]	[illegible]	[illegible]	[illegible]	[illegible]
[illegible]	[illegible]	[illegible]	[illegible]	[illegible]	[illegible]	[illegible]	[illegible]	[illegible]	[illegible]	[illegible]	[illegible]
[illegible]	[illegible]	[illegible]	[illegible]	[illegible]	[illegible]	[illegible]	[illegible]	[illegible]	[illegible]	[illegible]	[illegible]
[illegible]	[illegible]	[illegible]	[illegible]	[illegible]	[illegible]	[illegible]	[illegible]	[illegible]	[illegible]	[illegible]	[illegible]
[illegible]	[illegible]	[illegible]	[illegible]	[illegible]	[illegible]	[illegible]	[illegible]	[illegible]	[illegible]	[illegible]	[illegible]
[illegible]	[illegible]	[illegible]	[illegible]	[illegible]	[illegible]	[illegible]	[illegible]	[illegible]	[illegible]	[illegible]	[illegible]
[illegible]	[illegible]	[illegible]	[illegible]	[illegible]	[illegible]	[illegible]	[illegible]	[illegible]	[illegible]	[illegible]	[illegible]
[illegible]	[illegible]	[illegible]	[illegible]	[illegible]	[illegible]	[illegible]	[illegible]	[illegible]	[illegible]	[illegible]	[illegible]
[illegible]	[illegible]	[illegible]	[illegible]	[illegible]	[illegible]	[illegible]	[illegible]	[illegible]	[illegible]	[illegible]	[illegible]
[illegible]	[illegible]	[illegible]	[illegible]	[illegible]	[illegible]	[illegible]	[illegible]	[illegible]	[illegible]	[illegible]	[illegible]
[illegible]	[illegible]	[illegible]	[illegible]	[illegible]	[illegible]	[illegible]	[illegible]	[illegible]	[illegible]	[illegible]	[illegible]
[illegible]	[illegible]	[illegible]	[illegible]	[illegible]	[illegible]	[illegible]	[illegible]	[illegible]	[illegible]	[illegible]	[illegible]
[illegible]	[illegible]	[illegible]	[illegible]	[illegible]	[illegible]	[illegible]	[illegible]	[illegible]	[illegible]	[illegible]	[illegible]

[illegible]

AGES of the POPULATION in IRELAND according to the Census Returns of 1861, 1871, 1881, and 1891.

Year	Sexes.	Under 5.	[illegible]	[illegible]	[illegible]	[illegible]	[illegible]	[illegible]	[illegible]	[illegible]	[illegible]	[illegible]	[illegible]	[illegible]	[illegible]	Total.
1861	Males,	[illegible]	[illegible]	[illegible]	[illegible]	[illegible]	[illegible]	[illegible]	[illegible]	[illegible]	[illegible]	[illegible]	[illegible]	[illegible]	[illegible]	[illegible]
	Females,	[illegible]	[illegible]	[illegible]	[illegible]	[illegible]	[illegible]	[illegible]	[illegible]	[illegible]	[illegible]	[illegible]	[illegible]	[illegible]	[illegible]	[illegible]
	Total,	[illegible]	[illegible]	[illegible]	[illegible]	[illegible]	[illegible]	[illegible]	[illegible]	[illegible]	[illegible]	[illegible]	[illegible]	[illegible]	[illegible]	[illegible]
1871	Males,	[illegible]	[illegible]	[illegible]	[illegible]	[illegible]	[illegible]	[illegible]	[illegible]	[illegible]	[illegible]	[illegible]	[illegible]	[illegible]	[illegible]	[illegible]
	Females,	[illegible]	[illegible]	[illegible]	[illegible]	[illegible]	[illegible]	[illegible]	[illegible]	[illegible]	[illegible]	[illegible]	[illegible]	[illegible]	[illegible]	[illegible]
	Total,	[illegible]	[illegible]	[illegible]	[illegible]	[illegible]	[illegible]	[illegible]	[illegible]	[illegible]	[illegible]	[illegible]	[illegible]	[illegible]	[illegible]	[illegible]
1881	Males,	[illegible]	[illegible]	[illegible]	[illegible]	[illegible]	[illegible]	[illegible]	[illegible]	[illegible]	[illegible]	[illegible]	[illegible]	[illegible]	[illegible]	[illegible]
	Females,	[illegible]	[illegible]	[illegible]	[illegible]	[illegible]	[illegible]	[illegible]	[illegible]	[illegible]	[illegible]	[illegible]	[illegible]	[illegible]	[illegible]	[illegible]
	Total,	[illegible]	[illegible]	[illegible]	[illegible]	[illegible]	[illegible]	[illegible]	[illegible]	[illegible]	[illegible]	[illegible]	[illegible]	[illegible]	[illegible]	[illegible]
1891	Males,	[illegible]	[illegible]	[illegible]	[illegible]	[illegible]	[illegible]	[illegible]	[illegible]	[illegible]	[illegible]	[illegible]	[illegible]	[illegible]	[illegible]	[illegible]
	Females,	[illegible]	[illegible]	[illegible]	[illegible]	[illegible]	[illegible]	[illegible]	[illegible]	[illegible]	[illegible]	[illegible]	[illegible]	[illegible]	[illegible]	[illegible]
	Total,	[illegible]	[illegible]	[illegible]	[illegible]	[illegible]	[illegible]	[illegible]	[illegible]	[illegible]	[illegible]	[illegible]	[illegible]	[illegible]	[illegible]	[illegible]

ABSTRACT OF METEOROLOGICAL OBSERVATIONS taken at 40, Fitzwilliam-square, West, Dublin, Long. 6° 15′ W.; Lat. 53° 20′ N.; Thermometers, 4 feet above the ground.

Year and Month	Mean Pressure	Air Temperature									Tension of Vapour			Relative Humidity		
		9 a.m.	3 p.m.	Mean	[illegible]		Abs. Min.		Abs. Max.		9 a.m.	3 p.m.	Mean	9 a.m.	3 p.m.	Mean
					Min.	Max.	Temp.	Date	Temp.	Date						
[illegible]	Inch.	°	°	°	°	°	°		°		Ins.	Ins.	Ins.	%	%	%
January,	[illegible]	[illegible]	[illegible]	[illegible]	[illegible]	[illegible]	[illegible]	[illegible]	[illegible]	[illegible]	[illegible]	[illegible]	[illegible]	[illegible]	[illegible]	[illegible]
February,	[illegible]	[illegible]	[illegible]	[illegible]	[illegible]	[illegible]	[illegible]	[illegible]	[illegible]	[illegible]	[illegible]	[illegible]	[illegible]	[illegible]	[illegible]	[illegible]
March,	[illegible]	[illegible]	[illegible]	[illegible]	[illegible]	[illegible]	[illegible]	[illegible]	[illegible]	[illegible]	[illegible]	[illegible]	[illegible]	[illegible]	[illegible]	[illegible]
April,	[illegible]	[illegible]	[illegible]	[illegible]	[illegible]	[illegible]	[illegible]	[illegible]	[illegible]	[illegible]	[illegible]	[illegible]	[illegible]	[illegible]	[illegible]	[illegible]
May,	[illegible]	[illegible]	[illegible]	[illegible]	[illegible]	[illegible]	[illegible]	[illegible]	[illegible]	[illegible]	[illegible]	[illegible]	[illegible]	[illegible]	[illegible]	[illegible]
June,	[illegible]	[illegible]	[illegible]	[illegible]	[illegible]	[illegible]	[illegible]	[illegible]	[illegible]	[illegible]	[illegible]	[illegible]	[illegible]	[illegible]	[illegible]	[illegible]
July,	[illegible]	[illegible]	[illegible]	[illegible]	[illegible]	[illegible]	[illegible]	[illegible]	[illegible]	[illegible]	[illegible]	[illegible]	[illegible]	[illegible]	[illegible]	[illegible]
August,	[illegible]	[illegible]	[illegible]	[illegible]	[illegible]	[illegible]	[illegible]	[illegible]	[illegible]	[illegible]	[illegible]	[illegible]	[illegible]	[illegible]	[illegible]	[illegible]
September,	[illegible]	[illegible]	[illegible]	[illegible]	[illegible]	[illegible]	[illegible]	[illegible]	[illegible]	[illegible]	[illegible]	[illegible]	[illegible]	[illegible]	[illegible]	[illegible]
October,	[illegible]	[illegible]	[illegible]	[illegible]	[illegible]	[illegible]	[illegible]	[illegible]	[illegible]	[illegible]	[illegible]	[illegible]	[illegible]	[illegible]	[illegible]	[illegible]
November,	[illegible]	[illegible]	[illegible]	[illegible]	[illegible]	[illegible]	[illegible]	[illegible]	[illegible]	[illegible]	[illegible]	[illegible]	[illegible]	[illegible]	[illegible]	[illegible]
December,	[illegible]	[illegible]	[illegible]	[illegible]	[illegible]	[illegible]	[illegible]	[illegible]	[illegible]	[illegible]	[illegible]	[illegible]	[illegible]	[illegible]	[illegible]	[illegible]
Year,	[illegible]	[illegible]	[illegible]	[illegible]	[illegible]	[illegible]	[illegible]	[illegible]	[illegible]	[illegible]	[illegible]	[illegible]	[illegible]	[illegible]	[illegible]	[illegible]
[illegible]																
January,	[illegible]	[illegible]	[illegible]	[illegible]	[illegible]	[illegible]	[illegible]	[illegible]	[illegible]	[illegible]	[illegible]	[illegible]	[illegible]	[illegible]	[illegible]	[illegible]
February,	[illegible]	[illegible]	[illegible]	[illegible]	[illegible]	[illegible]	[illegible]	[illegible]	[illegible]	[illegible]	[illegible]	[illegible]	[illegible]	[illegible]	[illegible]	[illegible]
March,	[illegible]	[illegible]	[illegible]	[illegible]	[illegible]	[illegible]	[illegible]	[illegible]	[illegible]	[illegible]	[illegible]	[illegible]	[illegible]	[illegible]	[illegible]	[illegible]
April,	[illegible]	[illegible]	[illegible]	[illegible]	[illegible]	[illegible]	[illegible]	[illegible]	[illegible]	[illegible]	[illegible]	[illegible]	[illegible]	[illegible]	[illegible]	[illegible]
May,	[illegible]	[illegible]	[illegible]	[illegible]	[illegible]	[illegible]	[illegible]	[illegible]	[illegible]	[illegible]	[illegible]	[illegible]	[illegible]	[illegible]	[illegible]	[illegible]
June,	[illegible]	[illegible]	[illegible]	[illegible]	[illegible]	[illegible]	[illegible]	[illegible]	[illegible]	[illegible]	[illegible]	[illegible]	[illegible]	[illegible]	[illegible]	[illegible]
July,	[illegible]	[illegible]	[illegible]	[illegible]	[illegible]	[illegible]	[illegible]	[illegible]	[illegible]	[illegible]	[illegible]	[illegible]	[illegible]	[illegible]	[illegible]	[illegible]
August,	[illegible]	[illegible]	[illegible]	[illegible]	[illegible]	[illegible]	[illegible]	[illegible]	[illegible]	[illegible]	[illegible]	[illegible]	[illegible]	[illegible]	[illegible]	[illegible]
September,	[illegible]	[illegible]	[illegible]	[illegible]	[illegible]	[illegible]	[illegible]	[illegible]	[illegible]	[illegible]	[illegible]	[illegible]	[illegible]	[illegible]	[illegible]	[illegible]
October,	[illegible]	[illegible]	[illegible]	[illegible]	[illegible]	[illegible]	[illegible]	[illegible]	[illegible]	[illegible]	[illegible]	[illegible]	[illegible]	[illegible]	[illegible]	[illegible]
November,	[illegible]	[illegible]	[illegible]	[illegible]	[illegible]	[illegible]	[illegible]	[illegible]	[illegible]	[illegible]	[illegible]	[illegible]	[illegible]	[illegible]	[illegible]	[illegible]
December,	[illegible]	[illegible]	[illegible]	[illegible]	[illegible]	[illegible]	[illegible]	[illegible]	[illegible]	[illegible]	[illegible]	[illegible]	[illegible]	[illegible]	[illegible]	[illegible]

during the Ten Years 1881–90, by J. W. MOORE, M.D., Univ. Dub., F.R.C.P.I., F.R.Met.Soc.

For Height above Mean Sea Level and Rain Gauge, see Tables on pages 56–57.

Year and Month	Amount of Cloud.			Rainfall.			Weather. Number of days of							Wind. Number of Observations of								
	9 a.m.	9 p.m.	Mean.	Total.	Max.	Date.	[illegible]	[illegible]	[illegible]	[illegible]	[illegible]	[illegible]	[illegible]	N.	N.E.	E.	S.E.	S.	S.W.	W.	N.W.	Calm.
1881.				Ins.	Ins.																	
January,	[illegible]	[illegible]	[illegible]	[illegible]	[illegible]	[illegible]	[illegible]	[illegible]	[illegible]	[illegible]	[illegible]	[illegible]	[illegible]	[illegible]	[illegible]	[illegible]	[illegible]	[illegible]	[illegible]	[illegible]	[illegible]	[illegible]
February,	[illegible]	[illegible]	[illegible]	[illegible]	[illegible]	[illegible]	[illegible]	[illegible]	[illegible]	[illegible]	[illegible]	[illegible]	[illegible]	[illegible]	[illegible]	[illegible]	[illegible]	[illegible]	[illegible]	[illegible]	[illegible]	[illegible]
March,	[illegible]	[illegible]	[illegible]	[illegible]	[illegible]	[illegible]	[illegible]	[illegible]	[illegible]	[illegible]	[illegible]	[illegible]	[illegible]	[illegible]	[illegible]	[illegible]	[illegible]	[illegible]	[illegible]	[illegible]	[illegible]	[illegible]
April,	[illegible]	[illegible]	[illegible]	[illegible]	[illegible]	[illegible]	[illegible]	[illegible]	[illegible]	[illegible]	[illegible]	[illegible]	[illegible]	[illegible]	[illegible]	[illegible]	[illegible]	[illegible]	[illegible]	[illegible]	[illegible]	[illegible]
May,	[illegible]	[illegible]	[illegible]	[illegible]	[illegible]	[illegible]	[illegible]	[illegible]	[illegible]	[illegible]	[illegible]	[illegible]	[illegible]	[illegible]	[illegible]	[illegible]	[illegible]	[illegible]	[illegible]	[illegible]	[illegible]	[illegible]
June,	[illegible]	[illegible]	[illegible]	[illegible]	[illegible]	[illegible]	[illegible]	[illegible]	[illegible]	[illegible]	[illegible]	[illegible]	[illegible]	[illegible]	[illegible]	[illegible]	[illegible]	[illegible]	[illegible]	[illegible]	[illegible]	[illegible]
July,	[illegible]	[illegible]	[illegible]	[illegible]	[illegible]	[illegible]	[illegible]	[illegible]	[illegible]	[illegible]	[illegible]	[illegible]	[illegible]	[illegible]	[illegible]	[illegible]	[illegible]	[illegible]	[illegible]	[illegible]	[illegible]	[illegible]
August,	[illegible]	[illegible]	[illegible]	[illegible]	[illegible]	[illegible]	[illegible]	[illegible]	[illegible]	[illegible]	[illegible]	[illegible]	[illegible]	[illegible]	[illegible]	[illegible]	[illegible]	[illegible]	[illegible]	[illegible]	[illegible]	[illegible]
September,	[illegible]	[illegible]	[illegible]	[illegible]	[illegible]	[illegible]	[illegible]	[illegible]	[illegible]	[illegible]	[illegible]	[illegible]	[illegible]	[illegible]	[illegible]	[illegible]	[illegible]	[illegible]	[illegible]	[illegible]	[illegible]	[illegible]
October,	[illegible]	[illegible]	[illegible]	[illegible]	[illegible]	[illegible]	[illegible]	[illegible]	[illegible]	[illegible]	[illegible]	[illegible]	[illegible]	[illegible]	[illegible]	[illegible]	[illegible]	[illegible]	[illegible]	[illegible]	[illegible]	[illegible]
November,	[illegible]	[illegible]	[illegible]	[illegible]	[illegible]	[illegible]	[illegible]	[illegible]	[illegible]	[illegible]	[illegible]	[illegible]	[illegible]	[illegible]	[illegible]	[illegible]	[illegible]	[illegible]	[illegible]	[illegible]	[illegible]	[illegible]
December,	[illegible]	[illegible]	[illegible]	[illegible]	[illegible]	[illegible]	[illegible]	[illegible]	[illegible]	[illegible]	[illegible]	[illegible]	[illegible]	[illegible]	[illegible]	[illegible]	[illegible]	[illegible]	[illegible]	[illegible]	[illegible]	[illegible]
Year,	[illegible]	[illegible]	[illegible]	[illegible]	[illegible]	[illegible]	[illegible]	[illegible]	[illegible]	[illegible]	[illegible]	[illegible]	[illegible]	[illegible]	[illegible]	[illegible]	[illegible]	[illegible]	[illegible]	[illegible]	[illegible]	[illegible]
1882.																						
January,	[illegible]	[illegible]	[illegible]	[illegible]	[illegible]	[illegible]	[illegible]	[illegible]	[illegible]	[illegible]	[illegible]	[illegible]	[illegible]	[illegible]	[illegible]	[illegible]	[illegible]	[illegible]	[illegible]	[illegible]	[illegible]	[illegible]
February,	[illegible]	[illegible]	[illegible]	[illegible]	[illegible]	[illegible]	[illegible]	[illegible]	[illegible]	[illegible]	[illegible]	[illegible]	[illegible]	[illegible]	[illegible]	[illegible]	[illegible]	[illegible]	[illegible]	[illegible]	[illegible]	[illegible]
March,	[illegible]	[illegible]	[illegible]	[illegible]	[illegible]	[illegible]	[illegible]	[illegible]	[illegible]	[illegible]	[illegible]	[illegible]	[illegible]	[illegible]	[illegible]	[illegible]	[illegible]	[illegible]	[illegible]	[illegible]	[illegible]	[illegible]
April,	[illegible]	[illegible]	[illegible]	[illegible]	[illegible]	[illegible]	[illegible]	[illegible]	[illegible]	[illegible]	[illegible]	[illegible]	[illegible]	[illegible]	[illegible]	[illegible]	[illegible]	[illegible]	[illegible]	[illegible]	[illegible]	[illegible]
May,	[illegible]	[illegible]	[illegible]	[illegible]	[illegible]	[illegible]	[illegible]	[illegible]	[illegible]	[illegible]	[illegible]	[illegible]	[illegible]	[illegible]	[illegible]	[illegible]	[illegible]	[illegible]	[illegible]	[illegible]	[illegible]	[illegible]
June,	[illegible]	[illegible]	[illegible]	[illegible]	[illegible]	[illegible]	[illegible]	[illegible]	[illegible]	[illegible]	[illegible]	[illegible]	[illegible]	[illegible]	[illegible]	[illegible]	[illegible]	[illegible]	[illegible]	[illegible]	[illegible]	[illegible]
July,	[illegible]	[illegible]	[illegible]	[illegible]	[illegible]	[illegible]	[illegible]	[illegible]	[illegible]	[illegible]	[illegible]	[illegible]	[illegible]	[illegible]	[illegible]	[illegible]	[illegible]	[illegible]	[illegible]	[illegible]	[illegible]	[illegible]
August,	[illegible]	[illegible]	[illegible]	[illegible]	[illegible]	[illegible]	[illegible]	[illegible]	[illegible]	[illegible]	[illegible]	[illegible]	[illegible]	[illegible]	[illegible]	[illegible]	[illegible]	[illegible]	[illegible]	[illegible]	[illegible]	[illegible]
September,	[illegible]	[illegible]	[illegible]	[illegible]	[illegible]	[illegible]	[illegible]	[illegible]	[illegible]	[illegible]	[illegible]	[illegible]	[illegible]	[illegible]	[illegible]	[illegible]	[illegible]	[illegible]	[illegible]	[illegible]	[illegible]	[illegible]
October,	[illegible]	[illegible]	[illegible]	[illegible]	[illegible]	[illegible]	[illegible]	[illegible]	[illegible]	[illegible]	[illegible]	[illegible]	[illegible]	[illegible]	[illegible]	[illegible]	[illegible]	[illegible]	[illegible]	[illegible]	[illegible]	[illegible]
November,	[illegible]	[illegible]	[illegible]	[illegible]	[illegible]	[illegible]	[illegible]	[illegible]	[illegible]	[illegible]	[illegible]	[illegible]	[illegible]	[illegible]	[illegible]	[illegible]	[illegible]	[illegible]	[illegible]	[illegible]	[illegible]	[illegible]
December,	[illegible]	[illegible]	[illegible]	[illegible]	[illegible]	[illegible]	[illegible]	[illegible]	[illegible]	[illegible]	[illegible]	[illegible]	[illegible]	[illegible]	[illegible]	[illegible]	[illegible]	[illegible]	[illegible]	[illegible]	[illegible]	[illegible]
Year,	[illegible]	[illegible]	[illegible]	[illegible]	[illegible]	[illegible]	[illegible]	[illegible]	[illegible]	[illegible]	[illegible]	[illegible]	[illegible]	[illegible]	[illegible]	[illegible]	[illegible]	[illegible]	[illegible]	[illegible]	[illegible]	[illegible]
1883.																						
January,	[illegible]	[illegible]	[illegible]	[illegible]	[illegible]	[illegible]	[illegible]	[illegible]	[illegible]	[illegible]	[illegible]	[illegible]	[illegible]	[illegible]	[illegible]	[illegible]	[illegible]	[illegible]	[illegible]	[illegible]	[illegible]	[illegible]
February,	[illegible]	[illegible]	[illegible]	[illegible]	[illegible]	[illegible]	[illegible]	[illegible]	[illegible]	[illegible]	[illegible]	[illegible]	[illegible]	[illegible]	[illegible]	[illegible]	[illegible]	[illegible]	[illegible]	[illegible]	[illegible]	[illegible]
March,	[illegible]	[illegible]	[illegible]	[illegible]	[illegible]	[illegible]	[illegible]	[illegible]	[illegible]	[illegible]	[illegible]	[illegible]	[illegible]	[illegible]	[illegible]	[illegible]	[illegible]	[illegible]	[illegible]	[illegible]	[illegible]	[illegible]
April,	[illegible]	[illegible]	[illegible]	[illegible]	[illegible]	[illegible]	[illegible]	[illegible]	[illegible]	[illegible]	[illegible]	[illegible]	[illegible]	[illegible]	[illegible]	[illegible]	[illegible]	[illegible]	[illegible]	[illegible]	[illegible]	[illegible]
May,	[illegible]	[illegible]	[illegible]	[illegible]	[illegible]	[illegible]	[illegible]	[illegible]	[illegible]	[illegible]	[illegible]	[illegible]	[illegible]	[illegible]	[illegible]	[illegible]	[illegible]	[illegible]	[illegible]	[illegible]	[illegible]	[illegible]
June,	[illegible]	[illegible]	[illegible]	[illegible]	[illegible]	[illegible]	[illegible]	[illegible]	[illegible]	[illegible]	[illegible]	[illegible]	[illegible]	[illegible]	[illegible]	[illegible]	[illegible]	[illegible]	[illegible]	[illegible]	[illegible]	[illegible]
July,	[illegible]	[illegible]	[illegible]	[illegible]	[illegible]	[illegible]	[illegible]	[illegible]	[illegible]	[illegible]	[illegible]	[illegible]	[illegible]	[illegible]	[illegible]	[illegible]	[illegible]	[illegible]	[illegible]	[illegible]	[illegible]	[illegible]
August,	[illegible]	[illegible]	[illegible]	[illegible]	[illegible]	[illegible]	[illegible]	[illegible]	[illegible]	[illegible]	[illegible]	[illegible]	[illegible]	[illegible]	[illegible]	[illegible]	[illegible]	[illegible]	[illegible]	[illegible]	[illegible]	[illegible]
September,	[illegible]	[illegible]	[illegible]	[illegible]	[illegible]	[illegible]	[illegible]	[illegible]	[illegible]	[illegible]	[illegible]	[illegible]	[illegible]	[illegible]	[illegible]	[illegible]	[illegible]	[illegible]	[illegible]	[illegible]	[illegible]	[illegible]
October,	[illegible]	[illegible]	[illegible]	[illegible]	[illegible]	[illegible]	[illegible]	[illegible]	[illegible]	[illegible]	[illegible]	[illegible]	[illegible]	[illegible]	[illegible]	[illegible]	[illegible]	[illegible]	[illegible]	[illegible]	[illegible]	[illegible]
November,	[illegible]	[illegible]	[illegible]	[illegible]	[illegible]	[illegible]	[illegible]	[illegible]	[illegible]	[illegible]	[illegible]	[illegible]	[illegible]	[illegible]	[illegible]	[illegible]	[illegible]	[illegible]	[illegible]	[illegible]	[illegible]	[illegible]
December,	[illegible]	[illegible]	[illegible]	[illegible]	[illegible]	[illegible]	[illegible]	[illegible]	[illegible]	[illegible]	[illegible]	[illegible]	[illegible]	[illegible]	[illegible]	[illegible]	[illegible]	[illegible]	[illegible]	[illegible]	[illegible]	[illegible]
Year,	[illegible]	[illegible]	[illegible]	[illegible]	[illegible]	[illegible]	[illegible]	[illegible]	[illegible]	[illegible]	[illegible]	[illegible]	[illegible]	[illegible]	[illegible]	[illegible]	[illegible]	[illegible]	[illegible]	[illegible]	[illegible]	[illegible]

ABSTRACT OF METEOROLOGICAL OBSERVATIONS taken at 40, Fitzwilliam-square, West, Dublin, Long. 6° 15' W.; Lat. 53° 20' N.; Thermometers, 4 feet above the ground.

Year and Month	Mean Pressure	Air Temperature 9 a.m.	3 p.m.	Mean	Means of Min.	Means of Max.	Abs. Min. Temp.	Abs. Min. Date	Abs. Max. Temp.	Abs. Max. Date	Tension of Vapour 9 a.m.	3 p.m.	Mean	Relative Humidity 9 a.m.	3 p.m.	Mean
[illegible]	Ins.	°	°	°	°	°	°		°		Ins.	Ins.	Ins.			
January	[illegible]	[illegible]	[illegible]	[illegible]	[illegible]	[illegible]	[illegible]	[illegible]	[illegible]	[illegible]	[illegible]	[illegible]	[illegible]	[illegible]	[illegible]	[illegible]
February	[illegible]	[illegible]	[illegible]	[illegible]	[illegible]	[illegible]	[illegible]	[illegible]	[illegible]	[illegible]	[illegible]	[illegible]	[illegible]	[illegible]	[illegible]	[illegible]
March	[illegible]	[illegible]	[illegible]	[illegible]	[illegible]	[illegible]	[illegible]	[illegible]	[illegible]	[illegible]	[illegible]	[illegible]	[illegible]	[illegible]	[illegible]	[illegible]
April	[illegible]	[illegible]	[illegible]	[illegible]	[illegible]	[illegible]	[illegible]	[illegible]	[illegible]	[illegible]	[illegible]	[illegible]	[illegible]	[illegible]	[illegible]	[illegible]
May	[illegible]	[illegible]	[illegible]	[illegible]	[illegible]	[illegible]	[illegible]	[illegible]	[illegible]	[illegible]	[illegible]	[illegible]	[illegible]	[illegible]	[illegible]	[illegible]
June	[illegible]	[illegible]	[illegible]	[illegible]	[illegible]	[illegible]	[illegible]	[illegible]	[illegible]	[illegible]	[illegible]	[illegible]	[illegible]	[illegible]	[illegible]	[illegible]
July	[illegible]	[illegible]	[illegible]	[illegible]	[illegible]	[illegible]	[illegible]	[illegible]	[illegible]	[illegible]	[illegible]	[illegible]	[illegible]	[illegible]	[illegible]	[illegible]
August	[illegible]	[illegible]	[illegible]	[illegible]	[illegible]	[illegible]	[illegible]	[illegible]	[illegible]	[illegible]	[illegible]	[illegible]	[illegible]	[illegible]	[illegible]	[illegible]
September	[illegible]	[illegible]	[illegible]	[illegible]	[illegible]	[illegible]	[illegible]	[illegible]	[illegible]	[illegible]	[illegible]	[illegible]	[illegible]	[illegible]	[illegible]	[illegible]
October	[illegible]	[illegible]	[illegible]	[illegible]	[illegible]	[illegible]	[illegible]	[illegible]	[illegible]	[illegible]	[illegible]	[illegible]	[illegible]	[illegible]	[illegible]	[illegible]
November	[illegible]	[illegible]	[illegible]	[illegible]	[illegible]	[illegible]	[illegible]	[illegible]	[illegible]	[illegible]	[illegible]	[illegible]	[illegible]	[illegible]	[illegible]	[illegible]
December	[illegible]	[illegible]	[illegible]	[illegible]	[illegible]	[illegible]	[illegible]	[illegible]	[illegible]	[illegible]	[illegible]	[illegible]	[illegible]	[illegible]	[illegible]	[illegible]
Year	[illegible]	[illegible]	[illegible]	[illegible]	[illegible]	[illegible]	[illegible]	[illegible]	[illegible]	[illegible]	[illegible]	[illegible]	[illegible]	[illegible]	[illegible]	[illegible]
[illegible]																
January	[illegible]	[illegible]	[illegible]	[illegible]	[illegible]	[illegible]	[illegible]	[illegible]	[illegible]	[illegible]	[illegible]	[illegible]	[illegible]	[illegible]	[illegible]	[illegible]
February	[illegible]	[illegible]	[illegible]	[illegible]	[illegible]	[illegible]	[illegible]	[illegible]	[illegible]	[illegible]	[illegible]	[illegible]	[illegible]	[illegible]	[illegible]	[illegible]
March	[illegible]	[illegible]	[illegible]	[illegible]	[illegible]	[illegible]	[illegible]	[illegible]	[illegible]	[illegible]	[illegible]	[illegible]	[illegible]	[illegible]	[illegible]	[illegible]
April	[illegible]	[illegible]	[illegible]	[illegible]	[illegible]	[illegible]	[illegible]	[illegible]	[illegible]	[illegible]	[illegible]	[illegible]	[illegible]	[illegible]	[illegible]	[illegible]
May	[illegible]	[illegible]	[illegible]	[illegible]	[illegible]	[illegible]	[illegible]	[illegible]	[illegible]	[illegible]	[illegible]	[illegible]	[illegible]	[illegible]	[illegible]	[illegible]
June	[illegible]	[illegible]	[illegible]	[illegible]	[illegible]	[illegible]	[illegible]	[illegible]	[illegible]	[illegible]	[illegible]	[illegible]	[illegible]	[illegible]	[illegible]	[illegible]
July	[illegible]	[illegible]	[illegible]	[illegible]	[illegible]	[illegible]	[illegible]	[illegible]	[illegible]	[illegible]	[illegible]	[illegible]	[illegible]	[illegible]	[illegible]	[illegible]
August	[illegible]	[illegible]	[illegible]	[illegible]	[illegible]	[illegible]	[illegible]	[illegible]	[illegible]	[illegible]	[illegible]	[illegible]	[illegible]	[illegible]	[illegible]	[illegible]
September	[illegible]	[illegible]	[illegible]	[illegible]	[illegible]	[illegible]	[illegible]	[illegible]	[illegible]	[illegible]	[illegible]	[illegible]	[illegible]	[illegible]	[illegible]	[illegible]
October	[illegible]	[illegible]	[illegible]	[illegible]	[illegible]	[illegible]	[illegible]	[illegible]	[illegible]	[illegible]	[illegible]	[illegible]	[illegible]	[illegible]	[illegible]	[illegible]
November	[illegible]	[illegible]	[illegible]	[illegible]	[illegible]	[illegible]	[illegible]	[illegible]	[illegible]	[illegible]	[illegible]	[illegible]	[illegible]	[illegible]	[illegible]	[illegible]
December	[illegible]	[illegible]	[illegible]	[illegible]	[illegible]	[illegible]	[illegible]	[illegible]	[illegible]	[illegible]	[illegible]	[illegible]	[illegible]	[illegible]	[illegible]	[illegible]
Year	[illegible]	[illegible]	[illegible]	[illegible]	[illegible]	[illegible]	[illegible]	[illegible]	[illegible]	[illegible]	[illegible]	[illegible]	[illegible]	[illegible]	[illegible]	[illegible]
[illegible]																
January	[illegible]	[illegible]	[illegible]	[illegible]	[illegible]	[illegible]	[illegible]	[illegible]	[illegible]	[illegible]	[illegible]	[illegible]	[illegible]	[illegible]	[illegible]	[illegible]
February	[illegible]	[illegible]	[illegible]	[illegible]	[illegible]	[illegible]	[illegible]	[illegible]	[illegible]	[illegible]	[illegible]	[illegible]	[illegible]	[illegible]	[illegible]	[illegible]
March	[illegible]	[illegible]	[illegible]	[illegible]	[illegible]	[illegible]	[illegible]	[illegible]	[illegible]	[illegible]	[illegible]	[illegible]	[illegible]	[illegible]	[illegible]	[illegible]
April	[illegible]	[illegible]	[illegible]	[illegible]	[illegible]	[illegible]	[illegible]	[illegible]	[illegible]	[illegible]	[illegible]	[illegible]	[illegible]	[illegible]	[illegible]	[illegible]
May	[illegible]	[illegible]	[illegible]	[illegible]	[illegible]	[illegible]	[illegible]	[illegible]	[illegible]	[illegible]	[illegible]	[illegible]	[illegible]	[illegible]	[illegible]	[illegible]
June	[illegible]	[illegible]	[illegible]	[illegible]	[illegible]	[illegible]	[illegible]	[illegible]	[illegible]	[illegible]	[illegible]	[illegible]	[illegible]	[illegible]	[illegible]	[illegible]
July	[illegible]	[illegible]	[illegible]	[illegible]	[illegible]	[illegible]	[illegible]	[illegible]	[illegible]	[illegible]	[illegible]	[illegible]	[illegible]	[illegible]	[illegible]	[illegible]
August	[illegible]	[illegible]	[illegible]	[illegible]	[illegible]	[illegible]	[illegible]	[illegible]	[illegible]	[illegible]	[illegible]	[illegible]	[illegible]	[illegible]	[illegible]	[illegible]
September	[illegible]	[illegible]	[illegible]	[illegible]	[illegible]	[illegible]	[illegible]	[illegible]	[illegible]	[illegible]	[illegible]	[illegible]	[illegible]	[illegible]	[illegible]	[illegible]
October	[illegible]	[illegible]	[illegible]	[illegible]	[illegible]	[illegible]	[illegible]	[illegible]	[illegible]	[illegible]	[illegible]	[illegible]	[illegible]	[illegible]	[illegible]	[illegible]
November	[illegible]	[illegible]	[illegible]	[illegible]	[illegible]	[illegible]	[illegible]	[illegible]	[illegible]	[illegible]	[illegible]	[illegible]	[illegible]	[illegible]	[illegible]	[illegible]
December	[illegible]	[illegible]	[illegible]	[illegible]	[illegible]	[illegible]	[illegible]	[illegible]	[illegible]	[illegible]	[illegible]	[illegible]	[illegible]	[illegible]	[illegible]	[illegible]
Year	[illegible]	[illegible]	[illegible]	[illegible]	[illegible]	[illegible]	[illegible]	[illegible]	[illegible]	[illegible]	[illegible]	[illegible]	[illegible]	[illegible]	[illegible]	[illegible]

during the Ten Years 1851–60, by J. W. MOORE, M.D., Univ. Dub., F.R.Q.C.P.I., F.R.Met.Soc.—continued.

For Height above Mean Sea Level and Rain Gauge, see Tables on pages 56–57.

Year and Month.	Amount of Cloud.			Rainfall.			Weather. Number of days of							Wind. Number of Observations of								
	9 a.m.	9 p.m.	Mean.	Total.	Max.	Date.	[illegible]	[illegible]	[illegible]	[illegible]	[illegible]	[illegible]	[illegible]	N.	N.E.	E.	S.E.	S.	S.W.	W.	N.W.	Calm.
[illegible]				Ins.	Ins.																	
January.	[illegible]	[illegible]	[illegible]	[illegible]	[illegible]	[illegible]	[illegible]	[illegible]	[illegible]	–	[illegible]	[illegible]	[illegible]	–	[illegible]	[illegible]	[illegible]	[illegible]	[illegible]	[illegible]	[illegible]	–
February.	[illegible]	[illegible]	[illegible]	[illegible]	[illegible]	[illegible]	[illegible]	[illegible]	[illegible]	–	[illegible]	[illegible]	[illegible]	[illegible]	[illegible]	[illegible]	[illegible]	[illegible]	[illegible]	[illegible]	[illegible]	[illegible]
March.	[illegible]	[illegible]	[illegible]	[illegible]	[illegible]	[illegible]	[illegible]	[illegible]	[illegible]	–	[illegible]	[illegible]	[illegible]	–	[illegible]	[illegible]	[illegible]	[illegible]	[illegible]	[illegible]	[illegible]	[illegible]
April.	[illegible]	[illegible]	[illegible]	[illegible]	[illegible]	[illegible]	[illegible]	[illegible]	[illegible]	–	[illegible]	[illegible]	–	[illegible]	[illegible]	[illegible]	[illegible]	[illegible]	[illegible]	[illegible]	[illegible]	[illegible]
May.	[illegible]	[illegible]	[illegible]	[illegible]	[illegible]	[illegible]	[illegible]	–	[illegible]	[illegible]	[illegible]	[illegible]	[illegible]	–	[illegible]	[illegible]	[illegible]	[illegible]	[illegible]	[illegible]	[illegible]	[illegible]
June.	[illegible]	[illegible]	[illegible]	[illegible]	[illegible]	[illegible]	[illegible]	–	[illegible]	[illegible]	[illegible]	[illegible]	–	[illegible]	[illegible]	[illegible]	[illegible]	–	[illegible]	[illegible]	[illegible]	[illegible]
July.	[illegible]	[illegible]	[illegible]	[illegible]	[illegible]	[illegible]	[illegible]	–	[illegible]	[illegible]	[illegible]	[illegible]	–	[illegible]	[illegible]	[illegible]	[illegible]	[illegible]	[illegible]	[illegible]	[illegible]	[illegible]
August.	[illegible]	[illegible]	[illegible]	[illegible]	[illegible]	[illegible]	[illegible]	–	–	[illegible]	[illegible]	[illegible]	–	[illegible]	[illegible]	–	[illegible]	[illegible]	[illegible]	[illegible]	[illegible]	[illegible]
September.	[illegible]	[illegible]	[illegible]	[illegible]	[illegible]	[illegible]	[illegible]	[illegible]	[illegible]	[illegible]	[illegible]	[illegible]	[illegible]	–	[illegible]	[illegible]	[illegible]	[illegible]	[illegible]	[illegible]	[illegible]	[illegible]
October.	[illegible]	[illegible]	[illegible]	[illegible]	[illegible]	[illegible]	[illegible]	[illegible]	[illegible]	–	[illegible]	[illegible]	[illegible]	[illegible]	[illegible]	[illegible]	[illegible]	[illegible]	[illegible]	[illegible]	[illegible]	[illegible]
November.	[illegible]	[illegible]	[illegible]	[illegible]	[illegible]	[illegible]	[illegible]	[illegible]	[illegible]	–	[illegible]	[illegible]	[illegible]	[illegible]	[illegible]	[illegible]	[illegible]	[illegible]	[illegible]	[illegible]	[illegible]	[illegible]
December.	[illegible]	[illegible]	[illegible]	[illegible]	[illegible]	[illegible]	[illegible]	[illegible]	[illegible]	[illegible]	[illegible]	[illegible]	[illegible]	[illegible]	–	[illegible]	[illegible]	[illegible]	[illegible]	[illegible]	[illegible]	[illegible]
Year,	[illegible]	[illegible]	[illegible]	[illegible]	[illegible]	[illegible]	[illegible]	[illegible]	[illegible]	[illegible]	[illegible]	[illegible]	[illegible]	[illegible]	[illegible]	[illegible]	[illegible]	[illegible]	[illegible]	[illegible]	[illegible]	[illegible]
[illegible]																						
January.	[illegible]	[illegible]	[illegible]	[illegible]	[illegible]	[illegible]	[illegible]	[illegible]	[illegible]	–	[illegible]	[illegible]	[illegible]	[illegible]	[illegible]	[illegible]	[illegible]	[illegible]	[illegible]	[illegible]	[illegible]	[illegible]
February.	[illegible]	[illegible]	[illegible]	[illegible]	[illegible]	[illegible]	[illegible]	[illegible]	[illegible]	–	[illegible]	[illegible]	[illegible]	[illegible]	[illegible]	[illegible]	[illegible]	[illegible]	[illegible]	[illegible]	[illegible]	[illegible]
March.	[illegible]	[illegible]	[illegible]	[illegible]	[illegible]	[illegible]	[illegible]	[illegible]	[illegible]	–	[illegible]	[illegible]	[illegible]	[illegible]	[illegible]	[illegible]	[illegible]	[illegible]	[illegible]	[illegible]	[illegible]	[illegible]
April.	[illegible]	[illegible]	[illegible]	[illegible]	[illegible]	[illegible]	[illegible]	[illegible]	[illegible]	–	[illegible]	[illegible]	[illegible]	[illegible]	[illegible]	[illegible]	[illegible]	[illegible]	[illegible]	[illegible]	[illegible]	[illegible]
May.	[illegible]	[illegible]	[illegible]	[illegible]	[illegible]	[illegible]	[illegible]	[illegible]	[illegible]	[illegible]	[illegible]	[illegible]	–	[illegible]	[illegible]	[illegible]	[illegible]	[illegible]	[illegible]	[illegible]	[illegible]	[illegible]
June.	[illegible]	[illegible]	[illegible]	[illegible]	[illegible]	[illegible]	[illegible]	–	–	–	[illegible]	[illegible]	–	[illegible]	[illegible]	[illegible]	[illegible]	[illegible]	[illegible]	[illegible]	[illegible]	[illegible]
July.	[illegible]	[illegible]	[illegible]	[illegible]	[illegible]	[illegible]	[illegible]	–	–	–	[illegible]	[illegible]	–	[illegible]	[illegible]	[illegible]	[illegible]	[illegible]	[illegible]	[illegible]	[illegible]	[illegible]
August.	[illegible]	[illegible]	[illegible]	[illegible]	[illegible]	[illegible]	[illegible]	[illegible]	[illegible]	[illegible]	[illegible]	[illegible]	[illegible]	[illegible]	[illegible]	[illegible]	[illegible]	[illegible]	[illegible]	[illegible]	[illegible]	[illegible]
September.	[illegible]	[illegible]	[illegible]	[illegible]	[illegible]	[illegible]	[illegible]	–	[illegible]	–	[illegible]	[illegible]	[illegible]	[illegible]	–	[illegible]	[illegible]	[illegible]	[illegible]	[illegible]	[illegible]	[illegible]
October.	[illegible]	[illegible]	[illegible]	[illegible]	[illegible]	[illegible]	[illegible]	[illegible]	[illegible]	[illegible]	[illegible]	[illegible]	[illegible]	[illegible]	[illegible]	[illegible]	[illegible]	[illegible]	[illegible]	[illegible]	[illegible]	[illegible]
November.	[illegible]	[illegible]	[illegible]	[illegible]	[illegible]	[illegible]	[illegible]	[illegible]	[illegible]	–	[illegible]	[illegible]	[illegible]	–	[illegible]	[illegible]	[illegible]	[illegible]	[illegible]	[illegible]	[illegible]	[illegible]
December.	[illegible]	[illegible]	[illegible]	[illegible]	[illegible]	[illegible]	[illegible]	[illegible]	[illegible]	–	[illegible]	[illegible]	[illegible]	[illegible]	–	[illegible]	[illegible]	[illegible]	[illegible]	[illegible]	[illegible]	[illegible]
Year,	[illegible]	[illegible]	[illegible]	[illegible]	[illegible]	[illegible]	[illegible]	[illegible]	[illegible]	[illegible]	[illegible]	[illegible]	[illegible]	[illegible]	[illegible]	[illegible]	[illegible]	[illegible]	[illegible]	[illegible]	[illegible]	[illegible]
[illegible]																						
January.	[illegible]	[illegible]	[illegible]	[illegible]	[illegible]	[illegible]	[illegible]	[illegible]	[illegible]	–	[illegible]	[illegible]	[illegible]	[illegible]	[illegible]	[illegible]	[illegible]	[illegible]	[illegible]	[illegible]	[illegible]	[illegible]
February.	[illegible]	[illegible]	[illegible]	[illegible]	[illegible]	[illegible]	[illegible]	[illegible]	[illegible]	–	[illegible]	[illegible]	–	[illegible]	[illegible]	[illegible]	[illegible]	[illegible]	[illegible]	[illegible]	[illegible]	[illegible]
March.	[illegible]	[illegible]	[illegible]	[illegible]	[illegible]	[illegible]	[illegible]	[illegible]	[illegible]	–	[illegible]	[illegible]	[illegible]	[illegible]	[illegible]	[illegible]	[illegible]	[illegible]	[illegible]	[illegible]	[illegible]	[illegible]
April.	[illegible]	[illegible]	[illegible]	[illegible]	[illegible]	[illegible]	[illegible]	[illegible]	[illegible]	–	[illegible]	[illegible]	[illegible]	[illegible]	[illegible]	[illegible]	[illegible]	[illegible]	[illegible]	[illegible]	[illegible]	[illegible]
May.	[illegible]	[illegible]	[illegible]	[illegible]	[illegible]	[illegible]	[illegible]	[illegible]	[illegible]	–	[illegible]	[illegible]	[illegible]	[illegible]	[illegible]	[illegible]	[illegible]	[illegible]	[illegible]	[illegible]	[illegible]	[illegible]
June.	[illegible]	[illegible]	[illegible]	[illegible]	[illegible]	[illegible]	[illegible]	–	–	–	[illegible]	[illegible]	–	[illegible]	[illegible]	[illegible]	[illegible]	[illegible]	[illegible]	[illegible]	[illegible]	[illegible]
July.	[illegible]	[illegible]	[illegible]	[illegible]	[illegible]	[illegible]	[illegible]	–	–	–	[illegible]	[illegible]	[illegible]	[illegible]	[illegible]	[illegible]	[illegible]	[illegible]	[illegible]	[illegible]	[illegible]	[illegible]
August.	[illegible]	[illegible]	[illegible]	[illegible]	[illegible]	[illegible]	[illegible]	–	–	–	[illegible]	[illegible]	–	[illegible]	[illegible]	[illegible]	[illegible]	[illegible]	[illegible]	[illegible]	[illegible]	[illegible]
September.	[illegible]	[illegible]	[illegible]	[illegible]	[illegible]	[illegible]	[illegible]	–	–	[illegible]	[illegible]	[illegible]	[illegible]	[illegible]	[illegible]	[illegible]	[illegible]	[illegible]	[illegible]	[illegible]	[illegible]	[illegible]
October.	[illegible]	[illegible]	[illegible]	[illegible]	[illegible]	[illegible]	[illegible]	–	[illegible]	–	[illegible]	[illegible]	[illegible]	[illegible]	[illegible]	[illegible]	[illegible]	[illegible]	[illegible]	[illegible]	[illegible]	[illegible]
November.	[illegible]	[illegible]	[illegible]	[illegible]	[illegible]	[illegible]	[illegible]	[illegible]	–	–	[illegible]	[illegible]	[illegible]	[illegible]	[illegible]	[illegible]	[illegible]	[illegible]	[illegible]	[illegible]	[illegible]	[illegible]
December.	[illegible]	[illegible]	[illegible]	[illegible]	[illegible]	[illegible]	[illegible]	[illegible]	[illegible]	–	[illegible]	[illegible]	[illegible]	[illegible]	[illegible]	[illegible]	–	–	[illegible]	[illegible]	[illegible]	[illegible]
Year,	[illegible]	[illegible]	[illegible]	[illegible]	[illegible]	[illegible]	[illegible]	[illegible]	[illegible]	[illegible]	[illegible]	[illegible]	[illegible]	[illegible]	[illegible]	[illegible]	[illegible]	[illegible]	[illegible]	[illegible]	[illegible]	[illegible]

ABSTRACT OF METEOROLOGICAL OBSERVATIONS taken at 40, Fitzwilliam-square, West, Dublin, Long. 6° 15' W.; Lat. 53° 20' N.; Thermometers, 4 feet above the ground.

Year and Month.	Mean Pressure.	Air Temperature 9 a.m.	9 p.m.	Mean.	Means of Min.	Max.	Abs. Min. Temp.	Date.	Abs. Max. Temp.	Date.	Tension of Vapour 9 a.m.	9 p.m.	Mean.	Relative Humidity 9 a.m.	9 p.m.	Mean.
1867.	Ins.	°	°	°	°	°	°		°		Ins.	Ins.	Ins.	%	%	%
January,	[illegible]	[illegible]	[illegible]	[illegible]	[illegible]	[illegible]	[illegible]	[illegible]	[illegible]	[illegible]	[illegible]	[illegible]	[illegible]	[illegible]	[illegible]	[illegible]
February,	[illegible]	[illegible]	[illegible]	[illegible]	[illegible]	[illegible]	[illegible]	[illegible]	[illegible]	[illegible]	[illegible]	[illegible]	[illegible]	[illegible]	[illegible]	[illegible]
March,	[illegible]	[illegible]	[illegible]	[illegible]	[illegible]	[illegible]	[illegible]	[illegible]	[illegible]	[illegible]	[illegible]	[illegible]	[illegible]	[illegible]	[illegible]	[illegible]
April,	[illegible]	[illegible]	[illegible]	[illegible]	[illegible]	[illegible]	[illegible]	[illegible]	[illegible]	[illegible]	[illegible]	[illegible]	[illegible]	[illegible]	[illegible]	[illegible]
May,	[illegible]	[illegible]	[illegible]	[illegible]	[illegible]	[illegible]	[illegible]	[illegible]	[illegible]	[illegible]	[illegible]	[illegible]	[illegible]	[illegible]	[illegible]	[illegible]
June,	[illegible]	[illegible]	[illegible]	[illegible]	[illegible]	[illegible]	[illegible]	[illegible]	[illegible]	[illegible]	[illegible]	[illegible]	[illegible]	[illegible]	[illegible]	[illegible]
July,	[illegible]	[illegible]	[illegible]	[illegible]	[illegible]	[illegible]	[illegible]	[illegible]	[illegible]	[illegible]	[illegible]	[illegible]	[illegible]	[illegible]	[illegible]	[illegible]
August,	[illegible]	[illegible]	[illegible]	[illegible]	[illegible]	[illegible]	[illegible]	[illegible]	[illegible]	[illegible]	[illegible]	[illegible]	[illegible]	[illegible]	[illegible]	[illegible]
September,	[illegible]	[illegible]	[illegible]	[illegible]	[illegible]	[illegible]	[illegible]	[illegible]	[illegible]	[illegible]	[illegible]	[illegible]	[illegible]	[illegible]	[illegible]	[illegible]
October,	[illegible]	[illegible]	[illegible]	[illegible]	[illegible]	[illegible]	[illegible]	[illegible]	[illegible]	[illegible]	[illegible]	[illegible]	[illegible]	[illegible]	[illegible]	[illegible]
November,	[illegible]	[illegible]	[illegible]	[illegible]	[illegible]	[illegible]	[illegible]	[illegible]	[illegible]	[illegible]	[illegible]	[illegible]	[illegible]	[illegible]	[illegible]	[illegible]
December,	[illegible]	[illegible]	[illegible]	[illegible]	[illegible]	[illegible]	[illegible]	[illegible]	[illegible]	[illegible]	[illegible]	[illegible]	[illegible]	[illegible]	[illegible]	[illegible]
Year,	[illegible]	[illegible]	[illegible]	[illegible]	[illegible]	[illegible]	[illegible]	[illegible]	[illegible]	[illegible]	[illegible]	[illegible]	[illegible]	[illegible]	[illegible]	[illegible]
1868.																
January,	[illegible]	[illegible]	[illegible]	[illegible]	[illegible]	[illegible]	[illegible]	[illegible]	[illegible]	[illegible]	[illegible]	[illegible]	[illegible]	[illegible]	[illegible]	[illegible]
February,	[illegible]	[illegible]	[illegible]	[illegible]	[illegible]	[illegible]	[illegible]	[illegible]	[illegible]	[illegible]	[illegible]	[illegible]	[illegible]	[illegible]	[illegible]	[illegible]
March,	[illegible]	[illegible]	[illegible]	[illegible]	[illegible]	[illegible]	[illegible]	[illegible]	[illegible]	[illegible]	[illegible]	[illegible]	[illegible]	[illegible]	[illegible]	[illegible]
April,	[illegible]	[illegible]	[illegible]	[illegible]	[illegible]	[illegible]	[illegible]	[illegible]	[illegible]	[illegible]	[illegible]	[illegible]	[illegible]	[illegible]	[illegible]	[illegible]
May,	[illegible]	[illegible]	[illegible]	[illegible]	[illegible]	[illegible]	[illegible]	[illegible]	[illegible]	[illegible]	[illegible]	[illegible]	[illegible]	[illegible]	[illegible]	[illegible]
June,	[illegible]	[illegible]	[illegible]	[illegible]	[illegible]	[illegible]	[illegible]	[illegible]	[illegible]	[illegible]	[illegible]	[illegible]	[illegible]	[illegible]	[illegible]	[illegible]
July,	[illegible]	[illegible]	[illegible]	[illegible]	[illegible]	[illegible]	[illegible]	[illegible]	[illegible]	[illegible]	[illegible]	[illegible]	[illegible]	[illegible]	[illegible]	[illegible]
August,	[illegible]	[illegible]	[illegible]	[illegible]	[illegible]	[illegible]	[illegible]	[illegible]	[illegible]	[illegible]	[illegible]	[illegible]	[illegible]	[illegible]	[illegible]	[illegible]
September,	[illegible]	[illegible]	[illegible]	[illegible]	[illegible]	[illegible]	[illegible]	[illegible]	[illegible]	[illegible]	[illegible]	[illegible]	[illegible]	[illegible]	[illegible]	[illegible]
October,	[illegible]	[illegible]	[illegible]	[illegible]	[illegible]	[illegible]	[illegible]	[illegible]	[illegible]	[illegible]	[illegible]	[illegible]	[illegible]	[illegible]	[illegible]	[illegible]

during the Ten Years 1881–90, by J. W. MOORE, M.D., Univ. Dub., F.R.C.P.I., F.R.Met.Soc.—*continued.*
For Height above Mean Sea Level and Rain Gauge, see Tables on pages 44–47.

Year and Month.	Amount of Cloud.			Rainfall.			Weather. Number of days of							Wind. Number of Observations of								
	9 a.m.	9 p.m.	Mean.	Total.	Max.	Date.	[illegible]	[illegible]	[illegible]	[illegible]	[illegible]	[illegible]	[illegible]	N.	N.E.	E.	S.E.	S.	S.W.	W.	N.W.	Calm.
1887.				Ins.	Ins.																	
January,	[illegible]	[illegible]	[illegible]	[illegible]	[illegible]	[illegible]	[illegible]	[illegible]	[illegible]	[illegible]	[illegible]	[illegible]	[illegible]	[illegible]	[illegible]	[illegible]	[illegible]	[illegible]	[illegible]	[illegible]	[illegible]	[illegible]
February,	[illegible]	[illegible]	[illegible]	[illegible]	[illegible]	[illegible]	[illegible]	[illegible]	[illegible]	[illegible]	[illegible]	[illegible]	[illegible]	[illegible]	[illegible]	[illegible]	[illegible]	[illegible]	[illegible]	[illegible]	[illegible]	[illegible]
March,	[illegible]	[illegible]	[illegible]	[illegible]	[illegible]	[illegible]	[illegible]	[illegible]	[illegible]	[illegible]	[illegible]	[illegible]	[illegible]	[illegible]	[illegible]	[illegible]	[illegible]	[illegible]	[illegible]	[illegible]	[illegible]	[illegible]
April,	[illegible]	[illegible]	[illegible]	[illegible]	[illegible]	[illegible]	[illegible]	[illegible]	[illegible]	[illegible]	[illegible]	[illegible]	[illegible]	[illegible]	[illegible]	[illegible]	[illegible]	[illegible]	[illegible]	[illegible]	[illegible]	[illegible]
May,	[illegible]	[illegible]	[illegible]	[illegible]	[illegible]	[illegible]	[illegible]	[illegible]	[illegible]	[illegible]	[illegible]	[illegible]	[illegible]	[illegible]	[illegible]	[illegible]	[illegible]	[illegible]	[illegible]	[illegible]	[illegible]	[illegible]
June,	[illegible]	[illegible]	[illegible]	[illegible]	[illegible]	[illegible]	[illegible]	[illegible]	[illegible]	[illegible]	[illegible]	[illegible]	[illegible]	[illegible]	[illegible]	[illegible]	[illegible]	[illegible]	[illegible]	[illegible]	[illegible]	[illegible]
July,	[illegible]	[illegible]	[illegible]	[illegible]	[illegible]	[illegible]	[illegible]	[illegible]	[illegible]	[illegible]	[illegible]	[illegible]	[illegible]	[illegible]	[illegible]	[illegible]	[illegible]	[illegible]	[illegible]	[illegible]	[illegible]	[illegible]
August,	[illegible]	[illegible]	[illegible]	[illegible]	[illegible]	[illegible]	[illegible]	[illegible]	[illegible]	[illegible]	[illegible]	[illegible]	[illegible]	[illegible]	[illegible]	[illegible]	[illegible]	[illegible]	[illegible]	[illegible]	[illegible]	[illegible]
September,	[illegible]	[illegible]	[illegible]	[illegible]	[illegible]	[illegible]	[illegible]	[illegible]	[illegible]	[illegible]	[illegible]	[illegible]	[illegible]	[illegible]	[illegible]	[illegible]	[illegible]	[illegible]	[illegible]	[illegible]	[illegible]	[illegible]
October,	[illegible]	[illegible]	[illegible]	[illegible]	[illegible]	[illegible]	[illegible]	[illegible]	[illegible]	[illegible]	[illegible]	[illegible]	[illegible]	[illegible]	[illegible]	[illegible]	[illegible]	[illegible]	[illegible]	[illegible]	[illegible]	[illegible]
November,	[illegible]	[illegible]	[illegible]	[illegible]	[illegible]	[illegible]	[illegible]	[illegible]	[illegible]	[illegible]	[illegible]	[illegible]	[illegible]	[illegible]	[illegible]	[illegible]	[illegible]	[illegible]	[illegible]	[illegible]	[illegible]	[illegible]
December,	[illegible]	[illegible]	[illegible]	[illegible]	[illegible]	[illegible]	[illegible]	[illegible]	[illegible]	[illegible]	[illegible]	[illegible]	[illegible]	[illegible]	[illegible]	[illegible]	[illegible]	[illegible]	[illegible]	[illegible]	[illegible]	[illegible]
Year,	[illegible]	[illegible]	[illegible]	[illegible]	[illegible]	[illegible]	[illegible]	[illegible]	[illegible]	[illegible]	[illegible]	[illegible]	[illegible]	[illegible]	[illegible]	[illegible]	[illegible]	[illegible]	[illegible]	[illegible]	[illegible]	[illegible]
1888.																						
January,	[illegible]	[illegible]	[illegible]	[illegible]	[illegible]	[illegible]	[illegible]	[illegible]	[illegible]	[illegible]	[illegible]	[illegible]	[illegible]	[illegible]	[illegible]	[illegible]	[illegible]	[illegible]	[illegible]	[illegible]	[illegible]	[illegible]
February,	[illegible]	[illegible]	[illegible]	[illegible]	[illegible]	[illegible]	[illegible]	[illegible]	[illegible]	[illegible]	[illegible]	[illegible]	[illegible]	[illegible]	[illegible]	[illegible]	[illegible]	[illegible]	[illegible]	[illegible]	[illegible]	[illegible]
March,	[illegible]	[illegible]	[illegible]	[illegible]	[illegible]	[illegible]	[illegible]	[illegible]	[illegible]	[illegible]	[illegible]	[illegible]	[illegible]	[illegible]	[illegible]	[illegible]	[illegible]	[illegible]	[illegible]	[illegible]	[illegible]	[illegible]
April,	[illegible]	[illegible]	[illegible]	[illegible]	[illegible]	[illegible]	[illegible]	[illegible]	[illegible]	[illegible]	[illegible]	[illegible]	[illegible]	[illegible]	[illegible]	[illegible]	[illegible]	[illegible]	[illegible]	[illegible]	[illegible]	[illegible]
May,	[illegible]	[illegible]	[illegible]	[illegible]	[illegible]	[illegible]	[illegible]	[illegible]	[illegible]	[illegible]	[illegible]	[illegible]	[illegible]	[illegible]	[illegible]	[illegible]	[illegible]	[illegible]	[illegible]	[illegible]	[illegible]	[illegible]
June,	[illegible]	[illegible]	[illegible]	[illegible]	[illegible]	[illegible]	[illegible]	[illegible]	[illegible]	[illegible]	[illegible]	[illegible]	[illegible]	[illegible]	[illegible]	[illegible]	[illegible]	[illegible]	[illegible]	[illegible]	[illegible]	[illegible]
July,	[illegible]	[illegible]	[illegible]	[illegible]	[illegible]	[illegible]	[illegible]	[illegible]	[illegible]	[illegible]	[illegible]	[illegible]	[illegible]	[illegible]	[illegible]	[illegible]	[illegible]	[illegible]	[illegible]	[illegible]	[illegible]	[illegible]
August,	[illegible]	[illegible]	[illegible]	[illegible]	[illegible]	[illegible]	[illegible]	[illegible]	[illegible]	[illegible]	[illegible]	[illegible]	[illegible]	[illegible]	[illegible]	[illegible]	[illegible]	[illegible]	[illegible]	[illegible]	[illegible]	[illegible]
September,	[illegible]	[illegible]	[illegible]	[illegible]	[illegible]	[illegible]	[illegible]	[illegible]	[illegible]	[illegible]	[illegible]	[illegible]	[illegible]	[illegible]	[illegible]	[illegible]	[illegible]	[illegible]	[illegible]	[illegible]	[illegible]	[illegible]
October,	[illegible]	[illegible]	[illegible]	[illegible]	[illegible]	[illegible]	[illegible]	[illegible]	[illegible]	[illegible]	[illegible]	[illegible]	[illegible]	[illegible]	[illegible]	[illegible]	[illegible]	[illegible]	[illegible]	[illegible]	[illegible]	[illegible]
November,	[illegible]	[illegible]	[illegible]	[illegible]	[illegible]	[illegible]	[illegible]	[illegible]	[illegible]	[illegible]	[illegible]	[illegible]	[illegible]	[illegible]	[illegible]	[illegible]	[illegible]	[illegible]	[illegible]	[illegible]	[illegible]	[illegible]
December,	[illegible]	[illegible]	[illegible]	[illegible]	[illegible]	[illegible]	[illegible]	[illegible]	[illegible]	[illegible]	[illegible]	[illegible]	[illegible]	[illegible]	[illegible]	[illegible]	[illegible]	[illegible]	[illegible]	[illegible]	[illegible]	[illegible]
Year,	[illegible]	[illegible]	[illegible]	[illegible]	[illegible]	[illegible]	[illegible]	[illegible]	[illegible]	[illegible]	[illegible]	[illegible]	[illegible]	[illegible]	[illegible]	[illegible]	[illegible]	[illegible]	[illegible]	[illegible]	[illegible]	[illegible]
1889.																						
January,	[illegible]	[illegible]	[illegible]	[illegible]	[illegible]	[illegible]	[illegible]	[illegible]	[illegible]	[illegible]	[illegible]	[illegible]	[illegible]	[illegible]	[illegible]	[illegible]	[illegible]	[illegible]	[illegible]	[illegible]	[illegible]	[illegible]
February,	[illegible]	[illegible]	[illegible]	[illegible]	[illegible]	[illegible]	[illegible]	[illegible]	[illegible]	[illegible]	[illegible]	[illegible]	[illegible]	[illegible]	[illegible]	[illegible]	[illegible]	[illegible]	[illegible]	[illegible]	[illegible]	[illegible]
March,	[illegible]	[illegible]	[illegible]	[illegible]	[illegible]	[illegible]	[illegible]	[illegible]	[illegible]	[illegible]	[illegible]	[illegible]	[illegible]	[illegible]	[illegible]	[illegible]	[illegible]	[illegible]	[illegible]	[illegible]	[illegible]	[illegible]
April,	[illegible]	[illegible]	[illegible]	[illegible]	[illegible]	[illegible]	[illegible]	[illegible]	[illegible]	[illegible]	[illegible]	[illegible]	[illegible]	[illegible]	[illegible]	[illegible]	[illegible]	[illegible]	[illegible]	[illegible]	[illegible]	[illegible]
May,	[illegible]	[illegible]	[illegible]	[illegible]	[illegible]	[illegible]	[illegible]	[illegible]	[illegible]	[illegible]	[illegible]	[illegible]	[illegible]	[illegible]	[illegible]	[illegible]	[illegible]	[illegible]	[illegible]	[illegible]	[illegible]	[illegible]
June,	[illegible]	[illegible]	[illegible]	[illegible]	[illegible]	[illegible]	[illegible]	[illegible]	[illegible]	[illegible]	[illegible]	[illegible]	[illegible]	[illegible]	[illegible]	[illegible]	[illegible]	[illegible]	[illegible]	[illegible]	[illegible]	[illegible]
July,	[illegible]	[illegible]	[illegible]	[illegible]	[illegible]	[illegible]	[illegible]	[illegible]	[illegible]	[illegible]	[illegible]	[illegible]	[illegible]	[illegible]	[illegible]	[illegible]	[illegible]	[illegible]	[illegible]	[illegible]	[illegible]	[illegible]
August,	[illegible]	[illegible]	[illegible]	[illegible]	[illegible]	[illegible]	[illegible]	[illegible]	[illegible]	[illegible]	[illegible]	[illegible]	[illegible]	[illegible]	[illegible]	[illegible]	[illegible]	[illegible]	[illegible]	[illegible]	[illegible]	[illegible]
September,	[illegible]	[illegible]	[illegible]	[illegible]	[illegible]	[illegible]	[illegible]	[illegible]	[illegible]	[illegible]	[illegible]	[illegible]	[illegible]	[illegible]	[illegible]	[illegible]	[illegible]	[illegible]	[illegible]	[illegible]	[illegible]	[illegible]
October,	[illegible]	[illegible]	[illegible]	[illegible]	[illegible]	[illegible]	[illegible]	[illegible]	[illegible]	[illegible]	[illegible]	[illegible]	[illegible]	[illegible]	[illegible]	[illegible]	[illegible]	[illegible]	[illegible]	[illegible]	[illegible]	[illegible]
November,	[illegible]	[illegible]	[illegible]	[illegible]	[illegible]	[illegible]	[illegible]	[illegible]	[illegible]	[illegible]	[illegible]	[illegible]	[illegible]	[illegible]	[illegible]	[illegible]	[illegible]	[illegible]	[illegible]	[illegible]	[illegible]	[illegible]
December,	[illegible]	[illegible]	[illegible]	[illegible]	[illegible]	[illegible]	[illegible]	[illegible]	[illegible]	[illegible]	[illegible]	[illegible]	[illegible]	[illegible]	[illegible]	[illegible]	[illegible]	[illegible]	[illegible]	[illegible]	[illegible]	[illegible]
Year,	[illegible]	[illegible]	[illegible]	[illegible]	[illegible]	[illegible]	[illegible]	[illegible]	[illegible]	[illegible]	[illegible]	[illegible]	[illegible]	[illegible]	[illegible]	[illegible]	[illegible]	[illegible]	[illegible]	[illegible]	[illegible]	[illegible]

ABSTRACT OF METEOROLOGICAL OBSERVATIONS taken at 40, Fitzwilliam-square, West, Dublin.

Long. 6° 15′ W.; Lat. 53° 20′ N.; Thermometers, 4 feet above the ground.

Year and Month.	Mean Pressure.	Air Temperature. 9 a.m.	3 p.m.	Mean.	Means of Min.	Max.	Abs. Min. Temp.	Date.	Abs. Max. Temp.	Date.	Tension of Vapour. 9 a.m.	3 p.m.	Mean.	Relative Humidity. 9 a.m.	3 p.m.	Mean.
[illegible]	Ins.	°	°	°	°	°	°		°		Ins.	Ins.	Ins.	%	%	%
January,	[illegible]	[illegible]	[illegible]	[illegible]	[illegible]	[illegible]	[illegible]	[illegible]	[illegible]	[illegible]	[illegible]	[illegible]	[illegible]	[illegible]	[illegible]	[illegible]
February,	[illegible]	[illegible]	[illegible]	[illegible]	[illegible]	[illegible]	[illegible]	[illegible]	[illegible]	[illegible]	[illegible]	[illegible]	[illegible]	[illegible]	[illegible]	[illegible]
March,	[illegible]	[illegible]	[illegible]	[illegible]	[illegible]	[illegible]	[illegible]	[illegible]	[illegible]	[illegible]	[illegible]	[illegible]	[illegible]	[illegible]	[illegible]	[illegible]
April,	[illegible]	[illegible]	[illegible]	[illegible]	[illegible]	[illegible]	[illegible]	[illegible]	[illegible]	[illegible]	[illegible]	[illegible]	[illegible]	[illegible]	[illegible]	[illegible]
May,	[illegible]	[illegible]	[illegible]	[illegible]	[illegible]	[illegible]	[illegible]	[illegible]	[illegible]	[illegible]	[illegible]	[illegible]	[illegible]	[illegible]	[illegible]	[illegible]
June,	[illegible]	[illegible]	[illegible]	[illegible]	[illegible]	[illegible]	[illegible]	[illegible]	[illegible]	[illegible]	[illegible]	[illegible]	[illegible]	[illegible]	[illegible]	[illegible]
July,	[illegible]	[illegible]	[illegible]	[illegible]	[illegible]	[illegible]	[illegible]	[illegible]	[illegible]	[illegible]	[illegible]	[illegible]	[illegible]	[illegible]	[illegible]	[illegible]
August,	[illegible]	[illegible]	[illegible]	[illegible]	[illegible]	[illegible]	[illegible]	[illegible]	[illegible]	[illegible]	[illegible]	[illegible]	[illegible]	[illegible]	[illegible]	[illegible]
September,	[illegible]	[illegible]	[illegible]	[illegible]	[illegible]	[illegible]	[illegible]	[illegible]	[illegible]	[illegible]	[illegible]	[illegible]	[illegible]	[illegible]	[illegible]	[illegible]
October,	[illegible]	[illegible]	[illegible]	[illegible]	[illegible]	[illegible]	[illegible]	[illegible]	[illegible]	[illegible]	[illegible]	[illegible]	[illegible]	[illegible]	[illegible]	[illegible]
November,	[illegible]	[illegible]	[illegible]	[illegible]	[illegible]	[illegible]	[illegible]	[illegible]	[illegible]	[illegible]	[illegible]	[illegible]	[illegible]	[illegible]	[illegible]	[illegible]
December,	[illegible]	[illegible]	[illegible]	[illegible]	[illegible]	[illegible]	[illegible]	[illegible]	[illegible]	[illegible]	[illegible]	[illegible]	[illegible]	[illegible]	[illegible]	[illegible]
Year,	[illegible]	[illegible]	[illegible]	[illegible]	[illegible]	[illegible]	[illegible]	Dec. [illegible]	[illegible]	Aug. [illegible]	[illegible]	[illegible]	[illegible]	[illegible]	[illegible]	[illegible]

ABSTRACT OF METEOROLOGICAL OBSERVATIONS taken at 40, Fitzwilliam-square, West,

Long. 6° 15′ W.; Lat. 53° 20′ N. Height above Mean Sea Level, 51 feet for the years 1851–54, [illegible] feet for the years 1851–54, [illegible] feet for 1855–60.

Year.	Mean Pressure.	Air Temperature. 9 a.m.	3 p.m.	Mean.	Means of Min.	Max.	Absolute Min. and Max. Min.	Date.	Max.	Date.	Tension of Vapour. 9 a.m.	3 p.m.	Mean.	Relative Humidity. 9 a.m.	3 p.m.	Mean.
	Ins.	°	°	°	°	°	°		°		Ins.	Ins.	Ins.	%	%	%
[illegible]	[illegible]	[illegible]	[illegible]	[illegible]	[illegible]	[illegible]	[illegible]	January [illegible]	[illegible]	July [illegible]	[illegible]	[illegible]	[illegible]	[illegible]	[illegible]	[illegible]
[illegible]	[illegible]	[illegible]	[illegible]	[illegible]	[illegible]	[illegible]	[illegible]	December [illegible]	[illegible]	August [illegible]	[illegible]	[illegible]	[illegible]	[illegible]	[illegible]	[illegible]
[illegible]	[illegible]	[illegible]	[illegible]	[illegible]	[illegible]	[illegible]	[illegible]	March [illegible]	[illegible]	August [illegible]	[illegible]	[illegible]	[illegible]	[illegible]	[illegible]	[illegible]
[illegible]	[illegible]	[illegible]	[illegible]	[illegible]	[illegible]	[illegible]	[illegible]	December [illegible]	[illegible]	June [illegible]	[illegible]	[illegible]	[illegible]	[illegible]	[illegible]	[illegible]
[illegible]	[illegible]	[illegible]	[illegible]	[illegible]	[illegible]	[illegible]	[illegible]	December [illegible]	[illegible]	July [illegible]	[illegible]	[illegible]	[illegible]	[illegible]	[illegible]	[illegible]
[illegible]	[illegible]	[illegible]	[illegible]	[illegible]	[illegible]	[illegible]	[illegible]	December [illegible]	[illegible]	July 3rd,	[illegible]	[illegible]	[illegible]	[illegible]	[illegible]	[illegible]
[illegible]	[illegible]	[illegible]	[illegible]	[illegible]	[illegible]	[illegible]	[illegible]	January [illegible]	[illegible]	August [illegible]	[illegible]	[illegible]	[illegible]	[illegible]	[illegible]	[illegible]
[illegible]	[illegible]	[illegible]	[illegible]	[illegible]	[illegible]	[illegible]	[illegible]	February [illegible]	[illegible]	June [illegible]	[illegible]	[illegible]	[illegible]	[illegible]	[illegible]	[illegible]
[illegible]	[illegible]	[illegible]	[illegible]	[illegible]	[illegible]	[illegible]	[illegible]	February 19th,	[illegible]	July [illegible]	[illegible]	[illegible]	[illegible]	[illegible]	[illegible]	[illegible]
[illegible]	[illegible]	[illegible]	[illegible]	[illegible]	[illegible]	[illegible]	[illegible]	December [illegible]	[illegible]	August [illegible]	[illegible]	[illegible]	[illegible]	[illegible]	[illegible]	[illegible]
THE YEARS,	[illegible]	[illegible]	[illegible]	[illegible]	[illegible]	[illegible]	[illegible]	Dec. [illegible]	[illegible]	August [illegible]	[illegible]	[illegible]	[illegible]	[illegible]	[illegible]	[illegible]

during the Ten Years 1881-90, by J. W. MOORE, M.D., Univ. Dub., F.R.C.P.I., F.R.Met.Soc.—*continued.*

For Height above Mean Sea Level and Rain Gauge, see Tables on pages 56-57.

Year and Month.	Amount of Cloud.			Rainfall.			Weather. Number of Days of							Wind. Number of Observations of								
	9 a.m.	9 p.m.	Mean.	Total.	Max.	Date.	[illegible]	[illegible]	[illegible]	[illegible]	[illegible]	[illegible]	[illegible]	N.	N.E.	E.	S.E.	S.	S.W.	W.	N.W.	Calm.
1890.				In.	In.																	
January, .	[illegible]	[illegible]	[illegible]	[illegible]	[illegible]	[illegible]	[illegible]	[illegible]	[illegible]	-	[illegible]	[illegible]	[illegible]	[illegible]	[illegible]	[illegible]	[illegible]	[illegible]	[illegible]	[illegible]	[illegible]	[illegible]
February, .	[illegible]	[illegible]	[illegible]	[illegible]	[illegible]	[illegible]	[illegible]	[illegible]	[illegible]	-	[illegible]	[illegible]	[illegible]	[illegible]	[illegible]	[illegible]	[illegible]	[illegible]	[illegible]	[illegible]	[illegible]	[illegible]
March, .	[illegible]	[illegible]	[illegible]	[illegible]	[illegible]	[illegible]	[illegible]	[illegible]	[illegible]	[illegible]	[illegible]	[illegible]	[illegible]	[illegible]	[illegible]	[illegible]	[illegible]	[illegible]	[illegible]	[illegible]	[illegible]	[illegible]
April, .	[illegible]	[illegible]	[illegible]	[illegible]	[illegible]	[illegible]	[illegible]	[illegible]	[illegible]	[illegible]	[illegible]	[illegible]	[illegible]	[illegible]	[illegible]	[illegible]	[illegible]	[illegible]	[illegible]	[illegible]	[illegible]	[illegible]
May, .	[illegible]	[illegible]	[illegible]	[illegible]	[illegible]	[illegible]	[illegible]	-	[illegible]	-	[illegible]	[illegible]	-	[illegible]	[illegible]	[illegible]	[illegible]	[illegible]	[illegible]	[illegible]	[illegible]	[illegible]
June, .	[illegible]	[illegible]	[illegible]	[illegible]	[illegible]	[illegible]	[illegible]	-	[illegible]	[illegible]	-	[illegible]	[illegible]	[illegible]	[illegible]	-	[illegible]	[illegible]	[illegible]	[illegible]	[illegible]	[illegible]
July, .	[illegible]	[illegible]	[illegible]	[illegible]	[illegible]	[illegible]	[illegible]	-	-	-	-	[illegible]	[illegible]	[illegible]	[illegible]	[illegible]	[illegible]	[illegible]	[illegible]	[illegible]	[illegible]	[illegible]
August, .	[illegible]	[illegible]	[illegible]	[illegible]	[illegible]	[illegible]	[illegible]	-	[illegible]	-	[illegible]	[illegible]	[illegible]	[illegible]	[illegible]	[illegible]	[illegible]	-	[illegible]	[illegible]	[illegible]	[illegible]
September, .	[illegible]	[illegible]	[illegible]	[illegible]	[illegible]	[illegible]	[illegible]	-	-	-	[illegible]	[illegible]	[illegible]	[illegible]	-	-	[illegible]	[illegible]	[illegible]	[illegible]	[illegible]	[illegible]
October, .	[illegible]	[illegible]	[illegible]	[illegible]	[illegible]	[illegible]	[illegible]	[illegible]	[illegible]	-	[illegible]	[illegible]	[illegible]	[illegible]	[illegible]	-	[illegible]	-	[illegible]	[illegible]	[illegible]	[illegible]
November, .	[illegible]	[illegible]	[illegible]	[illegible]	[illegible]	[illegible]	[illegible]	[illegible]	[illegible]	-	[illegible]	[illegible]	[illegible]	[illegible]	[illegible]	-	[illegible]	[illegible]	[illegible]	[illegible]	[illegible]	[illegible]
December, .	[illegible]	[illegible]	[illegible]	[illegible]	[illegible]	[illegible]	[illegible]	[illegible]	[illegible]	-	[illegible]	[illegible]	[illegible]	[illegible]	[illegible]	[illegible]	[illegible]	[illegible]	[illegible]	[illegible]	[illegible]	[illegible]
Year, .	[illegible]	[illegible]	[illegible]	[illegible]	[illegible]	[illegible]	[illegible]	[illegible]	[illegible]	[illegible]	[illegible]	[illegible]	[illegible]	[illegible]	[illegible]	[illegible]	[illegible]	[illegible]	[illegible]	[illegible]	[illegible]	[illegible]

Dublin, during the Ten Years 1881-90, by J. W. MOORE, M.D., Univ. Dub., F.R.C.P.I., F.R.Met.Soc.

1885-89, and 50 feet for 1890. Thermometers 4 feet above ground. Rain gauge 3 feet 4 inches above ground 1 foot 4 inches for 1887-90.

Years.	Amount of Cloud.			Rainfall.			Weather. Number of Days of							Wind. Number of Observations of								
	[illegible]	[illegible]	[illegible]	Least.	Max.	Date.	[illegible]	[illegible]	[illegible]	[illegible]	[illegible]	[illegible]	[illegible]	N.	N.E.	E.	S.E.	S.	S.W.	W.	N.W.	Calm.
				Ins.	Ins.																	
[illegible]	[illegible]	[illegible]	[illegible]	[illegible]	[illegible]	October [illegible]	[illegible]	[illegible]	[illegible]	[illegible]	[illegible]	[illegible]	[illegible]	[illegible]	[illegible]	[illegible]	[illegible]	[illegible]	[illegible]	[illegible]	[illegible]	[illegible]
[illegible]	[illegible]	[illegible]	[illegible]	[illegible]	[illegible]	February [illegible]	[illegible]	[illegible]	[illegible]	[illegible]	[illegible]	[illegible]	[illegible]	[illegible]	[illegible]	[illegible]	[illegible]	[illegible]	[illegible]	[illegible]	[illegible]	[illegible]
[illegible]	[illegible]	[illegible]	[illegible]	[illegible]	[illegible]	April [illegible]	[illegible]	[illegible]	[illegible]	[illegible]	[illegible]	[illegible]	[illegible]	[illegible]	[illegible]	[illegible]	[illegible]	[illegible]	[illegible]	[illegible]	[illegible]	[illegible]
[illegible]	[illegible]	[illegible]	[illegible]	[illegible]	[illegible]	April [illegible]	[illegible]	[illegible]	[illegible]	[illegible]	[illegible]	[illegible]	[illegible]	[illegible]	[illegible]	[illegible]	[illegible]	[illegible]	[illegible]	[illegible]	[illegible]	[illegible]
[illegible]	[illegible]	[illegible]	[illegible]	[illegible]	[illegible]	August [illegible]	[illegible]	[illegible]	[illegible]	[illegible]	[illegible]	[illegible]	[illegible]	[illegible]	[illegible]	[illegible]	[illegible]	[illegible]	[illegible]	[illegible]	[illegible]	[illegible]
[illegible]	[illegible]	[illegible]	[illegible]	[illegible]	[illegible]	October [illegible]	[illegible]	[illegible]	[illegible]	[illegible]	[illegible]	[illegible]	[illegible]	[illegible]	[illegible]	[illegible]	[illegible]	[illegible]	[illegible]	[illegible]	[illegible]	[illegible]
[illegible]	[illegible]	[illegible]	[illegible]	[illegible]	[illegible]	November [illegible]	[illegible]	[illegible]	[illegible]	[illegible]	[illegible]	[illegible]	[illegible]	[illegible]	[illegible]	[illegible]	[illegible]	[illegible]	[illegible]	[illegible]	[illegible]	[illegible]
[illegible]	[illegible]	[illegible]	[illegible]	[illegible]	[illegible]	November [illegible]	[illegible]	[illegible]	[illegible]	[illegible]	[illegible]	[illegible]	[illegible]	[illegible]	[illegible]	[illegible]	[illegible]	[illegible]	[illegible]	[illegible]	[illegible]	[illegible]
[illegible]	[illegible]	[illegible]	[illegible]	[illegible]	[illegible]	August 19th,	[illegible]	[illegible]	[illegible]	[illegible]	[illegible]	[illegible]	[illegible]	[illegible]	[illegible]	[illegible]	[illegible]	[illegible]	[illegible]	[illegible]	[illegible]	[illegible]
[illegible]	[illegible]	[illegible]	[illegible]	[illegible]	[illegible]	March [illegible]	[illegible]	[illegible]	[illegible]	[illegible]	[illegible]	[illegible]	[illegible]	[illegible]	[illegible]	[illegible]	[illegible]	[illegible]	[illegible]	[illegible]	[illegible]	[illegible]
Ten Years.	[illegible]	[illegible]	[illegible]	[illegible]	[illegible]	August [illegible]	[illegible]	[illegible]	[illegible]	[illegible]	[illegible]	[illegible]	[illegible]	[illegible]	[illegible]	[illegible]	[illegible]	[illegible]	[illegible]	[illegible]	[illegible]	[illegible]

MONTHLY AND QUARTERLY ABSTRACT OF METEOROLOGICAL OBSERVATIONS taken at [illegible] F.R.C.P.I.; F.R.Met.Soc. Long. 6° 15' W.; Lat. 53° 20' N. Height above Mean Sea Level, 51 feet, 3 feet 4 inches above ground for the years 1881-84, 3 feet for 1885-86, 1 ft. 4 inches for 1887-90.

[illegible]	Mean Pressure in Inches	Air Temperature: 9 A.M.	9 P.M.	Mean	Means of Min.	Max.	Ran.	Abs. Min. Date	Max.	Date	Tension of Vapour: 9 A.M.	9 P.M.	Mean	Relative Humidity: 9 A.M.	9 P.M.	Mean
January	[illegible]	[illegible]	[illegible]	[illegible]	[illegible]	[illegible]	[illegible]	[illegible]	[illegible]	[illegible]	[illegible]	[illegible]	[illegible]	[illegible]	[illegible]	[illegible]
February	[illegible]	[illegible]	[illegible]	[illegible]	[illegible]	[illegible]	[illegible]	[illegible]	[illegible]	[illegible]	[illegible]	[illegible]	[illegible]	[illegible]	[illegible]	[illegible]
March	[illegible]	[illegible]	[illegible]	[illegible]	[illegible]	[illegible]	[illegible]	[illegible]	[illegible]	[illegible]	[illegible]	[illegible]	[illegible]	[illegible]	[illegible]	[illegible]
1st Quarter	[illegible]	[illegible]	[illegible]	[illegible]	[illegible]	[illegible]	[illegible]	[illegible]	[illegible]	[illegible]	[illegible]	[illegible]	[illegible]	[illegible]	[illegible]	[illegible]
April	[illegible]	[illegible]	[illegible]	[illegible]	[illegible]	[illegible]	[illegible]	[illegible]	[illegible]	[illegible]	[illegible]	[illegible]	[illegible]	[illegible]	[illegible]	[illegible]
May	[illegible]	[illegible]	[illegible]	[illegible]	[illegible]	[illegible]	[illegible]	[illegible]	[illegible]	[illegible]	[illegible]	[illegible]	[illegible]	[illegible]	[illegible]	[illegible]
June	[illegible]	[illegible]	[illegible]	[illegible]	[illegible]	[illegible]	[illegible]	[illegible]	[illegible]	[illegible]	[illegible]	[illegible]	[illegible]	[illegible]	[illegible]	[illegible]
2nd Quarter	[illegible]	[illegible]	[illegible]	[illegible]	[illegible]	[illegible]	[illegible]	[illegible]	[illegible]	[illegible]	[illegible]	[illegible]	[illegible]	[illegible]	[illegible]	[illegible]
July	[illegible]	[illegible]	[illegible]	[illegible]	[illegible]	[illegible]	[illegible]	[illegible]	[illegible]	[illegible]	[illegible]	[illegible]	[illegible]	[illegible]	[illegible]	[illegible]
August	[illegible]	[illegible]	[illegible]	[illegible]	[illegible]	[illegible]	[illegible]	[illegible]	[illegible]	[illegible]	[illegible]	[illegible]	[illegible]	[illegible]	[illegible]	[illegible]
September	[illegible]	[illegible]	[illegible]	[illegible]	[illegible]	[illegible]	[illegible]	[illegible]	[illegible]	[illegible]	[illegible]	[illegible]	[illegible]	[illegible]	[illegible]	[illegible]
3rd Quarter	[illegible]	[illegible]	[illegible]	[illegible]	[illegible]	[illegible]	[illegible]	[illegible]	[illegible]	[illegible]	[illegible]	[illegible]	[illegible]	[illegible]	[illegible]	[illegible]
October	[illegible]	[illegible]	[illegible]	[illegible]	[illegible]	[illegible]	[illegible]	[illegible]	[illegible]	[illegible]	[illegible]	[illegible]	[illegible]	[illegible]	[illegible]	[illegible]
November	[illegible]	[illegible]	[illegible]	[illegible]	[illegible]	[illegible]	[illegible]	[illegible]	[illegible]	[illegible]	[illegible]	[illegible]	[illegible]	[illegible]	[illegible]	[illegible]
December	[illegible]	[illegible]	[illegible]	[illegible]	[illegible]	[illegible]	[illegible]	[illegible]	[illegible]	[illegible]	[illegible]	[illegible]	[illegible]	[illegible]	[illegible]	[illegible]
4th Quarter	[illegible]	[illegible]	[illegible]	[illegible]	[illegible]	[illegible]	[illegible]	[illegible]	[illegible]	[illegible]	[illegible]	[illegible]	[illegible]	[illegible]	[illegible]	[illegible]
The Year	[illegible]	[illegible]	[illegible]	[illegible]	[illegible]	[illegible]	[illegible]	[illegible]	[illegible]	[illegible]	[illegible]	[illegible]	[illegible]	[illegible]	[illegible]	[illegible]

[illegible], Fitzwilliam-square, West, Dublin, during the Ten Years, 1881-90, by J. W. MOORE, M.D., Univ. Dub.; for the years 1881–84, [illegible] feet for 1885–89, and [illegible] feet for 1890, Thermometers 4 feet above ground. Rain-gauge

Ten Years, 1881–90.	Amount of Cloud			Rainfall			Weather — Number of Days of								Wind — Number of Observations at the each Point								
	[illegible]	[illegible]	[illegible]	Total. In.	Max. In.	Date.	[illegible]	[illegible]	[illegible]	[illegible]	[illegible]	[illegible]	[illegible]	[illegible]	N.	N.E.	E.	S.E.	S.	S.W.	W.	N.W.	Calm
January	[illegible]	[illegible]	[illegible]	[illegible]	[illegible]	[illegible]	[illegible]	[illegible]	[illegible]	[illegible]	[illegible]	[illegible]	[illegible]	[illegible]	[illegible]	[illegible]	[illegible]	[illegible]	[illegible]	[illegible]	[illegible]	[illegible]	[illegible]
February	[illegible]	[illegible]	[illegible]	[illegible]	[illegible]	[illegible]	[illegible]	[illegible]	[illegible]	[illegible]	[illegible]	[illegible]	[illegible]	[illegible]	[illegible]	[illegible]	[illegible]	[illegible]	[illegible]	[illegible]	[illegible]	[illegible]	[illegible]
March	[illegible]	[illegible]	[illegible]	[illegible]	[illegible]	[illegible]	[illegible]	[illegible]	[illegible]	[illegible]	[illegible]	[illegible]	[illegible]	[illegible]	[illegible]	[illegible]	[illegible]	[illegible]	[illegible]	[illegible]	[illegible]	[illegible]	[illegible]
1st Quarter	[illegible]	[illegible]	[illegible]	[illegible]	[illegible]	[illegible]	[illegible]	[illegible]	[illegible]	[illegible]	[illegible]	[illegible]	[illegible]	[illegible]	[illegible]	[illegible]	[illegible]	[illegible]	[illegible]	[illegible]	[illegible]	[illegible]	[illegible]
April	[illegible]	[illegible]	[illegible]	[illegible]	[illegible]	[illegible]	[illegible]	[illegible]	[illegible]	[illegible]	[illegible]	[illegible]	[illegible]	[illegible]	[illegible]	[illegible]	[illegible]	[illegible]	[illegible]	[illegible]	[illegible]	[illegible]	[illegible]
May	[illegible]	[illegible]	[illegible]	[illegible]	[illegible]	[illegible]	[illegible]	[illegible]	[illegible]	[illegible]	[illegible]	[illegible]	[illegible]	[illegible]	[illegible]	[illegible]	[illegible]	[illegible]	[illegible]	[illegible]	[illegible]	[illegible]	[illegible]
June	[illegible]	[illegible]	[illegible]	[illegible]	[illegible]	[illegible]	[illegible]	[illegible]	[illegible]	[illegible]	[illegible]	[illegible]	[illegible]	[illegible]	[illegible]	[illegible]	[illegible]	[illegible]	[illegible]	[illegible]	[illegible]	[illegible]	[illegible]
2nd Quarter	[illegible]	[illegible]	[illegible]	[illegible]	[illegible]	[illegible]	[illegible]	[illegible]	[illegible]	[illegible]	[illegible]	[illegible]	[illegible]	[illegible]	[illegible]	[illegible]	[illegible]	[illegible]	[illegible]	[illegible]	[illegible]	[illegible]	[illegible]
July	[illegible]	[illegible]	[illegible]	[illegible]	[illegible]	[illegible]	[illegible]	[illegible]	[illegible]	[illegible]	[illegible]	[illegible]	[illegible]	[illegible]	[illegible]	[illegible]	[illegible]	[illegible]	[illegible]	[illegible]	[illegible]	[illegible]	[illegible]
August	[illegible]	[illegible]	[illegible]	[illegible]	[illegible]	[illegible]	[illegible]	[illegible]	[illegible]	[illegible]	[illegible]	[illegible]	[illegible]	[illegible]	[illegible]	[illegible]	[illegible]	[illegible]	[illegible]	[illegible]	[illegible]	[illegible]	[illegible]
September	[illegible]	[illegible]	[illegible]	[illegible]	[illegible]	[illegible]	[illegible]	[illegible]	[illegible]	[illegible]	[illegible]	[illegible]	[illegible]	[illegible]	[illegible]	[illegible]	[illegible]	[illegible]	[illegible]	[illegible]	[illegible]	[illegible]	[illegible]
3rd Quarter	[illegible]	[illegible]	[illegible]	[illegible]	[illegible]	[illegible]	[illegible]	[illegible]	[illegible]	[illegible]	[illegible]	[illegible]	[illegible]	[illegible]	[illegible]	[illegible]	[illegible]	[illegible]	[illegible]	[illegible]	[illegible]	[illegible]	[illegible]
October	[illegible]	[illegible]	[illegible]	[illegible]	[illegible]	[illegible]	[illegible]	[illegible]	[illegible]	[illegible]	[illegible]	[illegible]	[illegible]	[illegible]	[illegible]	[illegible]	[illegible]	[illegible]	[illegible]	[illegible]	[illegible]	[illegible]	[illegible]
November	[illegible]	[illegible]	[illegible]	[illegible]	[illegible]	[illegible]	[illegible]	[illegible]	[illegible]	[illegible]	[illegible]	[illegible]	[illegible]	[illegible]	[illegible]	[illegible]	[illegible]	[illegible]	[illegible]	[illegible]	[illegible]	[illegible]	[illegible]
December	[illegible]	[illegible]	[illegible]	[illegible]	[illegible]	[illegible]	[illegible]	[illegible]	[illegible]	[illegible]	[illegible]	[illegible]	[illegible]	[illegible]	[illegible]	[illegible]	[illegible]	[illegible]	[illegible]	[illegible]	[illegible]	[illegible]	[illegible]
4th Quarter	[illegible]	[illegible]	[illegible]	[illegible]	[illegible]	[illegible]	[illegible]	[illegible]	[illegible]	[illegible]	[illegible]	[illegible]	[illegible]	[illegible]	[illegible]	[illegible]	[illegible]	[illegible]	[illegible]	[illegible]	[illegible]	[illegible]	[illegible]
Ten Years	[illegible]	[illegible]	[illegible]	[illegible]	[illegible]	[illegible]	[illegible]	[illegible]	[illegible]	[illegible]	[illegible]	[illegible]	[illegible]	[illegible]	[illegible]	[illegible]	[illegible]	[illegible]	[illegible]	[illegible]	[illegible]	[illegible]	[illegible]

ABSTRACT OF MARRIAGES.—Marriages Registered in Ireland, [illegible]

IRELAND,	[illegible]	[illegible]	[illegible]

Abstract of Marriages, 1881–90.

[illegible] the Acts 7 & 8 Vic., c. [illegible], and 26 & 27 Vic., c. [illegible], in the Ten Years 1881–90.

ABSTRACT OF MARRIAGES.—Marriages Registered in Ireland, [illegible]

in the Acts 7 and 8 Vic., c. 81, and 26 & 27 Vic., c. 90, in the Ten Years 1881–90—continued.

MARRIAGES. Registered in the Quarter ending: March	June	September	December	Condition of Parties: Bachelors and Spinsters	Bachelors and Widows	Widowers and Spinsters	Widowers and Widows	[illegible]: [illegible]	[illegible]	Of Persons under Full Age: Men	Women	Signed the Marriage Register with Marks: Men	Women	Couples where: Both signed	One signed	Superintendent Registrars' Districts, or Poor Law Unions
[illegible]	[illegible]	[illegible]	[illegible]	[illegible]	[illegible]	[illegible]	[illegible]	[illegible]	[illegible]	[illegible]	[illegible]	[illegible]	[illegible]	[illegible]	[illegible]	[illegible]
[illegible]	[illegible]	[illegible]	[illegible]	[illegible]	[illegible]	[illegible]	[illegible]	[illegible]	[illegible]	[illegible]	[illegible]	[illegible]	[illegible]	[illegible]	[illegible]	[illegible]
[illegible]	[illegible]	[illegible]	[illegible]	[illegible]	[illegible]	[illegible]	[illegible]	[illegible]	[illegible]	[illegible]	[illegible]	[illegible]	[illegible]	[illegible]	[illegible]	[illegible]
[illegible]	[illegible]	[illegible]	[illegible]	[illegible]	[illegible]	[illegible]	[illegible]	[illegible]	[illegible]	[illegible]	[illegible]	[illegible]	[illegible]	[illegible]	[illegible]	[illegible]
[illegible]	[illegible]	[illegible]	[illegible]	[illegible]	[illegible]	[illegible]	[illegible]	[illegible]	[illegible]	[illegible]	[illegible]	[illegible]	[illegible]	[illegible]	[illegible]	[illegible]
[illegible]	[illegible]	[illegible]	[illegible]	[illegible]	[illegible]	[illegible]	[illegible]	[illegible]	[illegible]	[illegible]	[illegible]	[illegible]	[illegible]	[illegible]	[illegible]	Downpatrick.
[illegible]	[illegible]	[illegible]	[illegible]	[illegible]	[illegible]	[illegible]	[illegible]	[illegible]	[illegible]	[illegible]	[illegible]	[illegible]	[illegible]	[illegible]	[illegible]	Drogheda.
[illegible]	[illegible]	[illegible]	[illegible]	[illegible]	[illegible]	[illegible]	[illegible]	[illegible]	[illegible]	[illegible]	[illegible]	[illegible]	[illegible]	[illegible]	[illegible]	Dromore, West.
[illegible]	[illegible]	[illegible]	[illegible]	[illegible]	[illegible]	[illegible]	[illegible]	[illegible]	[illegible]	[illegible]	[illegible]	[illegible]	[illegible]	[illegible]	[illegible]	Dublin, North.
[illegible]	[illegible]	[illegible]	[illegible]	[illegible]	[illegible]	[illegible]	[illegible]	[illegible]	[illegible]	[illegible]	[illegible]	[illegible]	[illegible]	[illegible]	[illegible]	Dublin, South.
[illegible]	[illegible]	[illegible]	[illegible]	[illegible]	[illegible]	[illegible]	[illegible]	[illegible]	[illegible]	[illegible]	[illegible]	[illegible]	[illegible]	[illegible]	[illegible]	Dundalk.
[illegible]	[illegible]	[illegible]	[illegible]	[illegible]	[illegible]	[illegible]	[illegible]	[illegible]	[illegible]	[illegible]	[illegible]	[illegible]	[illegible]	[illegible]	[illegible]	Dunfanaghy.
[illegible]	[illegible]	[illegible]	[illegible]	[illegible]	[illegible]	[illegible]	[illegible]	[illegible]	[illegible]	[illegible]	[illegible]	[illegible]	[illegible]	[illegible]	[illegible]	Dungannon.
[illegible]	[illegible]	[illegible]	[illegible]	[illegible]	[illegible]	[illegible]	[illegible]	[illegible]	[illegible]	[illegible]	[illegible]	[illegible]	[illegible]	[illegible]	[illegible]	Dungarvan.
[illegible]	[illegible]	[illegible]	[illegible]	[illegible]	[illegible]	[illegible]	[illegible]	[illegible]	[illegible]	[illegible]	[illegible]	[illegible]	[illegible]	[illegible]	[illegible]	Dunmanway.
[illegible]	[illegible]	[illegible]	[illegible]	[illegible]	[illegible]	[illegible]	[illegible]	[illegible]	[illegible]	[illegible]	[illegible]	[illegible]	[illegible]	[illegible]	[illegible]	Dunshaughlin.
[illegible]	[illegible]	[illegible]	[illegible]	[illegible]	[illegible]	[illegible]	[illegible]	[illegible]	[illegible]	[illegible]	[illegible]	[illegible]	[illegible]	[illegible]	[illegible]	Edenderry.
[illegible]	[illegible]	[illegible]	[illegible]	[illegible]	[illegible]	[illegible]	[illegible]	[illegible]	[illegible]	[illegible]	[illegible]	[illegible]	[illegible]	[illegible]	[illegible]	Ennis.
[illegible]	[illegible]	[illegible]	[illegible]	[illegible]	[illegible]	[illegible]	[illegible]	[illegible]	[illegible]	[illegible]	[illegible]	[illegible]	[illegible]	[illegible]	[illegible]	Enniscorthy.
[illegible]	[illegible]	[illegible]	[illegible]	[illegible]	[illegible]	[illegible]	[illegible]	[illegible]	[illegible]	[illegible]	[illegible]	[illegible]	[illegible]	[illegible]	[illegible]	Enniskillen.
[illegible]	[illegible]	[illegible]	[illegible]	[illegible]	[illegible]	[illegible]	[illegible]	[illegible]	[illegible]	[illegible]	[illegible]	[illegible]	[illegible]	[illegible]	[illegible]	Ennistymon.
[illegible]	[illegible]	[illegible]	[illegible]	[illegible]	[illegible]	[illegible]	[illegible]	[illegible]	[illegible]	[illegible]	[illegible]	[illegible]	[illegible]	[illegible]	[illegible]	Fermoy.
[illegible]	[illegible]	[illegible]	[illegible]	[illegible]	[illegible]	[illegible]	[illegible]	[illegible]	[illegible]	[illegible]	[illegible]	[illegible]	[illegible]	[illegible]	[illegible]	Galway.
[illegible]	[illegible]	[illegible]	[illegible]	[illegible]	[illegible]	[illegible]	[illegible]	[illegible]	[illegible]	[illegible]	[illegible]	[illegible]	[illegible]	[illegible]	[illegible]	Glenamaddy.
[illegible]	[illegible]	[illegible]	[illegible]	[illegible]	[illegible]	[illegible]	[illegible]	[illegible]	[illegible]	[illegible]	[illegible]	[illegible]	[illegible]	[illegible]	[illegible]	Glenties.
[illegible]	[illegible]	[illegible]	[illegible]	[illegible]	[illegible]	[illegible]	[illegible]	[illegible]	[illegible]	[illegible]	[illegible]	[illegible]	[illegible]	[illegible]	[illegible]	Glin.
[illegible]	[illegible]	[illegible]	[illegible]	[illegible]	[illegible]	[illegible]	[illegible]	[illegible]	[illegible]	[illegible]	[illegible]	[illegible]	[illegible]	[illegible]	[illegible]	Gorey.
[illegible]	[illegible]	[illegible]	[illegible]	[illegible]	[illegible]	[illegible]	[illegible]	[illegible]	[illegible]	[illegible]	[illegible]	[illegible]	[illegible]	[illegible]	[illegible]	Gort.
[illegible]	[illegible]	[illegible]	[illegible]	[illegible]	[illegible]	[illegible]	[illegible]	[illegible]	[illegible]	[illegible]	[illegible]	[illegible]	[illegible]	[illegible]	[illegible]	Granard.*
[illegible]	[illegible]	[illegible]	[illegible]	[illegible]	[illegible]	[illegible]	[illegible]	[illegible]	[illegible]	[illegible]	[illegible]	[illegible]	[illegible]	[illegible]	[illegible]	[illegible]
[illegible]	[illegible]	[illegible]	[illegible]	[illegible]	[illegible]	[illegible]	[illegible]	[illegible]	[illegible]	[illegible]	[illegible]	[illegible]	[illegible]	[illegible]	[illegible]	[illegible]
[illegible]	[illegible]	[illegible]	[illegible]	[illegible]	[illegible]	[illegible]	[illegible]	[illegible]	[illegible]	[illegible]	[illegible]	[illegible]	[illegible]	[illegible]	[illegible]	[illegible]
[illegible]	[illegible]	[illegible]	[illegible]	[illegible]	[illegible]	[illegible]	[illegible]	[illegible]	[illegible]	[illegible]	[illegible]	[illegible]	[illegible]	[illegible]	[illegible]	[illegible]
[illegible]	[illegible]	[illegible]	[illegible]	[illegible]	[illegible]	[illegible]	[illegible]	[illegible]	[illegible]	[illegible]	[illegible]	[illegible]	[illegible]	[illegible]	[illegible]	Kells.
[illegible]	[illegible]	[illegible]	[illegible]	[illegible]	[illegible]	[illegible]	[illegible]	[illegible]	[illegible]	[illegible]	[illegible]	[illegible]	[illegible]	[illegible]	[illegible]	Kenmare.
[illegible]	[illegible]	[illegible]	[illegible]	[illegible]	[illegible]	[illegible]	[illegible]	[illegible]	[illegible]	[illegible]	[illegible]	[illegible]	[illegible]	[illegible]	[illegible]	Kilkeel.
[illegible]	[illegible]	[illegible]	[illegible]	[illegible]	[illegible]	[illegible]	[illegible]	[illegible]	[illegible]	[illegible]	[illegible]	[illegible]	[illegible]	[illegible]	[illegible]	Kilkenny.
[illegible]	[illegible]	[illegible]	[illegible]	[illegible]	[illegible]	[illegible]	[illegible]	[illegible]	[illegible]	[illegible]	[illegible]	[illegible]	[illegible]	[illegible]	[illegible]	Killadysert.
[illegible]	[illegible]	[illegible]	[illegible]	[illegible]	[illegible]	[illegible]	[illegible]	[illegible]	[illegible]	[illegible]	[illegible]	[illegible]	[illegible]	[illegible]	[illegible]	Killala.
[illegible]	[illegible]	[illegible]	[illegible]	[illegible]	[illegible]	[illegible]	[illegible]	[illegible]	[illegible]	[illegible]	[illegible]	[illegible]	[illegible]	[illegible]	[illegible]	Killarney.
[illegible]	[illegible]	[illegible]	[illegible]	[illegible]	[illegible]	[illegible]	[illegible]	[illegible]	[illegible]	[illegible]	[illegible]	[illegible]	[illegible]	[illegible]	[illegible]	Kilmacthomas.
[illegible]	[illegible]	[illegible]	[illegible]	[illegible]	[illegible]	[illegible]	[illegible]	[illegible]	[illegible]	[illegible]	[illegible]	[illegible]	[illegible]	[illegible]	[illegible]	Kilmallock.
[illegible]	[illegible]	[illegible]	[illegible]	[illegible]	[illegible]	[illegible]	[illegible]	[illegible]	[illegible]	[illegible]	[illegible]	[illegible]	[illegible]	[illegible]	[illegible]	[illegible]
[illegible]	[illegible]	[illegible]	[illegible]	[illegible]	[illegible]	[illegible]	[illegible]	[illegible]	[illegible]	[illegible]	[illegible]	[illegible]	[illegible]	[illegible]	[illegible]	[illegible]
[illegible]	[illegible]	[illegible]	[illegible]	[illegible]	[illegible]	[illegible]	[illegible]	[illegible]	[illegible]	[illegible]	[illegible]	[illegible]	[illegible]	[illegible]	[illegible]	[illegible]
[illegible]	[illegible]	[illegible]	[illegible]	[illegible]	[illegible]	[illegible]	[illegible]	[illegible]	[illegible]	[illegible]	[illegible]	[illegible]	[illegible]	[illegible]	[illegible]	Letterkenny.
[illegible]	[illegible]	[illegible]	[illegible]	[illegible]	[illegible]	[illegible]	[illegible]	[illegible]	[illegible]	[illegible]	[illegible]	[illegible]	[illegible]	[illegible]	[illegible]	[illegible]
[illegible]	[illegible]	[illegible]	[illegible]	[illegible]	[illegible]	[illegible]	[illegible]	[illegible]	[illegible]	[illegible]	[illegible]	[illegible]	[illegible]	[illegible]	[illegible]	Limerick.
[illegible]	[illegible]	[illegible]	[illegible]	[illegible]	[illegible]	[illegible]	[illegible]	[illegible]	[illegible]	[illegible]	[illegible]	[illegible]	[illegible]	[illegible]	[illegible]	Lisburn.
[illegible]	[illegible]	[illegible]	[illegible]	[illegible]	[illegible]	[illegible]	[illegible]	[illegible]	[illegible]	[illegible]	[illegible]	[illegible]	[illegible]	[illegible]	[illegible]	Lismore.
[illegible]	[illegible]	[illegible]	[illegible]	[illegible]	[illegible]	[illegible]	[illegible]	[illegible]	[illegible]	[illegible]	[illegible]	[illegible]	[illegible]	[illegible]	[illegible]	Lisnaskea.
[illegible]	[illegible]	[illegible]	[illegible]	[illegible]	[illegible]	[illegible]	[illegible]	[illegible]	[illegible]	[illegible]	[illegible]	[illegible]	[illegible]	[illegible]	[illegible]	Listowel.
[illegible]	[illegible]	[illegible]	[illegible]	[illegible]	[illegible]	[illegible]	[illegible]	[illegible]	[illegible]	[illegible]	[illegible]	[illegible]	[illegible]	[illegible]	[illegible]	Londonderry.

* See note (*), pages 60–61.

Registration of Marriages, Births, and Deaths, Ireland

ABSTRACT OF MARRIAGES.—MARRIAGES REGISTERED IN IRELAND, [illegible]

[illegible]	[illegible]		[illegible]	[illegible]												
	[illegible]	[illegible]		[illegible]	Licence.	[illegible]	[illegible]	[illegible]	[illegible]	[illegible]	[illegible]	[illegible]	[illegible]	[illegible]	[illegible]	[illegible]
[illegible]	[illegible]	[illegible]	[illegible]	[illegible]	[illegible]	[illegible]	[illegible]	[illegible]	[illegible]	[illegible]	[illegible]	[illegible]	[illegible]	[illegible]	[illegible]	[illegible]
[illegible]	[illegible]	[illegible]	[illegible]	[illegible]	[illegible]	[illegible]	[illegible]	[illegible]	[illegible]	[illegible]	[illegible]	[illegible]	[illegible]	[illegible]	[illegible]	[illegible]
[illegible]	[illegible]	[illegible]	[illegible]	[illegible]	[illegible]	[illegible]	[illegible]	[illegible]	[illegible]	[illegible]	[illegible]	[illegible]	[illegible]	[illegible]	[illegible]	[illegible]
[illegible]	[illegible]	[illegible]	[illegible]	[illegible]	[illegible]	[illegible]	[illegible]	[illegible]	[illegible]	[illegible]	[illegible]	[illegible]	[illegible]	[illegible]	[illegible]	[illegible]
[illegible]	[illegible]	[illegible]	[illegible]	[illegible]	[illegible]	[illegible]	[illegible]	[illegible]	[illegible]	[illegible]	[illegible]	[illegible]	[illegible]	[illegible]	[illegible]	[illegible]

Ages of 103,418 Persons who were Married in Ireland in the Ten Years, 1881–90.

The Total Number of Marriages registered in Ireland in the Ten Years, 1881–90, was [illegible]; the precise Ages of both Parties were specified in 51,709 instances.

Ages of 51,709 Men and 51,709 Women married in Ireland in the Ten Years, 1881–90.

—	[illegible]	Total
Men,	[illegible]	[illegible]
Women,	[illegible]	[illegible]

Ages of 46,720 Bachelors and 49,264 Spinsters married in the Ten Years, 1881–90.

—	[illegible]	Total
Bachelors,	[illegible]	[illegible]
Spinsters,	[illegible]	[illegible]

Ages of 4,989 Widowers and 2,445 Widows married in the Ten Years, 1881–90.

—	[illegible]	Total
Widowers,	[illegible]	[illegible]
Widows,	[illegible]	[illegible]

Ages of 51,709 Husbands and their Wives in combination in the Ten Years, 1881–90.

Years	Ages of Wives	Total Husbands	
Ages of Husbands	[illegible]	[illegible]	[illegible]
Total Wives	[illegible]	[illegible]	Wives.

AGES of 1,263 BACHELORS and 1,263 WIDOWS who intermarried in the ten years 1881–90.

YEARS.	Ages of Widows. [illegible]	Total Bachelors.	
Ages of Bachelors. [illegible]	[illegible]	[illegible]	Ages of Bachelors. [illegible]
Total Widows.	[illegible]	1,263	Bachelors. / Widows.

AGES of 3,[illegible] WIDOWERS and 3,[illegible] SPINSTERS who intermarried in the ten years 1881–90.

YEARS.	Ages of Spinsters. [illegible]	Total Widowers.	
Ages of Widowers. [illegible]	[illegible]	[illegible]	Ages of Widowers. [illegible]
Total Spinsters.	[illegible]	[illegible]	Widowers. / Spinsters.

AGES of 1,0[illegible] WIDOWERS and 1,0[illegible] WIDOWS who intermarried in the ten years 1881–90.

YEARS.	Ages of Widows. [illegible]	Total Widowers.	
Ages of Widowers. [illegible]	[illegible]	[illegible]	Ages of Widowers. [illegible]
Total Widows.	[illegible]	[illegible]	Widowers. / Widows.

[illegible] Registered in each PROVINCE and COUNTY in IRELAND in the ten years 1881–90.

PROVINCES AND COUNTIES	Population, 1881	Population, 1891	TOTAL: Marriages	TOTAL: Births	TOTAL: Deaths	Births, including Illegitimate Births: Males	Births, including Illegitimate Births: Females	Illegitimate Births: Males	Illegitimate Births: Females	Deaths: Males	Deaths: Females
IRELAND,	[illegible]	[illegible]	[illegible]	[illegible]	[illegible]	[illegible]	[illegible]	[illegible]	[illegible]	[illegible]	[illegible]
PROVINCES.											
LEINSTER,	[illegible]	[illegible]	[illegible]	[illegible]	[illegible]	[illegible]	[illegible]	[illegible]	[illegible]	[illegible]	[illegible]
MUNSTER,	[illegible]	[illegible]	[illegible]	[illegible]	[illegible]	[illegible]	[illegible]	[illegible]	[illegible]	[illegible]	[illegible]
ULSTER,	[illegible]	[illegible]	[illegible]	[illegible]	[illegible]	[illegible]	[illegible]	[illegible]	[illegible]	[illegible]	[illegible]
CONNAUGHT,	[illegible]	[illegible]	[illegible]	[illegible]	[illegible]	[illegible]	[illegible]	[illegible]	[illegible]	[illegible]	[illegible]

[illegible]—MARRIAGES, BIRTHS, AND DEATHS, 1881–90—COUNTIES.

1 CARLOW,	[illegible]	[illegible]	1,777	[illegible]	[illegible]	[illegible]	[illegible]	[illegible]	[illegible]	[illegible]	[illegible]
2 DUBLIN,	[illegible]	[illegible]	[illegible]	[illegible]	[illegible]	[illegible]	[illegible]	[illegible]	[illegible]	[illegible]	[illegible]
3 KILDARE,	[illegible]	[illegible]	[illegible]	[illegible]	[illegible]	[illegible]	[illegible]	[illegible]	[illegible]	[illegible]	[illegible]
4 KILKENNY,	[illegible]	[illegible]	[illegible]	[illegible]	[illegible]	[illegible]	[illegible]	[illegible]	[illegible]	[illegible]	[illegible]
5 KING'S,	[illegible]	[illegible]	[illegible]	[illegible]	[illegible]	[illegible]	[illegible]	[illegible]	[illegible]	[illegible]	[illegible]
6 LONGFORD,	[illegible]	[illegible]	[illegible]	[illegible]	[illegible]	[illegible]	[illegible]	[illegible]	[illegible]	[illegible]	[illegible]
7 LOUTH, AND CO. OF THE TOWN OF DROGHEDA,	[illegible]	[illegible]	[illegible]	[illegible]	[illegible]	[illegible]	[illegible]	[illegible]	[illegible]	[illegible]	[illegible]
8 MEATH,	[illegible]	[illegible]	[illegible]	[illegible]	[illegible]	[illegible]	[illegible]	[illegible]	[illegible]	[illegible]	[illegible]
9 QUEEN'S,	[illegible]	[illegible]	[illegible]	[illegible]	[illegible]	[illegible]	[illegible]	[illegible]	[illegible]	[illegible]	[illegible]
10 WESTMEATH,	[illegible]	[illegible]	[illegible]	[illegible]	[illegible]	[illegible]	[illegible]	[illegible]	[illegible]	[illegible]	[illegible]

MARRIAGES, BIRTHS, and DEATHS registered in Ireland in the Ten Years, 1881-90.

I.—PROVINCE OF LEINSTER.—MARRIAGES, BIRTHS, AND DEATHS, 1881-90.

SUPERINTENDENT REGISTRARS' DISTRICTS, ARRANGED BY COUNTIES.

[illegible]

No.	Superintendent Registrars' Districts	Population 1881	Population 1891	Total Marriages	Total Births	Total Deaths	Births [illegible] Males	Births [illegible] Females	Births [illegible] Males	Births [illegible] Females	Deaths Males	Deaths Females	[illegible]
	1. Carlow Co.												
1	Baltinglass?, part of,	[illegible]	[illegible]	[illegible]	[illegible]	[illegible]	[illegible]	[illegible]	[illegible]	[illegible]	[illegible]	[illegible]	[illegible]
2	Carlow, do.	[illegible]	[illegible]	[illegible]	[illegible]	[illegible]	[illegible]	[illegible]	[illegible]	[illegible]	[illegible]	[illegible]	[illegible]
3	[illegible], do.	[illegible]	[illegible]	[illegible]	[illegible]	[illegible]	[illegible]	[illegible]	[illegible]	[illegible]	[illegible]	[illegible]	[illegible]
4	New Ross, do.	[illegible]	[illegible]	[illegible]	[illegible]	[illegible]	[illegible]	[illegible]	[illegible]	[illegible]	[illegible]	[illegible]	[illegible]
5	Shillelagh?, do.	[illegible]	[illegible]	[illegible]	[illegible]	[illegible]	[illegible]	[illegible]	[illegible]	[illegible]	[illegible]	[illegible]	[illegible]
	2. Dublin Co.												
6	Balrothery?,	[illegible]	[illegible]	[illegible]	[illegible]	[illegible]	[illegible]	[illegible]	[illegible]	[illegible]	[illegible]	[illegible]	[illegible]
7	Celbridge?, part of,	[illegible]	[illegible]	[illegible]	[illegible]	[illegible]	[illegible]	[illegible]	[illegible]	[illegible]	[illegible]	[illegible]	[illegible]
8	Dublin, North,	[illegible]	[illegible]	[illegible]	[illegible]	[illegible]	[illegible]	[illegible]	[illegible]	[illegible]	[illegible]	[illegible]	[illegible]
9	Dublin, South,	[illegible]	[illegible]	[illegible]	[illegible]	[illegible]	[illegible]	[illegible]	[illegible]	[illegible]	[illegible]	[illegible]	[illegible]
10	[illegible], part of,	[illegible]	[illegible]	[illegible]	[illegible]	[illegible]	[illegible]	[illegible]	[illegible]	[illegible]	[illegible]	[illegible]	[illegible]
11	Rathdown?, do.	[illegible]	[illegible]	[illegible]	[illegible]	[illegible]	[illegible]	[illegible]	[illegible]	[illegible]	[illegible]	[illegible]	[illegible]
	3. Kildare Co.												
12	Athy?, part of,	[illegible]	[illegible]	[illegible]	[illegible]	[illegible]	[illegible]	[illegible]	[illegible]	[illegible]	[illegible]	[illegible]	[illegible]
13	Baltinglass?, do.	[illegible]	[illegible]	[illegible]	[illegible]	[illegible]	[illegible]	[illegible]	[illegible]	[illegible]	[illegible]	[illegible]	[illegible]
14	Celbridge?, do.	[illegible]	[illegible]	[illegible]	[illegible]	[illegible]	[illegible]	[illegible]	[illegible]	[illegible]	[illegible]	[illegible]	[illegible]
15	[illegible], do.	[illegible]	[illegible]	[illegible]	[illegible]	[illegible]	[illegible]	[illegible]	[illegible]	[illegible]	[illegible]	[illegible]	[illegible]
16	Naas, do.	[illegible]	[illegible]	[illegible]	[illegible]	[illegible]	[illegible]	[illegible]	[illegible]	[illegible]	[illegible]	[illegible]	[illegible]
	4. Kilkenny Co.												
17	Callan, part of,	[illegible]	[illegible]	[illegible]	[illegible]	[illegible]	[illegible]	[illegible]	[illegible]	[illegible]	[illegible]	[illegible]	[illegible]
18	Carrick-on-Suir?, do.	[illegible]	[illegible]	[illegible]	[illegible]	[illegible]	[illegible]	[illegible]	[illegible]	[illegible]	[illegible]	[illegible]	[illegible]
19	Castlecomer?,	[illegible]	[illegible]	[illegible]	[illegible]	[illegible]	[illegible]	[illegible]	[illegible]	[illegible]	[illegible]	[illegible]	[illegible]
20	Kilkenny,	[illegible]	[illegible]	[illegible]	[illegible]	[illegible]	[illegible]	[illegible]	[illegible]	[illegible]	[illegible]	[illegible]	[illegible]
21	New Ross, part of,	[illegible]	[illegible]	[illegible]	[illegible]	[illegible]	[illegible]	[illegible]	[illegible]	[illegible]	[illegible]	[illegible]	[illegible]
22	Thomastown?,	[illegible]	[illegible]	[illegible]	[illegible]	[illegible]	[illegible]	[illegible]	[illegible]	[illegible]	[illegible]	[illegible]	[illegible]
23	Urlingford?, part of,*	[illegible]	[illegible]	[illegible]	[illegible]	[illegible]	[illegible]	[illegible]	[illegible]	[illegible]	[illegible]	[illegible]	[illegible]
24	Waterford?, do.	[illegible]	[illegible]	[illegible]	[illegible]	[illegible]	[illegible]	[illegible]	[illegible]	[illegible]	[illegible]	[illegible]	[illegible]
	5. King's Co.												
25	[illegible], part of,	[illegible]	[illegible]	[illegible]	[illegible]	[illegible]	[illegible]	[illegible]	[illegible]	[illegible]	[illegible]	[illegible]	[illegible]
26	Mountmellick?, do.	[illegible]	[illegible]	[illegible]	[illegible]	[illegible]	[illegible]	[illegible]	[illegible]	[illegible]	[illegible]	[illegible]	[illegible]
27	Parsonstown?, do.	[illegible]	[illegible]	[illegible]	[illegible]	[illegible]	[illegible]	[illegible]	[illegible]	[illegible]	[illegible]	[illegible]	[illegible]
28	Roscrea?,* do.	[illegible]	[illegible]	[illegible]	[illegible]	[illegible]	[illegible]	[illegible]	[illegible]	[illegible]	[illegible]	[illegible]	[illegible]
29	Tullamore, do.	[illegible]	[illegible]	[illegible]	[illegible]	[illegible]	[illegible]	[illegible]	[illegible]	[illegible]	[illegible]	[illegible]	[illegible]
	6. Longford Co.												
30	Ballymahon?, part of,	[illegible]	[illegible]	[illegible]	[illegible]	[illegible]	[illegible]	[illegible]	[illegible]	[illegible]	[illegible]	[illegible]	[illegible]
31	Granard, do.	[illegible]	[illegible]	[illegible]	[illegible]	[illegible]	[illegible]	[illegible]	[illegible]	[illegible]	[illegible]	[illegible]	[illegible]
32	Longford,	[illegible]	[illegible]	[illegible]	[illegible]	[illegible]	[illegible]	[illegible]	[illegible]	[illegible]	[illegible]	[illegible]	[illegible]
	7. Louth and Co. of Town of Drogheda.												
33	Ardee, part of,	[illegible]	[illegible]	[illegible]	[illegible]	[illegible]	[illegible]	[illegible]	[illegible]	[illegible]	[illegible]	[illegible]	[illegible]
34	Drogheda, do.	[illegible]	[illegible]	[illegible]	[illegible]	[illegible]	[illegible]	[illegible]	[illegible]	[illegible]	[illegible]	[illegible]	[illegible]
35	Dundalk, do.	[illegible]	[illegible]	[illegible]	[illegible]	[illegible]	[illegible]	[illegible]	[illegible]	[illegible]	[illegible]	[illegible]	[illegible]

* [illegible]

5.—PROVINCE OF LEINSTER.—MARRIAGES, BIRTHS, AND DEATHS, 1881-91.
SUPERINTENDENT REGISTRARS' DISTRICTS—*continued.*

No.	Superintendent Registrars' Districts	Population 1881	Population 1891	Total Marriages	Total Births	Total Deaths	Births (including Illegitimate Births) Males	Births (including Illegitimate Births) Females	Illegitimate Births Males	Illegitimate Births Females	Deaths Males	[illegible]
	8. Meath Co.											
36	Ardee, part of	[illegible]	[illegible]	[illegible]	[illegible]	[illegible]	[illegible]	[illegible]	[illegible]	[illegible]	[illegible]	
37	Celbridge, do.	[illegible]	[illegible]	4	[illegible]	[illegible]	[illegible]	[illegible]	.	.	[illegible]	
38	Drogheda, do.	[illegible]	[illegible]	[illegible]	[illegible]	[illegible]	[illegible]	[illegible]	[illegible]	[illegible]	[illegible]	[illegible]
39	Dunshaughlin, do.	[illegible]	[illegible]	[illegible]	[illegible]	[illegible]	[illegible]	[illegible]	[illegible]	[illegible]	[illegible]	
40	[illegible], do.	[illegible]	[illegible]	[illegible]	[illegible]	[illegible]	[illegible]	[illegible]	[illegible]	[illegible]	[illegible]	
41	Kells, do.	[illegible]	[illegible]	[illegible]	[illegible]	[illegible]	[illegible]	[illegible]	[illegible]	[illegible]	[illegible]	[illegible]
42	Navan,	[illegible]	[illegible]	[illegible]	[illegible]	[illegible]	[illegible]	[illegible]	[illegible]	[illegible]	[illegible]	[illegible]
43	Oldcastle, part of	[illegible]	[illegible]	[illegible]	[illegible]	[illegible]	[illegible]	[illegible]	[illegible]	[illegible]	[illegible]	
44	Trim	[illegible]	[illegible]	[illegible]	[illegible]	[illegible]	[illegible]	[illegible]	[illegible]	[illegible]	[illegible]	[illegible]
	9. Queen's Co.											
45	Abbeyleix	[illegible]	[illegible]	[illegible]	[illegible]	[illegible]	[illegible]	[illegible]	[illegible]	[illegible]	[illegible]	[illegible]
46	Athy, part of	[illegible]	[illegible]	[illegible]	[illegible]	[illegible]	[illegible]	[illegible]	[illegible]	[illegible]	[illegible]	
47	Carlow, do.	[illegible]	[illegible]	[illegible]	[illegible]	[illegible]	[illegible]	[illegible]	[illegible]	[illegible]	[illegible]	
48	Donaghmore	[illegible]	[illegible]	[illegible]	[illegible]	[illegible]	[illegible]	[illegible]	[illegible]	[illegible]	[illegible]	
49	Mountmellick, part of	[illegible]	[illegible]	[illegible]	[illegible]	[illegible]	[illegible]	[illegible]	[illegible]	[illegible]	[illegible]	[illegible]
50	Roscrea, do.	[illegible]	[illegible]	[illegible]	[illegible]	[illegible]	[illegible]	[illegible]	[illegible]	[illegible]	[illegible]	
51	Urlingford, do.	.	.	.	.	.	.	.	.	.	.	
	10. Westmeath Co.											
52	Athlone, part of	[illegible]	[illegible]	[illegible]	[illegible]	[illegible]	[illegible]	[illegible]	[illegible]	[illegible]	[illegible]	[illegible]
53	Ballymahon, do.	[illegible]	[illegible]	[illegible]	[illegible]	[illegible]	[illegible]	[illegible]	[illegible]	[illegible]	[illegible]	
54	Delvin	[illegible]	[illegible]	[illegible]	[illegible]	[illegible]	[illegible]	[illegible]	[illegible]	[illegible]	[illegible]	
55	Granard, part of	[illegible]	[illegible]	[illegible]	[illegible]	[illegible]	[illegible]	[illegible]	[illegible]	[illegible]	[illegible]	
56	Mullingar	[illegible]	[illegible]	[illegible]	[illegible]	[illegible]	[illegible]	[illegible]	[illegible]	[illegible]	[illegible]	[illegible]
57	Tullamore, part of	[illegible]	[illegible]	[illegible]	[illegible]	[illegible]	[illegible]	[illegible]	[illegible]	.	[illegible]	
	11. Wexford Co.											
58	Enniscorthy, part of	[illegible]	[illegible]	[illegible]	[illegible]	[illegible]	[illegible]	[illegible]	[illegible]	[illegible]	[illegible]	[illegible]
59	Gorey	[illegible]	[illegible]	[illegible]	[illegible]	[illegible]	[illegible]	[illegible]	[illegible]	[illegible]	[illegible]	[illegible]
60	New Ross, part of	[illegible]	[illegible]	[illegible]	[illegible]	[illegible]	[illegible]	[illegible]	[illegible]	[illegible]	[illegible]	[illegible]
61	Shillelagh, do.	[illegible]	[illegible]	1	[illegible]	[illegible]	[illegible]	[illegible]	[illegible]	[illegible]	[illegible]	
62	Wexford	[illegible]	[illegible]	[illegible]	[illegible]	[illegible]	[illegible]	[illegible]	[illegible]	[illegible]	[illegible]	
	12. Wicklow Co.											
63	Baltinglass, part of	[illegible]	[illegible]	[illegible]	[illegible]	[illegible]	[illegible]	[illegible]	[illegible]	[illegible]	[illegible]	
64	Naas, do.	[illegible]	[illegible]	[illegible]	[illegible]	[illegible]	[illegible]	[illegible]	1	[illegible]	[illegible]	
65	Rathdown, do.	[illegible]	[illegible]	[illegible]	[illegible]	[illegible]	[illegible]	[illegible]	[illegible]	[illegible]	[illegible]	
66	Rathdrum	[illegible]	[illegible]	[illegible]	[illegible]	[illegible]	[illegible]	[illegible]	[illegible]	[illegible]	[illegible]	
67	Shillelagh, part of	[illegible]	[illegible]	[illegible]	[illegible]	[illegible]	[illegible]	[illegible]	[illegible]	[illegible]	[illegible]	

[illegible]—PROVINCE OF MUNSTER.—MARRIAGES, BIRTHS, AND DEATHS, 1881–90—
Superintendent Registrars' Districts—*continued.*

No.	Superintendent Registrars' Districts.	Population, 1881.	Population, 1891.	Marriages.	Births.	Deaths.	Births, [illegible], Male.	Births, [illegible], Female.	Births, [illegible], Male.	Births, [illegible], Female.	Deaths, Male.	Deaths, Female.	[illegible]
	15. Cork Co.												
[illegible]	Bandon,	[illegible]	[illegible]	[illegible]	[illegible]	[illegible]	[illegible]	[illegible]	[illegible]	[illegible]	[illegible]	[illegible]	[illegible]
[illegible]	Bantry,	[illegible]	[illegible]	[illegible]	[illegible]	[illegible]	[illegible]	[illegible]	[illegible]	[illegible]	[illegible]	[illegible]	[illegible]
[illegible]	Castletown,	[illegible]	[illegible]	[illegible]	[illegible]	[illegible]	[illegible]	[illegible]	[illegible]	[illegible]	[illegible]	[illegible]	[illegible]
[illegible]	Clonakilty,	[illegible]	[illegible]	[illegible]	[illegible]	[illegible]	[illegible]	[illegible]	[illegible]	[illegible]	[illegible]	[illegible]	[illegible]
[illegible]	Cork,	[illegible]	[illegible]	[illegible]	[illegible]	[illegible]	[illegible]	[illegible]	[illegible]	[illegible]	[illegible]	[illegible]	[illegible]
[illegible]	Dunmanway,	[illegible]	[illegible]	[illegible]	[illegible]	[illegible]	[illegible]	[illegible]	[illegible]	[illegible]	[illegible]	[illegible]	[illegible]
[illegible]	Fermoy,	[illegible]	[illegible]	[illegible]	[illegible]	[illegible]	[illegible]	[illegible]	[illegible]	[illegible]	[illegible]	[illegible]	[illegible]
[illegible]	Kanturk,	[illegible]	[illegible]	[illegible]	[illegible]	[illegible]	[illegible]	[illegible]	[illegible]	[illegible]	[illegible]	[illegible]	[illegible]
[illegible]	Kilmallock, part of,	[illegible]	[illegible]	[illegible]	[illegible]	[illegible]	[illegible]	[illegible]	[illegible]	[illegible]	[illegible]	[illegible]	[illegible]
[illegible]	Kinsale,	[illegible]	[illegible]	[illegible]	[illegible]	[illegible]	[illegible]	[illegible]	[illegible]	[illegible]	[illegible]	[illegible]	[illegible]
[illegible]	Macroom,	[illegible]	[illegible]	[illegible]	[illegible]	[illegible]	[illegible]	[illegible]	[illegible]	[illegible]	[illegible]	[illegible]	[illegible]
[illegible]	Mallow,	[illegible]	[illegible]	[illegible]	[illegible]	[illegible]	[illegible]	[illegible]	[illegible]	[illegible]	[illegible]	[illegible]	[illegible]
[illegible]	Midleton,	[illegible]	[illegible]	[illegible]	[illegible]	[illegible]	[illegible]	[illegible]	[illegible]	[illegible]	[illegible]	[illegible]	[illegible]
[illegible]	Millstreet,	[illegible]	[illegible]	[illegible]	[illegible]	[illegible]	[illegible]	[illegible]	[illegible]	[illegible]	[illegible]	[illegible]	[illegible]
[illegible]	Mitchelstown, part of,	[illegible]	[illegible]	[illegible]	[illegible]	[illegible]	[illegible]	[illegible]	[illegible]	[illegible]	[illegible]	[illegible]	[illegible]
[illegible]	Skibbereen,	[illegible]	[illegible]	[illegible]	[illegible]	[illegible]	[illegible]	[illegible]	[illegible]	[illegible]	[illegible]	[illegible]	[illegible]
[illegible]	Skull,	[illegible]	[illegible]	[illegible]	[illegible]	[illegible]	[illegible]	[illegible]	[illegible]	[illegible]	[illegible]	[illegible]	[illegible]
[illegible]	Youghal, part of,	[illegible]	[illegible]	[illegible]	[illegible]	[illegible]	[illegible]	[illegible]	[illegible]	[illegible]	[illegible]	[illegible]	[illegible]
	16. Kerry Co.												
[illegible]	Cahersiveen,	[illegible]	[illegible]	[illegible]	[illegible]	[illegible]	[illegible]	[illegible]	[illegible]	[illegible]	[illegible]	[illegible]	[illegible]
[illegible]	Dingle,	[illegible]	[illegible]	[illegible]	[illegible]	[illegible]	[illegible]	[illegible]	[illegible]	[illegible]	[illegible]	[illegible]	[illegible]
[illegible]	Glin, part of,	[illegible]	[illegible]	[illegible]	[illegible]	[illegible]	[illegible]	[illegible]	[illegible]	[illegible]	[illegible]	[illegible]	[illegible]
[illegible]	Kenmare,	[illegible]	[illegible]	[illegible]	[illegible]	[illegible]	[illegible]	[illegible]	[illegible]	[illegible]	[illegible]	[illegible]	[illegible]
[illegible]	Killarney,	[illegible]	[illegible]	[illegible]	[illegible]	[illegible]	[illegible]	[illegible]	[illegible]	[illegible]	[illegible]	[illegible]	[illegible]
[illegible]	Listowel,	[illegible]	[illegible]	[illegible]	[illegible]	[illegible]	[illegible]	[illegible]	[illegible]	[illegible]	[illegible]	[illegible]	[illegible]
[illegible]	Tralee,	[illegible]	[illegible]	[illegible]	[illegible]	[illegible]	[illegible]	[illegible]	[illegible]	[illegible]	[illegible]	[illegible]	[illegible]
	16. Limerick Co.												
[illegible]	Croom,	[illegible]	[illegible]	[illegible]	[illegible]	[illegible]	[illegible]	[illegible]	[illegible]	[illegible]	[illegible]	[illegible]	[illegible]
[illegible]	Glin, part of,	[illegible]	[illegible]	[illegible]	[illegible]	[illegible]	[illegible]	[illegible]	[illegible]	[illegible]	[illegible]	[illegible]	[illegible]
[illegible]	Kilmallock, do.,	[illegible]	[illegible]	[illegible]	[illegible]	[illegible]	[illegible]	[illegible]	[illegible]	[illegible]	[illegible]	[illegible]	[illegible]
[illegible]	Limerick, do.,	[illegible]	[illegible]	[illegible]	[illegible]	[illegible]	[illegible]	[illegible]	[illegible]	[illegible]	[illegible]	[illegible]	[illegible]
[illegible]	Mitchelstown, do.,	[illegible]	[illegible]	[illegible]	[illegible]	[illegible]	[illegible]	[illegible]	[illegible]	[illegible]	[illegible]	[illegible]	[illegible]
[illegible]	Newcastle,	[illegible]	[illegible]	[illegible]	[illegible]	[illegible]	[illegible]	[illegible]	[illegible]	[illegible]	[illegible]	[illegible]	[illegible]
[illegible]	Rathkeale,	[illegible]	[illegible]	[illegible]	[illegible]	[illegible]	[illegible]	[illegible]	[illegible]	[illegible]	[illegible]	[illegible]	[illegible]
[illegible]	Tipperary, part of,	[illegible]	[illegible]	[illegible]	[illegible]	[illegible]	[illegible]	[illegible]	[illegible]	[illegible]	[illegible]	[illegible]	[illegible]
	17. Tipperary Co.												
[illegible]	Borrisokane,	[illegible]	[illegible]	[illegible]	[illegible]	[illegible]	[illegible]	[illegible]	[illegible]	[illegible]	[illegible]	[illegible]	[illegible]
[illegible]	Callan, part of,	[illegible]	[illegible]	[illegible]	[illegible]	[illegible]	[illegible]	[illegible]	[illegible]	[illegible]	[illegible]	[illegible]	[illegible]
[illegible]	Carrick-on-Suir, do.,	[illegible]	[illegible]	[illegible]	[illegible]	[illegible]	[illegible]	[illegible]	[illegible]	[illegible]	[illegible]	[illegible]	[illegible]
[illegible]	Cashel,	[illegible]	[illegible]	[illegible]	[illegible]	[illegible]	[illegible]	[illegible]	[illegible]	[illegible]	[illegible]	[illegible]	[illegible]
[illegible]	Clogheen,	[illegible]	[illegible]	[illegible]	[illegible]	[illegible]	[illegible]	[illegible]	[illegible]	[illegible]	[illegible]	[illegible]	[illegible]
[illegible]	Clonmel, part of,	[illegible]	[illegible]	[illegible]	[illegible]	[illegible]	[illegible]	[illegible]	[illegible]	[illegible]	[illegible]	[illegible]	[illegible]
[illegible]	Nenagh,	[illegible]	[illegible]	[illegible]	[illegible]	[illegible]	[illegible]	[illegible]	[illegible]	[illegible]	[illegible]	[illegible]	[illegible]
[illegible]	Parsonstown, part of,	[illegible]	[illegible]	[illegible]	[illegible]	[illegible]	[illegible]	[illegible]	[illegible]	[illegible]	[illegible]	[illegible]	[illegible]
[illegible]	Roscrea,* do.,	[illegible]	[illegible]	[illegible]	[illegible]	[illegible]	[illegible]	[illegible]	[illegible]	[illegible]	[illegible]	[illegible]	[illegible]
[illegible]	Thurles,	[illegible]	[illegible]	[illegible]	[illegible]	[illegible]	[illegible]	[illegible]	[illegible]	[illegible]	[illegible]	[illegible]	[illegible]
[illegible]	Tipperary, part of,	[illegible]	[illegible]	[illegible]	[illegible]	[illegible]	[illegible]	[illegible]	[illegible]	[illegible]	[illegible]	[illegible]	[illegible]
[illegible]	Urlingford,* do.,	[illegible]	[illegible]	[illegible]	[illegible]	[illegible]	[illegible]	[illegible]	[illegible]	[illegible]	[illegible]	[illegible]	[illegible]

XXI.—[illegible] OF [illegible].—MARRIAGES, BIRTHS, AND DEATHS, 1881-90—

SUPERINTENDENT REGISTRARS' DISTRICTS.

	19. Antrim Co.												
[illegible]	ANTRIM, . . .	[illegible]	[illegible]	[illegible]	[illegible]	[illegible]	[illegible]	[illegible]	[illegible]	771	[illegible]	[illegible]
[illegible]	BALLYCASTLE, . .	[illegible]	[illegible]	[illegible]	[illegible]	[illegible]	[illegible]	[illegible]	[illegible]	117	[illegible]	[illegible]
[illegible]	BALLYMENA, . .	[illegible]	[illegible]	[illegible]	[illegible]	[illegible]	[illegible]	[illegible]	[illegible]	[illegible]	[illegible]	[illegible]
[illegible]	BALLYMONEY, part of,	[illegible]	[illegible]	[illegible]	[illegible]	[illegible]	[illegible]	[illegible]	[illegible]	[illegible]	[illegible]	[illegible]
[illegible]	BELFAST, do. .	[illegible]	[illegible]	[illegible]	[illegible]	[illegible]	[illegible]	[illegible]	[illegible]	[illegible]	[illegible]	[illegible]
[illegible]	COLERAINE, do. .	[illegible]	[illegible]	[illegible]	[illegible]	[illegible]	[illegible]	779	[illegible]	[illegible]	[illegible]	[illegible]
[illegible]	LARNE, . . .	[illegible]	[illegible]	[illegible]	[illegible]	[illegible]	[illegible]	[illegible]	[illegible]	[illegible]	[illegible]	[illegible]
[illegible]	LISBURN, part of, .	[illegible]	[illegible]	[illegible]	[illegible]	[illegible]	[illegible]	[illegible]	[illegible]	[illegible]	[illegible]	[illegible]
[illegible]	LURGAN, do. .	[illegible]	[illegible]	[illegible]	[illegible]	[illegible]	[illegible]	[illegible]	[illegible]	[illegible]	[illegible]	[illegible]
	20. Armagh Co.												
[illegible]	ARMAGH, part of,	[illegible]	[illegible]	[illegible]	[illegible]	[illegible]	[illegible]	[illegible]	[illegible]	[illegible]	[illegible]	[illegible]
[illegible]	BANBRIDGE, do.	[illegible]	[illegible]	[illegible]	[illegible]	[illegible]	[illegible]	[illegible]	[illegible]	[illegible]	[illegible]	[illegible]
[illegible]	CASTLEBLAYNEY, do.	[illegible]	[illegible]	[illegible]	[illegible]	[illegible]	[illegible]	[illegible]	[illegible]	[illegible]	[illegible]	[illegible]
[illegible]	DUNDALK, do.	[illegible]	[illegible]	6	[illegible]	[illegible]	[illegible]	[illegible]	[illegible]	1	[illegible]	[illegible]
[illegible]	LURGAN, do.	[illegible]	[illegible]	[illegible]	[illegible]	[illegible]	[illegible]	[illegible]	[illegible]	[illegible]	[illegible]	[illegible]
[illegible]	NEWRY, do.	[illegible]	[illegible]	[illegible]	[illegible]	[illegible]	[illegible]	[illegible]	[illegible]	[illegible]	[illegible]	[illegible]
	21. Cavan Co.												
[illegible]	BAILIEBOROUGH, .	[illegible]	[illegible]	[illegible]	[illegible]	[illegible]	[illegible]	[illegible]	[illegible]	[illegible]	[illegible]	[illegible]
[illegible]	BAWNBOY, part of,	[illegible]	[illegible]	[illegible]	[illegible]	[illegible]	[illegible]	[illegible]	[illegible]	[illegible]	[illegible]	[illegible]
[illegible]	CAVAN, . . .	[illegible]	[illegible]	[illegible]	[illegible]	[illegible]	[illegible]	[illegible]	[illegible]	[illegible]	[illegible]	[illegible]
[illegible]	COOTEHILL, part of, .	[illegible]	[illegible]	[illegible]	[illegible]	[illegible]	[illegible]	[illegible]	[illegible]	[illegible]	[illegible]	[illegible]
[illegible]	ENNISKILLEN, do. .	[illegible]	[illegible]	[illegible]	[illegible]	[illegible]	[illegible]	[illegible]	7	6	[illegible]	[illegible]
[illegible]	GRANARD, do. .	[illegible]	[illegible]	[illegible]	[illegible]	[illegible]	[illegible]	[illegible]	[illegible]	7	[illegible]	[illegible]
[illegible]	KELLS, do. .	[illegible]	[illegible]	[illegible]	[illegible]	[illegible]	[illegible]	[illegible]	[illegible]	—	[illegible]	[illegible]
[illegible]	OLDCASTLE, do. .	[illegible]	[illegible]	[illegible]	[illegible]	[illegible]	[illegible]	[illegible]	[illegible]	[illegible]	[illegible]	[illegible]
	22. Donegal Co.												
[illegible]	BALLYSHANNON, part of,	[illegible]	[illegible]	[illegible]	[illegible]	[illegible]	[illegible]	[illegible]	[illegible]	[illegible]	[illegible]	[illegible]
[illegible]	DONEGAL, . .	[illegible]	[illegible]	[illegible]	[illegible]	[illegible]	[illegible]	[illegible]	[illegible]	[illegible]	[illegible]	[illegible]
[illegible]	DUNFANAGHY, .	[illegible]	[illegible]	[illegible]	[illegible]	[illegible]	[illegible]	[illegible]	[illegible]	[illegible]	[illegible]	[illegible]
[illegible]	GLENTIES, . .	[illegible]	[illegible]	[illegible]	[illegible]	[illegible]	[illegible]	[illegible]	[illegible]	[illegible]	[illegible]	[illegible]
[illegible]	INISHOWEN, . .	[illegible]	[illegible]	[illegible]	[illegible]	[illegible]	[illegible]	[illegible]	[illegible]	[illegible]	[illegible]	[illegible]
[illegible]	LETTERKENNY, .	[illegible]	[illegible]	[illegible]	[illegible]	[illegible]	[illegible]	[illegible]	[illegible]	[illegible]	[illegible]	[illegible]
[illegible]	LONDONDERRY, part of,	[illegible]	[illegible]	[illegible]	[illegible]	[illegible]	[illegible]	[illegible]	[illegible]	[illegible]	[illegible]	[illegible]
[illegible]	MILFORD, .	[illegible]	[illegible]	[illegible]	[illegible]	[illegible]	[illegible]	[illegible]	[illegible]	[illegible]	[illegible]	[illegible]
[illegible]	STRABANE, part of,* .	[illegible]	[illegible]	[illegible]	[illegible]	[illegible]	[illegible]	[illegible]	[illegible]	[illegible]	[illegible]	[illegible]
[illegible]	STRANORLAR, . .	[illegible]	[illegible]	771	[illegible]	[illegible]	[illegible]	[illegible]	[illegible]	[illegible]	[illegible]	[illegible]

III.—PROVINCE OF ULSTER.—MARRIAGES, BIRTHS, AND DEATHS, 1881–1890.
SUPERINTENDENT REGISTRARS' DISTRICTS—*continued.*

No.	Superintendent Registrars' Districts.	Population 1881.	Population 1891.	Total: Marriages.	Total: Births.	Total: Deaths.	Births: Legitimate: Males.	Births: Legitimate: Females.	Births: Illegitimate: Males.	Births: Illegitimate: Females.	Deaths: Males.	Deaths: Females.	[illegible]
	33. Down Co.												
[illegible]	Banbridge, part of,	[illegible]	[illegible]	[illegible]	[illegible]	[illegible]	[illegible]	[illegible]	[illegible]	[illegible]	[illegible]	[illegible]	[illegible]
[illegible]	Belfast, do.	[illegible]	[illegible]	[illegible]	[illegible]	[illegible]	[illegible]	[illegible]	[illegible]	[illegible]	[illegible]	[illegible]	[illegible]
[illegible]	Downpatrick,	[illegible]	[illegible]	[illegible]	[illegible]	[illegible]	[illegible]	[illegible]	[illegible]	[illegible]	[illegible]	[illegible]	[illegible]
[illegible]	Kilkeel,	[illegible]	[illegible]	[illegible]	[illegible]	[illegible]	[illegible]	[illegible]	[illegible]	[illegible]	[illegible]	[illegible]	[illegible]
[illegible]	Lisburn, part of,	[illegible]	[illegible]	[illegible]	[illegible]	[illegible]	[illegible]	[illegible]	[illegible]	[illegible]	[illegible]	[illegible]	[illegible]
[illegible]	Lurgan, do.	[illegible]	[illegible]	[illegible]	[illegible]	[illegible]	[illegible]	[illegible]	[illegible]	[illegible]	[illegible]	[illegible]	[illegible]
[illegible]	Newry, do.	[illegible]	[illegible]	[illegible]	[illegible]	[illegible]	[illegible]	[illegible]	[illegible]	[illegible]	[illegible]	[illegible]	[illegible]
[illegible]	Newtownards,	[illegible]	[illegible]	[illegible]	[illegible]	[illegible]	[illegible]	[illegible]	[illegible]	[illegible]	[illegible]	[illegible]	[illegible]
	34. Fermanagh Co.												
[illegible]	Ballyshannon, part of,	[illegible]	[illegible]	[illegible]	[illegible]	[illegible]	[illegible]	[illegible]	[illegible]	[illegible]	[illegible]	[illegible]	[illegible]
[illegible]	Clones, do.	[illegible]	[illegible]	[illegible]	[illegible]	[illegible]	[illegible]	[illegible]	[illegible]	[illegible]	[illegible]	[illegible]	[illegible]
[illegible]	Enniskillen, do.	[illegible]	[illegible]	[illegible]	[illegible]	[illegible]	[illegible]	[illegible]	[illegible]	[illegible]	[illegible]	[illegible]	[illegible]
[illegible]	Irvinestown, do.	[illegible]	[illegible]	[illegible]	[illegible]	[illegible]	[illegible]	[illegible]	[illegible]	[illegible]	[illegible]	[illegible]	[illegible]
[illegible]	Lisnaskea,	[illegible]	[illegible]	[illegible]	[illegible]	[illegible]	[illegible]	[illegible]	[illegible]	[illegible]	[illegible]	[illegible]	[illegible]
	35. Londonderry Co.												
[illegible]	Ballymoney, part of,	[illegible]	[illegible]	[illegible]	[illegible]	[illegible]	[illegible]	[illegible]	[illegible]	[illegible]	[illegible]	[illegible]	[illegible]
[illegible]	Coleraine, do.	[illegible]	[illegible]	[illegible]	[illegible]	[illegible]	[illegible]	[illegible]	[illegible]	[illegible]	[illegible]	[illegible]	[illegible]
[illegible]	Limavady,	[illegible]	[illegible]	[illegible]	[illegible]	[illegible]	[illegible]	[illegible]	[illegible]	[illegible]	[illegible]	[illegible]	[illegible]
[illegible]	Londonderry, part of,	[illegible]	[illegible]	[illegible]	[illegible]	[illegible]	[illegible]	[illegible]	[illegible]	[illegible]	[illegible]	[illegible]	[illegible]
[illegible]	Magherafelt,	[illegible]	[illegible]	[illegible]	[illegible]	[illegible]	[illegible]	[illegible]	[illegible]	[illegible]	[illegible]	[illegible]	[illegible]
	36. Monaghan Co.												
[illegible]	Carrickmacross,	[illegible]	[illegible]	[illegible]	[illegible]	[illegible]	[illegible]	[illegible]	[illegible]	[illegible]	[illegible]	[illegible]	[illegible]
[illegible]	Castleblayney, part of,	[illegible]	[illegible]	[illegible]	[illegible]	[illegible]	[illegible]	[illegible]	[illegible]	[illegible]	[illegible]	[illegible]	[illegible]
[illegible]	Clogher, do.	[illegible]	[illegible]	[illegible]	[illegible]	[illegible]	[illegible]	[illegible]	[illegible]	[illegible]	[illegible]	[illegible]	[illegible]
[illegible]	Clones, do.	[illegible]	[illegible]	[illegible]	[illegible]	[illegible]	[illegible]	[illegible]	[illegible]	[illegible]	[illegible]	[illegible]	[illegible]
[illegible]	Cootehill, do.	[illegible]	[illegible]	[illegible]	[illegible]	[illegible]	[illegible]	[illegible]	[illegible]	[illegible]	[illegible]	[illegible]	[illegible]
[illegible]	Dundalk, do.	[illegible]	[illegible]	[illegible]	[illegible]	[illegible]	[illegible]	[illegible]	[illegible]	[illegible]	[illegible]	[illegible]	[illegible]
[illegible]	Monaghan, do.	[illegible]	[illegible]	[illegible]	[illegible]	[illegible]	[illegible]	[illegible]	[illegible]	[illegible]	[illegible]	[illegible]	[illegible]
	37. Tyrone Co.												
[illegible]	Armagh, part of,	[illegible]	[illegible]	[illegible]	[illegible]	[illegible]	[illegible]	[illegible]	[illegible]	[illegible]	[illegible]	[illegible]	[illegible]
[illegible]	Castlederg,	[illegible]	[illegible]	[illegible]	[illegible]	[illegible]	[illegible]	[illegible]	[illegible]	[illegible]	[illegible]	[illegible]	[illegible]
[illegible]	Clogher, part of,	[illegible]	[illegible]	[illegible]	[illegible]	[illegible]	[illegible]	[illegible]	[illegible]	[illegible]	[illegible]	[illegible]	[illegible]
[illegible]	Cookstown,	[illegible]	[illegible]	[illegible]	[illegible]	[illegible]	[illegible]	[illegible]	[illegible]	[illegible]	[illegible]	[illegible]	[illegible]
[illegible]	Dungannon,	[illegible]	[illegible]	[illegible]	[illegible]	[illegible]	[illegible]	[illegible]	[illegible]	[illegible]	[illegible]	[illegible]	[illegible]
[illegible]	Enniskillen, part of,	[illegible]	[illegible]	[illegible]	[illegible]	[illegible]	[illegible]	[illegible]	[illegible]	[illegible]	[illegible]	[illegible]	[illegible]
[illegible]	Gortin,*	[illegible]	[illegible]	[illegible]	[illegible]	[illegible]	[illegible]	[illegible]	[illegible]	[illegible]	[illegible]	[illegible]	[illegible]
[illegible]	Irvinestown, do.	[illegible]	[illegible]	[illegible]	[illegible]	[illegible]	[illegible]	[illegible]	[illegible]	[illegible]	[illegible]	[illegible]	[illegible]
[illegible]	Omagh,*	[illegible]	[illegible]	[illegible]	[illegible]	[illegible]	[illegible]	[illegible]	[illegible]	[illegible]	[illegible]	[illegible]	[illegible]
[illegible]	Strabane, part of,*	[illegible]	[illegible]	[illegible]	[illegible]	[illegible]	[illegible]	[illegible]	[illegible]	[illegible]	[illegible]	[illegible]	[illegible]

* See note (*) [illegible]

IV.—PROVINCE OF CONNAUGHT.—MARRIAGES, BIRTHS, AND DEATHS, 1881-90—SUPERINTENDENT REGISTRARS' DISTRICTS.

No.	Superintendent Registrars' Districts.	Population 1881.	Population 1871.	Total: Marriages.	Total: Births.	Total: Deaths.	Births, including Illegitimate Births: Males.	Births, including Illegitimate Births: Females.	Illegitimate Births: Males.	Illegitimate Births: Females.	Deaths: Males.	Deaths: Females.
	28. Galway Co.											
[illegible]	Ballinasloe, part of,	[illegible]	[illegible]	[illegible]	[illegible]	[illegible]	[illegible]	[illegible]	[illegible]	[illegible]	[illegible]	[illegible]
[illegible]	Ballyvaughan, do.	[illegible]	[illegible]	[illegible]	[illegible]	[illegible]	[illegible]	[illegible]	[illegible]	[illegible]	[illegible]	[illegible]
[illegible]	Clifden,	[illegible]	[illegible]	[illegible]	[illegible]	[illegible]	[illegible]	[illegible]	[illegible]	[illegible]	[illegible]	[illegible]
[illegible]	Galway,	[illegible]	[illegible]	[illegible]	[illegible]	[illegible]	[illegible]	[illegible]	[illegible]	[illegible]	[illegible]	[illegible]
[illegible]	Glennamaddy,	[illegible]	[illegible]	[illegible]	[illegible]	[illegible]	[illegible]	[illegible]	[illegible]	[illegible]	[illegible]	[illegible]
[illegible]	Gort,	[illegible]	[illegible]	[illegible]	[illegible]	[illegible]	[illegible]	[illegible]	[illegible]	[illegible]	[illegible]	[illegible]
[illegible]	Loughrea,	[illegible]	[illegible]	[illegible]	[illegible]	[illegible]	[illegible]	[illegible]	[illegible]	[illegible]	[illegible]	[illegible]
[illegible]	Mount Bellew,	[illegible]	[illegible]	[illegible]	[illegible]	[illegible]	[illegible]	[illegible]	[illegible]	[illegible]	[illegible]	[illegible]
[illegible]	Oughterard,	[illegible]	[illegible]	[illegible]	[illegible]	[illegible]	[illegible]	[illegible]	[illegible]	[illegible]	[illegible]	[illegible]
[illegible]	Portumna,	[illegible]	[illegible]	[illegible]	[illegible]	[illegible]	[illegible]	[illegible]	[illegible]	[illegible]	[illegible]	[illegible]
[illegible]	Roscommon, part of,	[illegible]	[illegible]	[illegible]	[illegible]	[illegible]	[illegible]	[illegible]	[illegible]	[illegible]	[illegible]	[illegible]
[illegible]	Scarriff, do.	[illegible]	[illegible]	[illegible]	[illegible]	[illegible]	[illegible]	[illegible]	[illegible]	[illegible]	[illegible]	[illegible]
[illegible]	Tuam,	[illegible]	[illegible]	[illegible]	[illegible]	[illegible]	[illegible]	[illegible]	[illegible]	[illegible]	[illegible]	[illegible]
	29. Leitrim Co.											
[illegible]	Ballyshannon, part of,	[illegible]	[illegible]	[illegible]	[illegible]	[illegible]	[illegible]	[illegible]	[illegible]	[illegible]	[illegible]	[illegible]
[illegible]	Bawnboy, do.	[illegible]	[illegible]	[illegible]	[illegible]	[illegible]	[illegible]	[illegible]	[illegible]	[illegible]	[illegible]	[illegible]
[illegible]	Carrick-on-Shannon, do.	[illegible]	[illegible]	[illegible]	[illegible]	[illegible]	[illegible]	[illegible]	[illegible]	[illegible]	[illegible]	[illegible]
[illegible]	Manorhamilton,	[illegible]	[illegible]	[illegible]	[illegible]	[illegible]	[illegible]	[illegible]	[illegible]	[illegible]	[illegible]	[illegible]
[illegible]	Mohill,	[illegible]	[illegible]	[illegible]	[illegible]	[illegible]	[illegible]	[illegible]	[illegible]	[illegible]	[illegible]	[illegible]
	30. Mayo Co.											
[illegible]	Ballina, part of,	[illegible]	[illegible]	[illegible]	[illegible]	[illegible]	[illegible]	[illegible]	[illegible]	[illegible]	[illegible]	[illegible]
[illegible]	Ballinrobe, do.	[illegible]	[illegible]	[illegible]	[illegible]	[illegible]	[illegible]	[illegible]	[illegible]	[illegible]	[illegible]	[illegible]
[illegible]	Belmullet,	[illegible]	[illegible]	[illegible]	[illegible]	[illegible]	[illegible]	[illegible]	[illegible]	[illegible]	[illegible]	[illegible]
[illegible]	Castlebar,	[illegible]	[illegible]	[illegible]	[illegible]	[illegible]	[illegible]	[illegible]	[illegible]	[illegible]	[illegible]	[illegible]
[illegible]	Castlerea, part of,	[illegible]	[illegible]	[illegible]	[illegible]	[illegible]	[illegible]	[illegible]	[illegible]	[illegible]	[illegible]	[illegible]
[illegible]	Claremorris,	[illegible]	[illegible]	[illegible]	[illegible]	[illegible]	[illegible]	[illegible]	[illegible]	[illegible]	[illegible]	[illegible]
[illegible]	Killala,	[illegible]	[illegible]	[illegible]	[illegible]	[illegible]	[illegible]	[illegible]	[illegible]	[illegible]	[illegible]	[illegible]
[illegible]	Newport,	[illegible]	[illegible]	[illegible]	[illegible]	[illegible]	[illegible]	[illegible]	[illegible]	[illegible]	[illegible]	[illegible]
[illegible]	Swinford,	[illegible]	[illegible]	[illegible]	[illegible]	[illegible]	[illegible]	[illegible]	[illegible]	[illegible]	[illegible]	[illegible]
[illegible]	Westport,	[illegible]	[illegible]	[illegible]	[illegible]	[illegible]	[illegible]	[illegible]	[illegible]	[illegible]	[illegible]	[illegible]
	31. Roscommon Co.											
[illegible]	Athlone, part of,	[illegible]	[illegible]	[illegible]	[illegible]	[illegible]	[illegible]	[illegible]	[illegible]	[illegible]	[illegible]	[illegible]
[illegible]	Ballinasloe, do.	[illegible]	[illegible]	[illegible]	[illegible]	[illegible]	[illegible]	[illegible]	[illegible]	[illegible]	[illegible]	[illegible]
[illegible]	Boyle, do.	[illegible]	[illegible]	[illegible]	[illegible]	[illegible]	[illegible]	[illegible]	[illegible]	[illegible]	[illegible]	[illegible]
[illegible]	Carrick-on-Shannon, do.	[illegible]	[illegible]	[illegible]	[illegible]	[illegible]	[illegible]	[illegible]	[illegible]	[illegible]	[illegible]	[illegible]
[illegible]	Castlerea, do.	[illegible]	[illegible]	[illegible]	[illegible]	[illegible]	[illegible]	[illegible]	[illegible]	[illegible]	[illegible]	[illegible]
[illegible]	Roscommon, do.	[illegible]	[illegible]	[illegible]	[illegible]	[illegible]	[illegible]	[illegible]	[illegible]	[illegible]	[illegible]	[illegible]
[illegible]	Strokestown, do.	[illegible]	[illegible]	[illegible]	[illegible]	[illegible]	[illegible]	[illegible]	[illegible]	[illegible]	[illegible]	[illegible]
	32. Sligo Co.											
[illegible]	Ballina, part of,	[illegible]	[illegible]	[illegible]	[illegible]	[illegible]	[illegible]	[illegible]	[illegible]	[illegible]	[illegible]	[illegible]
[illegible]	Boyle, do.	[illegible]	[illegible]	[illegible]	[illegible]	[illegible]	[illegible]	[illegible]	[illegible]	[illegible]	[illegible]	[illegible]
[illegible]	Dromore West,	[illegible]	[illegible]	[illegible]	[illegible]	[illegible]	[illegible]	[illegible]	[illegible]	[illegible]	[illegible]	[illegible]
[illegible]	Sligo,	[illegible]	[illegible]	[illegible]	[illegible]	[illegible]	[illegible]	[illegible]	[illegible]	[illegible]	[illegible]	[illegible]
[illegible]	Tobercurry,	[illegible]	[illegible]	[illegible]	[illegible]	[illegible]	[illegible]	[illegible]	[illegible]	[illegible]	[illegible]	[illegible]

VACCINATION.

RETURN showing by UNIONS or SUPERINTENDENT REGISTRARS' DISTRICTS the NUMBER of PRIMARY SUCCESSFUL VACCINATIONS for the NINE YEARS, 1882-90. These Statistics were first collected in the year 1882.

Unions or Superintendent Registrars' Districts.	Primary Vaccinations.
IRELAND,	[illegible]
Abbeyleix,*	[illegible]
Antrim,	[illegible]
Ardee,	[illegible]
Armagh,	[illegible]
Athlone,	[illegible]
Athy,	[illegible]
Bailieborough,	[illegible]
Ballina,	[illegible]
Ballinasloe,	[illegible]
Ballinrobe,	[illegible]
Ballycastle,	[illegible]
Ballymahon,	[illegible]
Ballymena,	[illegible]
Ballymoney,	[illegible]
Ballyshannon,	[illegible]
Ballyvaghan,	[illegible]
Balrothery,	[illegible]
Baltinglass,	[illegible]
Banbridge,	[illegible]
Bandon,	[illegible]
Bantry,	[illegible]
Bawnboy,	[illegible]
Belfast,	[illegible]
Belmullet,	[illegible]
Borrisokane,	[illegible]
Boyle,	[illegible]
Cahersiveen,	[illegible]
Callan,	[illegible]
Carlow,	[illegible]
Carrickmacross,	[illegible]
Carrick-on-Shannon,	[illegible]
Carrick-on-Suir,	[illegible]
Cashel,	[illegible]
Castlebar,	[illegible]
Castleblayney,	[illegible]
Castlecomer,	[illegible]
Castlederg,	[illegible]
Castlereagh,	[illegible]
Castletown,	[illegible]
Cavan,	[illegible]
Celbridge,	[illegible]
Claremorris,	[illegible]
Clifden,	[illegible]
Clogheen,	[illegible]
Clogher,	[illegible]
Clonakilty,	[illegible]
Clones,	[illegible]
Clonmel,	[illegible]
Coleraine,	[illegible]
Cookstown,	[illegible]
Cootehill,	[illegible]
Cork,	[illegible]
Corrofin,	[illegible]
Croom,	[illegible]
Delvin,	[illegible]
Dingle,	[illegible]
Donaghmore,*	[illegible]
Donegal,	[illegible]
Downpatrick,	[illegible]
Drogheda,	[illegible]
Dromore West,	[illegible]
Dublin North,	[illegible]
Dublin South,	[illegible]
Dundalk,	[illegible]
Dunfanaghy,	[illegible]
Dungannon,	[illegible]
Dunmanway,	[illegible]
Dunshaughlin,	[illegible]
Edenderry,	[illegible]
Ennis,	[illegible]
Enniscorthy,	[illegible]
Enniskillen,	[illegible]
Ennistymon,	[illegible]
Fermoy,	[illegible]
Galway,	[illegible]
Glenamaddy,	[illegible]
Glenties,	[illegible]
Glin,	[illegible]
Gorey,	[illegible]
Gort,	[illegible]
Gortin,*	[illegible]
Granard,	[illegible]
Inishowen,	[illegible]
Irvinestown,	[illegible]
Kanturk,	[illegible]
Kells,	[illegible]
Kenmare,	[illegible]
Kilkeel,	[illegible]
Kilkenny,	[illegible]
Killadysert,	[illegible]
Killala,	[illegible]
Killarney,	[illegible]
Kilmacthomas,	[illegible]
Kilmallock,	[illegible]
Kilrush,	[illegible]
Kinsale,	[illegible]
Larne,	[illegible]
Letterkenny,	[illegible]
Limavady,	[illegible]
Limerick,	[illegible]
Lisburn,	[illegible]
Lismore,	[illegible]
Lisnaskea,	[illegible]
Listowel,	[illegible]
Londonderry,	[illegible]
Longford,	[illegible]
Loughrea,	[illegible]
Lurgan,	[illegible]
Macroom,	[illegible]
Magherafelt,	[illegible]
Mallow,	[illegible]
Manorhamilton,	[illegible]
Midleton,	[illegible]
Millford,	[illegible]
Millstreet,	[illegible]
Mitchelstown,	[illegible]
Mohill,	[illegible]
Monaghan,	[illegible]
Mountbellew,	[illegible]
Mountmellick,	[illegible]
Mullingar,	[illegible]
Naas,	[illegible]
Navan,	[illegible]
Nenagh,	[illegible]
Newcastle,	[illegible]
Newport,*	[illegible]
New Ross,	[illegible]
Newry,	[illegible]
Newtownards,	[illegible]
Oldcastle,	[illegible]
Omagh,*	[illegible]
Oughterard,	[illegible]
Parsonstown,	[illegible]
Portumna,	[illegible]
Rathdown,	[illegible]
Rathdrum,	[illegible]
Rathkeale,	[illegible]
Roscommon,	[illegible]
Roscrea,*	[illegible]
Scarriff,	[illegible]
Shillelagh,	[illegible]
Skibbereen,	[illegible]
Skull,	[illegible]
Sligo,	[illegible]
Strabane,*	[illegible]
Stranorlar,	[illegible]
Strokestown,	[illegible]
Swineford,	[illegible]
Thomastown,	[illegible]
Thurles,	[illegible]
Tipperary,	[illegible]
Tobercurry,	[illegible]
Tralee,	[illegible]
Trim,	[illegible]
Tuam,	[illegible]
Tulla,	[illegible]
Tullamore,	[illegible]
Waterford,*	[illegible]
Westport,	[illegible]
Wexford,*	[illegible]
Wicklow,	[illegible]
Youghal,	[illegible]

* See Note (*) pages 66-67.

BIRTHS Registered in each of the Ten

Provinces and Counties.	Population.		BIRTHS.												
			Total in the Ten Years [illegible]			In each Year.									
	[illegible]	[illegible]	Males and Females.	Males.	Females.	[illegible]	[illegible]	[illegible]	[illegible]	[illegible]	[illegible]	[illegible]	[illegible]	[illegible]	[illegible]
IRELAND,	[illegible]	[illegible]	[illegible]	[illegible]	[illegible]	[illegible]	[illegible]	[illegible]	[illegible]	[illegible]	[illegible]	[illegible]	[illegible]	[illegible]	[illegible]
PROVINCES.															
I. LEINSTER,	[illegible]	[illegible]	[illegible]	[illegible]	[illegible]	[illegible]	[illegible]	[illegible]	[illegible]	[illegible]	[illegible]	[illegible]	[illegible]	[illegible]	[illegible]
II. MUNSTER,	[illegible]	[illegible]	[illegible]	[illegible]	[illegible]	[illegible]	[illegible]	[illegible]	[illegible]	[illegible]	[illegible]	[illegible]	[illegible]	[illegible]	[illegible]
III. ULSTER,	[illegible]	[illegible]	[illegible]	[illegible]	[illegible]	[illegible]	[illegible]	[illegible]	[illegible]	[illegible]	[illegible]	[illegible]	[illegible]	[illegible]	[illegible]
IV. CONNAUGHT,	[illegible]	[illegible]	[illegible]	[illegible]	[illegible]	[illegible]	[illegible]	[illegible]	[illegible]	[illegible]	[illegible]	[illegible]	[illegible]	[illegible]	[illegible]
I. LEINSTER.															
CARLOW,	[illegible]	[illegible]	[illegible]	[illegible]	[illegible]	[illegible]	[illegible]	[illegible]	[illegible]	[illegible]	[illegible]	[illegible]	[illegible]	[illegible]	[illegible]
DUBLIN,	[illegible]	[illegible]	[illegible]	[illegible]	[illegible]	[illegible]	[illegible]	[illegible]	[illegible]	[illegible]	[illegible]	[illegible]	[illegible]	[illegible]	[illegible]
KILDARE,	[illegible]	[illegible]	[illegible]	[illegible]	[illegible]	[illegible]	[illegible]	[illegible]	[illegible]	[illegible]	[illegible]	[illegible]	[illegible]	[illegible]	[illegible]
KILKENNY,	[illegible]	[illegible]	[illegible]	[illegible]	[illegible]	[illegible]	[illegible]	[illegible]	[illegible]	[illegible]	[illegible]	[illegible]	[illegible]	[illegible]	[illegible]
KING'S,	[illegible]	[illegible]	[illegible]	[illegible]	[illegible]	[illegible]	[illegible]	[illegible]	[illegible]	[illegible]	[illegible]	[illegible]	[illegible]	[illegible]	[illegible]
LONGFORD,	[illegible]	[illegible]	[illegible]	[illegible]	[illegible]	[illegible]	[illegible]	[illegible]	[illegible]	[illegible]	[illegible]	[illegible]	[illegible]	[illegible]	[illegible]
LOUTH,	[illegible]	[illegible]	[illegible]	[illegible]	[illegible]	[illegible]	[illegible]	[illegible]	[illegible]	[illegible]	[illegible]	[illegible]	[illegible]	[illegible]	[illegible]
MEATH,	[illegible]	[illegible]	[illegible]	[illegible]	[illegible]	[illegible]	[illegible]	[illegible]	[illegible]	[illegible]	[illegible]	[illegible]	[illegible]	[illegible]	[illegible]
[illegible]	[illegible]	[illegible]	[illegible]	[illegible]	[illegible]	[illegible]	[illegible]	[illegible]	[illegible]	[illegible]	[illegible]	[illegible]	[illegible]	[illegible]	[illegible]
[illegible]	[illegible]	[illegible]	[illegible]	[illegible]	[illegible]	[illegible]	[illegible]	[illegible]	[illegible]	[illegible]	[illegible]	[illegible]	[illegible]	[illegible]	[illegible]
WEXFORD,	[illegible]	[illegible]	[illegible]	[illegible]	[illegible]	[illegible]	[illegible]	[illegible]	[illegible]	[illegible]	[illegible]	[illegible]	[illegible]	[illegible]	[illegible]
WICKLOW,	[illegible]	[illegible]	[illegible]	[illegible]	[illegible]	[illegible]	[illegible]	[illegible]	[illegible]	[illegible]	[illegible]	[illegible]	[illegible]	[illegible]	[illegible]
II. MUNSTER.															
CLARE,	[illegible]	[illegible]	[illegible]	[illegible]	[illegible]	[illegible]	[illegible]	[illegible]	[illegible]	[illegible]	[illegible]	[illegible]	[illegible]	[illegible]	[illegible]
CORK,	[illegible]	[illegible]	[illegible]	[illegible]	[illegible]	[illegible]	[illegible]	[illegible]	[illegible]	[illegible]	[illegible]	[illegible]	[illegible]	[illegible]	[illegible]
KERRY,	[illegible]	[illegible]	[illegible]	[illegible]	[illegible]	[illegible]	[illegible]	[illegible]	[illegible]	[illegible]	[illegible]	[illegible]	[illegible]	[illegible]	[illegible]
LIMERICK,	[illegible]	[illegible]	[illegible]	[illegible]	[illegible]	[illegible]	[illegible]	[illegible]	[illegible]	[illegible]	[illegible]	[illegible]	[illegible]	[illegible]	[illegible]
TIPPERARY,	[illegible]	[illegible]	[illegible]	[illegible]	[illegible]	[illegible]	[illegible]	[illegible]	[illegible]	[illegible]	[illegible]	[illegible]	[illegible]	[illegible]	[illegible]
WATERFORD,	[illegible]	[illegible]	[illegible]	[illegible]	[illegible]	[illegible]	[illegible]	[illegible]	[illegible]	[illegible]	[illegible]	[illegible]	[illegible]	[illegible]	[illegible]
III. ULSTER.															
ANTRIM,	[illegible]	[illegible]	[illegible]	[illegible]	[illegible]	[illegible]	[illegible]	[illegible]	[illegible]	[illegible]	[illegible]	[illegible]	[illegible]	[illegible]	[illegible]
ARMAGH,	[illegible]	[illegible]	[illegible]	[illegible]	[illegible]	[illegible]	[illegible]	[illegible]	[illegible]	[illegible]	[illegible]	[illegible]	[illegible]	[illegible]	[illegible]
CAVAN,	[illegible]	[illegible]	[illegible]	[illegible]	[illegible]	[illegible]	[illegible]	[illegible]	[illegible]	[illegible]	[illegible]	[illegible]	[illegible]	[illegible]	[illegible]
DONEGAL,	[illegible]	[illegible]	[illegible]	[illegible]	[illegible]	[illegible]	[illegible]	[illegible]	[illegible]	[illegible]	[illegible]	[illegible]	[illegible]	[illegible]	[illegible]
DOWN,	[illegible]	[illegible]	[illegible]	[illegible]	[illegible]	[illegible]	[illegible]	[illegible]	[illegible]	[illegible]	[illegible]	[illegible]	[illegible]	[illegible]	[illegible]
FERMANAGH,	[illegible]	[illegible]	[illegible]	[illegible]	[illegible]	[illegible]	[illegible]	[illegible]	[illegible]	[illegible]	[illegible]	[illegible]	[illegible]	[illegible]	[illegible]
LONDONDERRY,	[illegible]	[illegible]	[illegible]	[illegible]	[illegible]	[illegible]	[illegible]	[illegible]	[illegible]	[illegible]	[illegible]	[illegible]	[illegible]	[illegible]	[illegible]
MONAGHAN,	[illegible]	[illegible]	[illegible]	[illegible]	[illegible]	[illegible]	[illegible]	[illegible]	[illegible]	[illegible]	[illegible]	[illegible]	[illegible]	[illegible]	[illegible]
TYRONE,	[illegible]	[illegible]	[illegible]	[illegible]	[illegible]	[illegible]	[illegible]	[illegible]	[illegible]	[illegible]	[illegible]	[illegible]	[illegible]	[illegible]	[illegible]
IV. CONNAUGHT.															
GALWAY,	[illegible]	[illegible]	[illegible]	[illegible]	[illegible]	[illegible]	[illegible]	[illegible]	[illegible]	[illegible]	[illegible]	[illegible]	[illegible]	[illegible]	[illegible]
LEITRIM,	[illegible]	[illegible]	[illegible]	[illegible]	[illegible]	[illegible]	[illegible]	[illegible]	[illegible]	[illegible]	[illegible]	[illegible]	[illegible]	[illegible]	[illegible]
MAYO,	[illegible]	[illegible]	[illegible]	[illegible]	[illegible]	[illegible]	[illegible]	[illegible]	[illegible]	[illegible]	[illegible]	[illegible]	[illegible]	[illegible]	[illegible]
ROSCOMMON,	[illegible]	[illegible]	[illegible]	[illegible]	[illegible]	[illegible]	[illegible]	[illegible]	[illegible]	[illegible]	[illegible]	[illegible]	[illegible]	[illegible]	[illegible]
SLIGO,	[illegible]	[illegible]	[illegible]	[illegible]	[illegible]	[illegible]	[illegible]	[illegible]	[illegible]	[illegible]	[illegible]	[illegible]	[illegible]	[illegible]	[illegible]

							I. LEINSTER.
[illegible]	[illegible]	[illegible]	[illegible]	[illegible]	[illegible]	[illegible]	Carlow.
[illegible]	[illegible]	[illegible]	[illegible]	[illegible]	[illegible]	[illegible]	Dublin.
[illegible]	[illegible]	[illegible]	[illegible]	[illegible]	[illegible]	[illegible]	Kildare.
[illegible]	[illegible]	[illegible]	[illegible]	[illegible]	[illegible]	[illegible]	Kilkenny.
[illegible]	[illegible]	[illegible]	[illegible]	[illegible]	[illegible]	[illegible]	King's.
[illegible]	[illegible]	[illegible]	[illegible]	[illegible]	[illegible]	[illegible]	Longford.
[illegible]	[illegible]	[illegible]	[illegible]	[illegible]	[illegible]	[illegible]	Louth.
[illegible]	[illegible]	[illegible]	[illegible]	[illegible]	[illegible]	[illegible]	Meath.
[illegible]	[illegible]	[illegible]	[illegible]	[illegible]	[illegible]	[illegible]	Queen's.
[illegible]	[illegible]	[illegible]	[illegible]	[illegible]	[illegible]	[illegible]	Westmeath.
[illegible]	[illegible]	[illegible]	[illegible]	[illegible]	[illegible]	[illegible]	Wexford.
[illegible]	[illegible]	[illegible]	[illegible]	[illegible]	[illegible]	[illegible]	Wicklow.
							II. MUNSTER.
[illegible]	[illegible]	[illegible]	[illegible]	[illegible]	[illegible]	[illegible]	Clare.
[illegible]	[illegible]	[illegible]	[illegible]	[illegible]	[illegible]	[illegible]	Cork.
[illegible]	[illegible]	[illegible]	[illegible]	[illegible]	[illegible]	[illegible]	Kerry.
[illegible]	[illegible]	[illegible]	[illegible]	[illegible]	[illegible]	[illegible]	Limerick.
[illegible]	[illegible]	[illegible]	[illegible]	[illegible]	[illegible]	[illegible]	Tipperary.
[illegible]	[illegible]	[illegible]	[illegible]	[illegible]	[illegible]	[illegible]	Waterford.
							III. ULSTER.
[illegible]	[illegible]	[illegible]	[illegible]	[illegible]	[illegible]	[illegible]	Antrim.
[illegible]	[illegible]	[illegible]	[illegible]	[illegible]	[illegible]	[illegible]	Armagh.
[illegible]	[illegible]	[illegible]	[illegible]	[illegible]	[illegible]	[illegible]	Cavan.
[illegible]	[illegible]	[illegible]	[illegible]	[illegible]	[illegible]	[illegible]	Donegal.
[illegible]	[illegible]	[illegible]	[illegible]	[illegible]	[illegible]	[illegible]	Down.
[illegible]	[illegible]	[illegible]	[illegible]	[illegible]	[illegible]	[illegible]	Fermanagh.
[illegible]	[illegible]	[illegible]	[illegible]	[illegible]	[illegible]	[illegible]	Londonderry.
[illegible]	[illegible]	[illegible]	[illegible]	[illegible]	[illegible]	[illegible]	Monaghan.
[illegible]	[illegible]	[illegible]	[illegible]	[illegible]	[illegible]	[illegible]	Tyrone.
							IV. CONNAUGHT.
[illegible]	[illegible]	[illegible]	[illegible]	[illegible]	[illegible]	[illegible]	Galway.
[illegible]	[illegible]	[illegible]	[illegible]	[illegible]	[illegible]	[illegible]	Leitrim.
[illegible]	[illegible]	[illegible]	[illegible]	[illegible]	[illegible]	[illegible]	Mayo.
[illegible]	[illegible]	[illegible]	[illegible]	[illegible]	[illegible]	[illegible]	Roscommon.

DEATHS Registered in each of the Ten

Provinces and Counties.	Population.		Deaths.													
	[illegible]	[illegible]	Total in the Ten Years [illegible]			Males and Females.										
	[illegible]	[illegible]	Persons.	Males.	Females.	[illegible]	[illegible]	[illegible]	[illegible]	[illegible]	[illegible]	[illegible]	[illegible]	[illegible]	[illegible]
IRELAND,	[illegible]	[illegible]	[illegible]	[illegible]	[illegible]	[illegible]	[illegible]	[illegible]	[illegible]	[illegible]	[illegible]	[illegible]	[illegible]	[illegible]	[illegible]
PROVINCES.															
I. LEINSTER,	[illegible]	[illegible]	[illegible]	[illegible]	[illegible]	[illegible]	[illegible]	[illegible]	[illegible]	[illegible]	[illegible]	[illegible]	[illegible]	[illegible]	[illegible]
II. MUNSTER,	[illegible]	[illegible]	[illegible]	[illegible]	[illegible]	[illegible]	[illegible]	[illegible]	[illegible]	[illegible]	[illegible]	[illegible]	[illegible]	[illegible]	[illegible]
III. ULSTER,	[illegible]	[illegible]	[illegible]	[illegible]	[illegible]	[illegible]	[illegible]	[illegible]	[illegible]	[illegible]	[illegible]	[illegible]	[illegible]	[illegible]	[illegible]
IV. CONNAUGHT,	[illegible]	[illegible]	[illegible]	[illegible]	[illegible]	[illegible]	[illegible]	[illegible]	[illegible]	[illegible]	[illegible]	[illegible]	[illegible]	[illegible]	[illegible]
I. LEINSTER.															
Carlow,	[illegible]	[illegible]	[illegible]	[illegible]	[illegible]	[illegible]	[illegible]	[illegible]	[illegible]	[illegible]	[illegible]	[illegible]	[illegible]	[illegible]	[illegible]
Dublin,	[illegible]	[illegible]	[illegible]	[illegible]	[illegible]	[illegible]	[illegible]	[illegible]	[illegible]	[illegible]	[illegible]	[illegible]	[illegible]	[illegible]	[illegible]
Kildare,	[illegible]	[illegible]	[illegible]	[illegible]	[illegible]	[illegible]	[illegible]	[illegible]	[illegible]	[illegible]	[illegible]	[illegible]	[illegible]	[illegible]	[illegible]
Kilkenny,	[illegible]	[illegible]	[illegible]	[illegible]	[illegible]	[illegible]	[illegible]	[illegible]	[illegible]	[illegible]	[illegible]	[illegible]	[illegible]	[illegible]	[illegible]
King's,	[illegible]	[illegible]	[illegible]	[illegible]	[illegible]	[illegible]	[illegible]	[illegible]	[illegible]	[illegible]	[illegible]	[illegible]	[illegible]	[illegible]	[illegible]
Longford,	[illegible]	[illegible]	[illegible]	[illegible]	[illegible]	[illegible]	[illegible]	[illegible]	[illegible]	[illegible]	[illegible]	[illegible]	[illegible]	[illegible]	[illegible]
Louth,	[illegible]	[illegible]	[illegible]	[illegible]	[illegible]	[illegible]	[illegible]	[illegible]	[illegible]	[illegible]	[illegible]	[illegible]	[illegible]	[illegible]	[illegible]
Meath,	[illegible]	[illegible]	[illegible]	[illegible]	[illegible]	[illegible]	[illegible]	[illegible]	[illegible]	[illegible]	[illegible]	[illegible]	[illegible]	[illegible]	[illegible]
Queen's,	[illegible]	[illegible]	[illegible]	[illegible]	[illegible]	[illegible]	[illegible]	[illegible]	[illegible]	[illegible]	[illegible]	[illegible]	[illegible]	[illegible]	[illegible]
Westmeath,	[illegible]	[illegible]	[illegible]	[illegible]	[illegible]	[illegible]	[illegible]	[illegible]	[illegible]	[illegible]	[illegible]	[illegible]	[illegible]	[illegible]	[illegible]
Wexford,	[illegible]	[illegible]	[illegible]	[illegible]	[illegible]	[illegible]	[illegible]	[illegible]	[illegible]	[illegible]	[illegible]	[illegible]	[illegible]	[illegible]	[illegible]
Wicklow,	[illegible]	[illegible]	[illegible]	[illegible]	[illegible]	[illegible]	[illegible]	[illegible]	[illegible]	[illegible]	[illegible]	[illegible]	[illegible]	[illegible]	[illegible]
II. MUNSTER.															
Clare,	[illegible]	[illegible]	[illegible]	[illegible]	[illegible]	[illegible]	[illegible]	[illegible]	[illegible]	[illegible]	[illegible]	[illegible]	[illegible]	[illegible]	[illegible]
Cork,	[illegible]	[illegible]	[illegible]	[illegible]	[illegible]	[illegible]	[illegible]	[illegible]	[illegible]	[illegible]	[illegible]	[illegible]	[illegible]	[illegible]	[illegible]
Kerry,	[illegible]	[illegible]	[illegible]	[illegible]	[illegible]	[illegible]	[illegible]	[illegible]	[illegible]	[illegible]	[illegible]	[illegible]	[illegible]	[illegible]	[illegible]
Limerick,	[illegible]	[illegible]	[illegible]	[illegible]	[illegible]	[illegible]	[illegible]	[illegible]	[illegible]	[illegible]	[illegible]	[illegible]	[illegible]	[illegible]	[illegible]
Tipperary,	[illegible]	[illegible]	[illegible]	[illegible]	[illegible]	[illegible]	[illegible]	[illegible]	[illegible]	[illegible]	[illegible]	[illegible]	[illegible]	[illegible]	[illegible]
Waterford,	[illegible]	[illegible]	[illegible]	[illegible]	[illegible]	[illegible]	[illegible]	[illegible]	[illegible]	[illegible]	[illegible]	[illegible]	[illegible]	[illegible]	[illegible]
III. ULSTER.															
Antrim,	[illegible]	[illegible]	[illegible]	[illegible]	[illegible]	[illegible]	[illegible]	[illegible]	[illegible]	[illegible]	[illegible]	[illegible]	[illegible]	[illegible]	[illegible]
Armagh,	[illegible]	[illegible]	[illegible]	[illegible]	[illegible]	[illegible]	[illegible]	[illegible]	[illegible]	[illegible]	[illegible]	[illegible]	[illegible]	[illegible]	[illegible]
Cavan,	[illegible]	[illegible]	[illegible]	[illegible]	[illegible]	[illegible]	[illegible]	[illegible]	[illegible]	[illegible]	[illegible]	[illegible]	[illegible]	[illegible]	[illegible]
Donegal,	[illegible]	[illegible]	[illegible]	[illegible]	[illegible]	[illegible]	[illegible]	[illegible]	[illegible]	[illegible]	[illegible]	[illegible]	[illegible]	[illegible]	[illegible]
Down,	[illegible]	[illegible]	[illegible]	[illegible]	[illegible]	[illegible]	[illegible]	[illegible]	[illegible]	[illegible]	[illegible]	[illegible]	[illegible]	[illegible]	[illegible]
Fermanagh,	[illegible]	[illegible]	[illegible]	[illegible]	[illegible]	[illegible]	[illegible]	[illegible]	[illegible]	[illegible]	[illegible]	[illegible]	[illegible]	[illegible]	[illegible]
Londonderry,	[illegible]	[illegible]	[illegible]	[illegible]	[illegible]	[illegible]	[illegible]	[illegible]	[illegible]	[illegible]	[illegible]	[illegible]	[illegible]	[illegible]	[illegible]
Monaghan,	[illegible]	[illegible]	[illegible]	[illegible]	[illegible]	[illegible]	[illegible]	[illegible]	[illegible]	[illegible]	[illegible]	[illegible]	[illegible]	[illegible]	[illegible]
Tyrone,	[illegible]	[illegible]	[illegible]	[illegible]	[illegible]	[illegible]	[illegible]	[illegible]	[illegible]	[illegible]	[illegible]	[illegible]	[illegible]	[illegible]	[illegible]
IV. CONNAUGHT.															
Galway,	[illegible]	[illegible]	[illegible]	[illegible]	[illegible]	[illegible]	[illegible]	[illegible]	[illegible]	[illegible]	[illegible]	[illegible]	[illegible]	[illegible]	[illegible]
Leitrim,	[illegible]	[illegible]	[illegible]	[illegible]	[illegible]	[illegible]	[illegible]	[illegible]	[illegible]	[illegible]	[illegible]	[illegible]	[illegible]	[illegible]	[illegible]
Mayo,	[illegible]	[illegible]	[illegible]	[illegible]	[illegible]	[illegible]	[illegible]	[illegible]	[illegible]	[illegible]	[illegible]	[illegible]	[illegible]	[illegible]	[illegible]
Roscommon,	[illegible]	[illegible]	[illegible]	[illegible]	[illegible]	[illegible]	[illegible]	[illegible]	[illegible]	[illegible]	[illegible]	[illegible]	[illegible]	[illegible]	[illegible]
Sligo,	[illegible]	[illegible]	[illegible]	[illegible]	[illegible]	[illegible]	[illegible]	[illegible]	[illegible]	[illegible]	[illegible]	[illegible]	[illegible]	[illegible]	[illegible]

[illegible]	[illegible]	[illegible]	[illegible]	[illegible]	[illegible]	[illegible]	[illegible]	[illegible]	[illegible]	[illegible]	[illegible]	[illegible]	[illegible]	[illegible]	[illegible]	Ireland.
[illegible]	[illegible]	[illegible]	[illegible]	[illegible]	[illegible]	[illegible]	[illegible]	[illegible]	[illegible]	[illegible]	[illegible]	[illegible]	[illegible]	[illegible]	[illegible]	[illegible]
																Leinster.
[illegible]	[illegible]	[illegible]	[illegible]	[illegible]	[illegible]	[illegible]	[illegible]	[illegible]	[illegible]	[illegible]	[illegible]	[illegible]	[illegible]	[illegible]	[illegible]	Carlow.
[illegible]	[illegible]	[illegible]	[illegible]	[illegible]	[illegible]	[illegible]	[illegible]	[illegible]	[illegible]	[illegible]	[illegible]	[illegible]	[illegible]	[illegible]	[illegible]	Dublin.
[illegible]	[illegible]	[illegible]	[illegible]	[illegible]	[illegible]	[illegible]	[illegible]	[illegible]	[illegible]	[illegible]	[illegible]	[illegible]	[illegible]	[illegible]	[illegible]	Kildare.
[illegible]	[illegible]	[illegible]	[illegible]	[illegible]	[illegible]	[illegible]	[illegible]	[illegible]	[illegible]	[illegible]	[illegible]	[illegible]	[illegible]	[illegible]	[illegible]	Kilkenny.
[illegible]	[illegible]	[illegible]	[illegible]	[illegible]	[illegible]	[illegible]	[illegible]	[illegible]	[illegible]	[illegible]	[illegible]	[illegible]	[illegible]	[illegible]	[illegible]	King's.
[illegible]	[illegible]	[illegible]	[illegible]	[illegible]	[illegible]	[illegible]	[illegible]	[illegible]	[illegible]	[illegible]	[illegible]	[illegible]	[illegible]	[illegible]	[illegible]	Longford.
[illegible]	[illegible]	[illegible]	[illegible]	[illegible]	[illegible]	[illegible]	[illegible]	[illegible]	[illegible]	[illegible]	[illegible]	[illegible]	[illegible]	[illegible]	[illegible]	Louth.
[illegible]	[illegible]	[illegible]	[illegible]	[illegible]	[illegible]	[illegible]	[illegible]	[illegible]	[illegible]	[illegible]	[illegible]	[illegible]	[illegible]	[illegible]	[illegible]	Meath.
[illegible]	[illegible]	[illegible]	[illegible]	[illegible]	[illegible]	[illegible]	[illegible]	[illegible]	[illegible]	[illegible]	[illegible]	[illegible]	[illegible]	[illegible]	[illegible]	Queen's.
[illegible]	[illegible]	[illegible]	[illegible]	[illegible]	[illegible]	[illegible]	[illegible]	[illegible]	[illegible]	[illegible]	[illegible]	[illegible]	[illegible]	[illegible]	[illegible]	Westmeath.
[illegible]	[illegible]	[illegible]	[illegible]	[illegible]	[illegible]	[illegible]	[illegible]	[illegible]	[illegible]	[illegible]	[illegible]	[illegible]	[illegible]	[illegible]	[illegible]	Wexford.
[illegible]	[illegible]	[illegible]	[illegible]	[illegible]	[illegible]	[illegible]	[illegible]	[illegible]	[illegible]	[illegible]	[illegible]	[illegible]	[illegible]	[illegible]	[illegible]	Wicklow.
																Munster.
[illegible]	[illegible]	[illegible]	[illegible]	[illegible]	[illegible]	[illegible]	[illegible]	[illegible]	[illegible]	[illegible]	[illegible]	[illegible]	[illegible]	[illegible]	[illegible]	Clare.
[illegible]	[illegible]	[illegible]	[illegible]	[illegible]	[illegible]	[illegible]	[illegible]	[illegible]	[illegible]	[illegible]	[illegible]	[illegible]	[illegible]	[illegible]	[illegible]	Cork.
[illegible]	[illegible]	[illegible]	[illegible]	[illegible]	[illegible]	[illegible]	[illegible]	[illegible]	[illegible]	[illegible]	[illegible]	[illegible]	[illegible]	[illegible]	[illegible]	Kerry.
[illegible]	[illegible]	[illegible]	[illegible]	[illegible]	[illegible]	[illegible]	[illegible]	[illegible]	[illegible]	[illegible]	[illegible]	[illegible]	[illegible]	[illegible]	[illegible]	Limerick.
[illegible]	[illegible]	[illegible]	[illegible]	[illegible]	[illegible]	[illegible]	[illegible]	[illegible]	[illegible]	[illegible]	[illegible]	[illegible]	[illegible]	[illegible]	[illegible]	Tipperary.
[illegible]	[illegible]	[illegible]	[illegible]	[illegible]	[illegible]	[illegible]	[illegible]	[illegible]	[illegible]	[illegible]	[illegible]	[illegible]	[illegible]	[illegible]	[illegible]	Waterford.
																Ulster.
[illegible]	[illegible]	[illegible]	[illegible]	[illegible]	[illegible]	[illegible]	[illegible]	[illegible]	[illegible]	[illegible]	[illegible]	[illegible]	[illegible]	[illegible]	[illegible]	Antrim.
[illegible]	[illegible]	[illegible]	[illegible]	[illegible]	[illegible]	[illegible]	[illegible]	[illegible]	[illegible]	[illegible]	[illegible]	[illegible]	[illegible]	[illegible]	[illegible]	Armagh.
[illegible]	[illegible]	[illegible]	[illegible]	[illegible]	[illegible]	[illegible]	[illegible]	[illegible]	[illegible]	[illegible]	[illegible]	[illegible]	[illegible]	[illegible]	[illegible]	Cavan.
[illegible]	[illegible]	[illegible]	[illegible]	[illegible]	[illegible]	[illegible]	[illegible]	[illegible]	[illegible]	[illegible]	[illegible]	[illegible]	[illegible]	[illegible]	[illegible]	Donegal.
[illegible]	[illegible]	[illegible]	[illegible]	[illegible]	[illegible]	[illegible]	[illegible]	[illegible]	[illegible]	[illegible]	[illegible]	[illegible]	[illegible]	[illegible]	[illegible]	Down.
[illegible]	[illegible]	[illegible]	[illegible]	[illegible]	[illegible]	[illegible]	[illegible]	[illegible]	[illegible]	[illegible]	[illegible]	[illegible]	[illegible]	[illegible]	[illegible]	Fermanagh.
[illegible]	[illegible]	[illegible]	[illegible]	[illegible]	[illegible]	[illegible]	[illegible]	[illegible]	[illegible]	[illegible]	[illegible]	[illegible]	[illegible]	[illegible]	[illegible]	Londonderry.
[illegible]	[illegible]	[illegible]	[illegible]	[illegible]	[illegible]	[illegible]	[illegible]	[illegible]	[illegible]	[illegible]	[illegible]	[illegible]	[illegible]	[illegible]	[illegible]	Monaghan.
[illegible]	[illegible]	[illegible]	[illegible]	[illegible]	[illegible]	[illegible]	[illegible]	[illegible]	[illegible]	[illegible]	[illegible]	[illegible]	[illegible]	[illegible]	[illegible]	Tyrone.
																Connaught.
[illegible]	[illegible]	[illegible]	[illegible]	[illegible]	[illegible]	[illegible]	[illegible]	[illegible]	[illegible]	[illegible]	[illegible]	[illegible]	[illegible]	[illegible]	[illegible]	Galway.
[illegible]	[illegible]	[illegible]	[illegible]	[illegible]	[illegible]	[illegible]	[illegible]	[illegible]	[illegible]	[illegible]	[illegible]	[illegible]	[illegible]	[illegible]	[illegible]	Leitrim.
[illegible]	[illegible]	[illegible]	[illegible]	[illegible]	[illegible]	[illegible]	[illegible]	[illegible]	[illegible]	[illegible]	[illegible]	[illegible]	[illegible]	[illegible]	[illegible]	Mayo.
[illegible]	[illegible]	[illegible]	[illegible]	[illegible]	[illegible]	[illegible]	[illegible]	[illegible]	[illegible]	[illegible]	[illegible]	[illegible]	[illegible]	[illegible]	[illegible]	Roscommon.
[illegible]	[illegible]	[illegible]	[illegible]	[illegible]	[illegible]	[illegible]	[illegible]	[illegible]	[illegible]	[illegible]	[illegible]	[illegible]	[illegible]	[illegible]	[illegible]	Sligo.

IRELAND.—DEATHS at different AGES registered in the Ten Years 1881-90—in the SUPERINTENDENT REGISTRARS' DISTRICTS—MALES.

Superintendent Registrars' Districts.	MALES.																						
	[illegible]	[illegible]	AGE AT DEATH.																				
			[illegible]	1	2	3	4	[illegible]	5–	10–	15–	20–	25–	35–	45–	55–	65–	75–	85–	95–	[illegible]		
IRELAND,	[illegible]	[illegible]	[illegible]	[illegible]	[illegible]	[illegible]	[illegible]	[illegible]	[illegible]	[illegible]	[illegible]	[illegible]	[illegible]	[illegible]	[illegible]	[illegible]	[illegible]	[illegible]	[illegible]	[illegible]	[illegible]	[illegible]	

REGISTRARS' DISTRICTS—FEMALES.

FEMALES.

AGES AT DEATH.

[illegible]	1	2	3	4	Under 5 Years	5-	10-	15-	20-	25-	35-	45-	55-	65-	75-	85-	[illegible]
[illegible]	[illegible]	[illegible]	[illegible]	[illegible]	[illegible]	[illegible]	[illegible]	[illegible]	[illegible]	[illegible]	[illegible]	[illegible]	[illegible]	[illegible]	[illegible]	[illegible]	[illegible]
[illegible]	[illegible]	[illegible]	[illegible]	[illegible]	[illegible]	[illegible]	[illegible]	[illegible]	[illegible]	[illegible]	[illegible]	[illegible]	[illegible]	[illegible]	[illegible]	[illegible]	[illegible]
[illegible]	[illegible]	[illegible]	[illegible]	[illegible]	[illegible]	[illegible]	[illegible]	[illegible]	[illegible]	[illegible]	[illegible]	[illegible]	[illegible]	[illegible]	[illegible]	[illegible]	[illegible]
[illegible]	[illegible]	[illegible]	[illegible]	[illegible]	[illegible]	[illegible]	[illegible]	[illegible]	[illegible]	[illegible]	[illegible]	[illegible]	[illegible]	[illegible]	[illegible]	[illegible]	[illegible]
[illegible]	[illegible]	[illegible]	[illegible]	[illegible]	[illegible]	[illegible]	[illegible]	[illegible]	[illegible]	[illegible]	[illegible]	[illegible]	[illegible]	[illegible]	[illegible]	[illegible]	[illegible]
[illegible]	[illegible]	[illegible]	[illegible]	[illegible]	[illegible]	[illegible]	[illegible]	[illegible]	[illegible]	[illegible]	[illegible]	[illegible]	[illegible]	[illegible]	[illegible]	[illegible]	[illegible]

IRELAND.—[illegible] at different AGES registered in the Ten Years 18[illegible]—in the SUPERINTENDENT REGISTRARS' DISTRICTS.—MALES—*continued.*

Superintendent Registrars' Districts	MALES																						
	[illegible]	[illegible]	Ages at Death																				
			[illegible]	[illegible]	[illegible]	[illegible]	[illegible]	[illegible]	[illegible]	[illegible]	[illegible]	[illegible]	[illegible]	[illegible]	[illegible]	[illegible]	[illegible]	[illegible]	[illegible]	[illegible]	[illegible]	[illegible]	[illegible]
[illegible]	[illegible]	[illegible]	[illegible]	[illegible]	[illegible]	[illegible]	[illegible]	[illegible]	[illegible]	[illegible]	[illegible]	[illegible]	[illegible]	[illegible]	[illegible]	[illegible]	[illegible]	[illegible]	[illegible]	[illegible]	[illegible]	[illegible]	[illegible]
[illegible]	[illegible]	[illegible]	[illegible]	[illegible]	[illegible]	[illegible]	[illegible]	[illegible]	[illegible]	[illegible]	[illegible]	[illegible]	[illegible]	[illegible]	[illegible]	[illegible]	[illegible]	[illegible]	[illegible]	[illegible]	[illegible]	[illegible]	[illegible]
[illegible]	[illegible]	[illegible]	[illegible]	[illegible]	[illegible]	[illegible]	[illegible]	[illegible]	[illegible]	[illegible]	[illegible]	[illegible]	[illegible]	[illegible]	[illegible]	[illegible]	[illegible]	[illegible]	[illegible]	[illegible]	[illegible]	[illegible]	[illegible]
[illegible]	[illegible]	[illegible]	[illegible]	[illegible]	[illegible]	[illegible]	[illegible]	[illegible]	[illegible]	[illegible]	[illegible]	[illegible]	[illegible]	[illegible]	[illegible]	[illegible]	[illegible]	[illegible]	[illegible]	[illegible]	[illegible]	[illegible]	[illegible]
[illegible]	[illegible]	[illegible]	[illegible]	[illegible]	[illegible]	[illegible]	[illegible]	[illegible]	[illegible]	[illegible]	[illegible]	[illegible]	[illegible]	[illegible]	[illegible]	[illegible]	[illegible]	[illegible]	[illegible]	[illegible]	[illegible]	[illegible]	[illegible]

IRELAND.—Deaths at different Ages registered in the Ten Years, 1881-90—in the Superintendent Registrars' Districts.—Females—*continued*.

Superintendent Registrars' Districts	[illegible]	[illegible]	Under 1 Year	1	2	3	4	Total under 5 Years	5-	10-	15-	20-	25-	35-	45-	55-	65-	75-	85-	95 and upwards
[illegible]	[illegible]	[illegible]	[illegible]	[illegible]	[illegible]	[illegible]	[illegible]	[illegible]	[illegible]	[illegible]	[illegible]	[illegible]	[illegible]	[illegible]	[illegible]	[illegible]	[illegible]	[illegible]	[illegible]	[illegible]
[illegible]	[illegible]	[illegible]	[illegible]	[illegible]	[illegible]	[illegible]	[illegible]	[illegible]	[illegible]	[illegible]	[illegible]	[illegible]	[illegible]	[illegible]	[illegible]	[illegible]	[illegible]	[illegible]	[illegible]	[illegible]
[illegible]	[illegible]	[illegible]	[illegible]	[illegible]	[illegible]	[illegible]	[illegible]	[illegible]	[illegible]	[illegible]	[illegible]	[illegible]	[illegible]	[illegible]	[illegible]	[illegible]	[illegible]	[illegible]	[illegible]	[illegible]
[illegible]	[illegible]	[illegible]	[illegible]	[illegible]	[illegible]	[illegible]	[illegible]	[illegible]	[illegible]	[illegible]	[illegible]	[illegible]	[illegible]	[illegible]	[illegible]	[illegible]	[illegible]	[illegible]	[illegible]	[illegible]
[illegible]	[illegible]	[illegible]	[illegible]	[illegible]	[illegible]	[illegible]	[illegible]	[illegible]	[illegible]	[illegible]	[illegible]	[illegible]	[illegible]	[illegible]	[illegible]	[illegible]	[illegible]	[illegible]	[illegible]	[illegible]

[illegible]	[illegible]	[illegible]	[illegible]	[illegible]	[illegible]	[illegible]	[illegible]	[illegible]	[illegible]	[illegible]	[illegible]	[illegible]	[illegible]	[illegible]	[illegible]	[illegible]
[illegible]	[illegible]	[illegible]	[illegible]	[illegible]	[illegible]	180	[illegible]	[illegible]	[illegible]	[illegible]	[illegible]	[illegible]	[illegible]	[illegible]	[illegible]	[illegible]
[illegible]	[illegible]	[illegible]	[illegible]	[illegible]	[illegible]	[illegible]	[illegible]	[illegible]	[illegible]	[illegible]	[illegible]	[illegible]	[illegible]	[illegible]	[illegible]	[illegible]
[illegible]	[illegible]	[illegible]	[illegible]	[illegible]	[illegible]	[illegible]	[illegible]	[illegible]	[illegible]	[illegible]	[illegible]	[illegible]	[illegible]	[illegible]	[illegible]	[illegible]
[illegible]	[illegible]	[illegible]	1,323	[illegible]	[illegible]	[illegible]	[illegible]	[illegible]	[illegible]	[illegible]	[illegible]	[illegible]	[illegible]	[illegible]	[illegible]	[illegible]
[illegible]	[illegible]	[illegible]	1,272	[illegible]	[illegible]	[illegible]	[illegible]	[illegible]	[illegible]	[illegible]	[illegible]	[illegible]	[illegible]	[illegible]	[illegible]	[illegible]

IRELAND.—DEATHS at different AGES registered in the Ten Years, 1881–90—in the SUPERINTENDENT REGISTRARS' DISTRICTS.—FEMALES—*continued.*

[illegible]	[illegible]	[illegible]	Ages at Death																				
			[illegible]	[illegible]	[illegible]	[illegible]	[illegible]	[illegible]	[illegible]	[illegible]	[illegible]	[illegible]	[illegible]	[illegible]	[illegible]	[illegible]	[illegible]	[illegible]	[illegible]	[illegible]	[illegible]	[illegible]	[illegible]
[illegible]	[illegible]	[illegible]	[illegible]	[illegible]	[illegible]	[illegible]	[illegible]	[illegible]	[illegible]	[illegible]	[illegible]	[illegible]	[illegible]	[illegible]	[illegible]	[illegible]	[illegible]	[illegible]	[illegible]	[illegible]	[illegible]	[illegible]	[illegible]
[illegible]	[illegible]	[illegible]	[illegible]	[illegible]	[illegible]	[illegible]	[illegible]	[illegible]	[illegible]	[illegible]	[illegible]	[illegible]	[illegible]	[illegible]	[illegible]	[illegible]	[illegible]	[illegible]	[illegible]	[illegible]	[illegible]	[illegible]	[illegible]
[illegible]	[illegible]	[illegible]	[illegible]	[illegible]	[illegible]	[illegible]	[illegible]	[illegible]	[illegible]	[illegible]	[illegible]	[illegible]	[illegible]	[illegible]	[illegible]	[illegible]	[illegible]	[illegible]	[illegible]	[illegible]	[illegible]	[illegible]	[illegible]
[illegible]	[illegible]	[illegible]	[illegible]	[illegible]	[illegible]	[illegible]	[illegible]	[illegible]	[illegible]	[illegible]	[illegible]	[illegible]	[illegible]	[illegible]	[illegible]	[illegible]	[illegible]	[illegible]	[illegible]	[illegible]	[illegible]	[illegible]	[illegible]
[illegible]	[illegible]	[illegible]	[illegible]	[illegible]	[illegible]	[illegible]	[illegible]	[illegible]	[illegible]	[illegible]	[illegible]	[illegible]	[illegible]	[illegible]	[illegible]	[illegible]	[illegible]	[illegible]	[illegible]	[illegible]	[illegible]	[illegible]	[illegible]
[illegible]	[illegible]	[illegible]	[illegible]	[illegible]	[illegible]	[illegible]	[illegible]	[illegible]	[illegible]	[illegible]	[illegible]	[illegible]	[illegible]	[illegible]	[illegible]	[illegible]	[illegible]	[illegible]	[illegible]	[illegible]	[illegible]	[illegible]	[illegible]
[illegible]	[illegible]	[illegible]	[illegible]	[illegible]	[illegible]	[illegible]	[illegible]	[illegible]	[illegible]	[illegible]	[illegible]	[illegible]	[illegible]	[illegible]	[illegible]	[illegible]	[illegible]	[illegible]	[illegible]	[illegible]	[illegible]	[illegible]	[illegible]
[illegible]	[illegible]	[illegible]	[illegible]	[illegible]	[illegible]	[illegible]	[illegible]	[illegible]	[illegible]	[illegible]	[illegible]	[illegible]	[illegible]	[illegible]	[illegible]	[illegible]	[illegible]	[illegible]	[illegible]	[illegible]	[illegible]	[illegible]	[illegible]
[illegible]	[illegible]	[illegible]	[illegible]	[illegible]	[illegible]	[illegible]	[illegible]	[illegible]	[illegible]	[illegible]	[illegible]	[illegible]	[illegible]	[illegible]	[illegible]	[illegible]	[illegible]	[illegible]	[illegible]	[illegible]	[illegible]	[illegible]	[illegible]
[illegible]	[illegible]	[illegible]	[illegible]	[illegible]	[illegible]	[illegible]	[illegible]	[illegible]	[illegible]	[illegible]	[illegible]	[illegible]	[illegible]	[illegible]	[illegible]	[illegible]	[illegible]	[illegible]	[illegible]	[illegible]	[illegible]	[illegible]	[illegible]
[illegible]	[illegible]	[illegible]	[illegible]	[illegible]	[illegible]	[illegible]	[illegible]	[illegible]	[illegible]	[illegible]	[illegible]	[illegible]	[illegible]	[illegible]	[illegible]	[illegible]	[illegible]	[illegible]	[illegible]	[illegible]	[illegible]	[illegible]	[illegible]
[illegible]	[illegible]	[illegible]	[illegible]	[illegible]	[illegible]	[illegible]	[illegible]	[illegible]	[illegible]	[illegible]	[illegible]	[illegible]	[illegible]	[illegible]	[illegible]	[illegible]	[illegible]	[illegible]	[illegible]	[illegible]	[illegible]	[illegible]	[illegible]
[illegible]	[illegible]	[illegible]	[illegible]	[illegible]	[illegible]	[illegible]	[illegible]	[illegible]	[illegible]	[illegible]	[illegible]	[illegible]	[illegible]	[illegible]	[illegible]	[illegible]	[illegible]	[illegible]	[illegible]	[illegible]	[illegible]	[illegible]	[illegible]
[illegible]	[illegible]	[illegible]	[illegible]	[illegible]	[illegible]	[illegible]	[illegible]	[illegible]	[illegible]	[illegible]	[illegible]	[illegible]	[illegible]	[illegible]	[illegible]	[illegible]	[illegible]	[illegible]	[illegible]	[illegible]	[illegible]	[illegible]	[illegible]
[illegible]	[illegible]	[illegible]	[illegible]	[illegible]	[illegible]	[illegible]	[illegible]	[illegible]	[illegible]	[illegible]	[illegible]	[illegible]	[illegible]	[illegible]	[illegible]	[illegible]	[illegible]	[illegible]	[illegible]	[illegible]	[illegible]	[illegible]	[illegible]
[illegible]	[illegible]	[illegible]	[illegible]	[illegible]	[illegible]	[illegible]	[illegible]	[illegible]	[illegible]	[illegible]	[illegible]	[illegible]	[illegible]	[illegible]	[illegible]	[illegible]	[illegible]	[illegible]	[illegible]	[illegible]	[illegible]	[illegible]	[illegible]
[illegible]	[illegible]	[illegible]	[illegible]	[illegible]	[illegible]	[illegible]	[illegible]	[illegible]	[illegible]	[illegible]	[illegible]	[illegible]	[illegible]	[illegible]	[illegible]	[illegible]	[illegible]	[illegible]	[illegible]	[illegible]	[illegible]	[illegible]	[illegible]
[illegible]	[illegible]	[illegible]	[illegible]	[illegible]	[illegible]	[illegible]	[illegible]	[illegible]	[illegible]	[illegible]	[illegible]	[illegible]	[illegible]	[illegible]	[illegible]	[illegible]	[illegible]	[illegible]	[illegible]	[illegible]	[illegible]	[illegible]	[illegible]
[illegible]	[illegible]	[illegible]	[illegible]	[illegible]	[illegible]	[illegible]	[illegible]	[illegible]	[illegible]	[illegible]	[illegible]	[illegible]	[illegible]	[illegible]	[illegible]	[illegible]	[illegible]	[illegible]	[illegible]	[illegible]	[illegible]	[illegible]	[illegible]
[illegible]	[illegible]	[illegible]	[illegible]	[illegible]	[illegible]	[illegible]	[illegible]	[illegible]	[illegible]	[illegible]	[illegible]	[illegible]	[illegible]	[illegible]	[illegible]	[illegible]	[illegible]	[illegible]	[illegible]	[illegible]	[illegible]	[illegible]	[illegible]
[illegible]	[illegible]	[illegible]	[illegible]	[illegible]	[illegible]	[illegible]	[illegible]	[illegible]	[illegible]	[illegible]	[illegible]	[illegible]	[illegible]	[illegible]	[illegible]	[illegible]	[illegible]	[illegible]	[illegible]	[illegible]	[illegible]	[illegible]	[illegible]
[illegible]	[illegible]	[illegible]	[illegible]	[illegible]	[illegible]	[illegible]	[illegible]	[illegible]	[illegible]	[illegible]	[illegible]	[illegible]	[illegible]	[illegible]	[illegible]	[illegible]	[illegible]	[illegible]	[illegible]	[illegible]	[illegible]	[illegible]	[illegible]
[illegible]	[illegible]	[illegible]	[illegible]	[illegible]	[illegible]	[illegible]	[illegible]	[illegible]	[illegible]	[illegible]	[illegible]	[illegible]	[illegible]	[illegible]	[illegible]	[illegible]	[illegible]	[illegible]	[illegible]	[illegible]	[illegible]	[illegible]	[illegible]
[illegible]	[illegible]	[illegible]	[illegible]	[illegible]	[illegible]	[illegible]	[illegible]	[illegible]	[illegible]	[illegible]	[illegible]	[illegible]	[illegible]	[illegible]	[illegible]	[illegible]	[illegible]	[illegible]	[illegible]	[illegible]	[illegible]	[illegible]	[illegible]
[illegible]	[illegible]	[illegible]	[illegible]	[illegible]	[illegible]	[illegible]	[illegible]	[illegible]	[illegible]	[illegible]	[illegible]	[illegible]	[illegible]	[illegible]	[illegible]	[illegible]	[illegible]	[illegible]	[illegible]	[illegible]	[illegible]	[illegible]	[illegible]
[illegible]	[illegible]	[illegible]	[illegible]	[illegible]	[illegible]	[illegible]	[illegible]	[illegible]	[illegible]	[illegible]	[illegible]	[illegible]	[illegible]	[illegible]	[illegible]	[illegible]	[illegible]	[illegible]	[illegible]	[illegible]	[illegible]	[illegible]	[illegible]
[illegible]	[illegible]	[illegible]	[illegible]	[illegible]	[illegible]	[illegible]	[illegible]	[illegible]	[illegible]	[illegible]	[illegible]	[illegible]	[illegible]	[illegible]	[illegible]	[illegible]	[illegible]	[illegible]	[illegible]	[illegible]	[illegible]	[illegible]	[illegible]
[illegible]	[illegible]	[illegible]	[illegible]	[illegible]	[illegible]	[illegible]	[illegible]	[illegible]	[illegible]	[illegible]	[illegible]	[illegible]	[illegible]	[illegible]	[illegible]	[illegible]	[illegible]	[illegible]	[illegible]	[illegible]	[illegible]	[illegible]	[illegible]
[illegible]	[illegible]	[illegible]	[illegible]	[illegible]	[illegible]	[illegible]	[illegible]	[illegible]	[illegible]	[illegible]	[illegible]	[illegible]	[illegible]	[illegible]	[illegible]	[illegible]	[illegible]	[illegible]	[illegible]	[illegible]	[illegible]	[illegible]	[illegible]
[illegible]	[illegible]	[illegible]	[illegible]	[illegible]	[illegible]	[illegible]	[illegible]	[illegible]	[illegible]	[illegible]	[illegible]	[illegible]	[illegible]	[illegible]	[illegible]	[illegible]	[illegible]	[illegible]	[illegible]	[illegible]	[illegible]	[illegible]	[illegible]
[illegible]	[illegible]	[illegible]	[illegible]	[illegible]	[illegible]	[illegible]	[illegible]	[illegible]	[illegible]	[illegible]	[illegible]	[illegible]	[illegible]	[illegible]	[illegible]	[illegible]	[illegible]	[illegible]	[illegible]	[illegible]	[illegible]	[illegible]	[illegible]
[illegible]	[illegible]	[illegible]	[illegible]	[illegible]	[illegible]	[illegible]	[illegible]	[illegible]	[illegible]	[illegible]	[illegible]	[illegible]	[illegible]	[illegible]	[illegible]	[illegible]	[illegible]	[illegible]	[illegible]	[illegible]	[illegible]	[illegible]	[illegible]
[illegible]	[illegible]	[illegible]	[illegible]	[illegible]	[illegible]	[illegible]	[illegible]	[illegible]	[illegible]	[illegible]	[illegible]	[illegible]	[illegible]	[illegible]	[illegible]	[illegible]	[illegible]	[illegible]	[illegible]	[illegible]	[illegible]	[illegible]	[illegible]
[illegible]	[illegible]	[illegible]	[illegible]	[illegible]	[illegible]	[illegible]	[illegible]	[illegible]	[illegible]	[illegible]	[illegible]	[illegible]	[illegible]	[illegible]	[illegible]	[illegible]	[illegible]	[illegible]	[illegible]	[illegible]	[illegible]	[illegible]	[illegible]
[illegible]	[illegible]	[illegible]	[illegible]	[illegible]	[illegible]	[illegible]	[illegible]	[illegible]	[illegible]	[illegible]	[illegible]	[illegible]	[illegible]	[illegible]	[illegible]	[illegible]	[illegible]	[illegible]	[illegible]	[illegible]	[illegible]	[illegible]	[illegible]
[illegible]	[illegible]	[illegible]	[illegible]	[illegible]	[illegible]	[illegible]	[illegible]	[illegible]	[illegible]	[illegible]	[illegible]	[illegible]	[illegible]	[illegible]	[illegible]	[illegible]	[illegible]	[illegible]	[illegible]	[illegible]	[illegible]	[illegible]	[illegible]
[illegible]	[illegible]	[illegible]	[illegible]	[illegible]	[illegible]	[illegible]	[illegible]	[illegible]	[illegible]	[illegible]	[illegible]	[illegible]	[illegible]	[illegible]	[illegible]	[illegible]	[illegible]	[illegible]	[illegible]	[illegible]	[illegible]	[illegible]	[illegible]
[illegible]	[illegible]	[illegible]	[illegible]	[illegible]	[illegible]	[illegible]	[illegible]	[illegible]	[illegible]	[illegible]	[illegible]	[illegible]	[illegible]	[illegible]	[illegible]	[illegible]	[illegible]	[illegible]	[illegible]	[illegible]	[illegible]	[illegible]	[illegible]
[illegible]	[illegible]	[illegible]	[illegible]	[illegible]	[illegible]	[illegible]	[illegible]	[illegible]	[illegible]	[illegible]	[illegible]	[illegible]	[illegible]	[illegible]	[illegible]	[illegible]	[illegible]	[illegible]	[illegible]	[illegible]	[illegible]	[illegible]	[illegible]
[illegible]	[illegible]	[illegible]	[illegible]	[illegible]	[illegible]	[illegible]	[illegible]	[illegible]	[illegible]	[illegible]	[illegible]	[illegible]	[illegible]	[illegible]	[illegible]	[illegible]	[illegible]	[illegible]	[illegible]	[illegible]	[illegible]	[illegible]	[illegible]
[illegible]	[illegible]	[illegible]	[illegible]	[illegible]	[illegible]	[illegible]	[illegible]	[illegible]	[illegible]	[illegible]	[illegible]	[illegible]	[illegible]	[illegible]	[illegible]	[illegible]	[illegible]	[illegible]	[illegible]	[illegible]	[illegible]	[illegible]	[illegible]
[illegible]	[illegible]	[illegible]	[illegible]	[illegible]	[illegible]	[illegible]	[illegible]	[illegible]	[illegible]	[illegible]	[illegible]	[illegible]	[illegible]	[illegible]	[illegible]	[illegible]	[illegible]	[illegible]	[illegible]	[illegible]	[illegible]	[illegible]	[illegible]

IRELAND.—CAUSES of DEATHS at different Periods of Life in the Ten Years 1881–90.—Males.

Class.	CAUSES OF DEATH.	All Ages.	Under 1 Year.	1	2	3	4	Total under 5 years.	5-	10-	15-	20-	25-	35-	45-	55-	65-	75-	85-	95 and upwards.
	ALL CAUSES	[illegible]	[illegible]	[illegible]	[illegible]	[illegible]	[illegible]	[illegible]	[illegible]	[illegible]	[illegible]	[illegible]	[illegible]	[illegible]	[illegible]	[illegible]	[illegible]	[illegible]	[illegible]	[illegible]
	(CLASSES.)																			
I.	SPECIFIC FEBRILE OR ZYMOTIC DISEASES	[illegible]	[illegible]	[illegible]	[illegible]	[illegible]	[illegible]	[illegible]	[illegible]	[illegible]	[illegible]	[illegible]	[illegible]	[illegible]	[illegible]	[illegible]	[illegible]	[illegible]	[illegible]	[illegible]
II.	PARASITIC DISEASES	[illegible]	[illegible]	[illegible]	[illegible]	[illegible]	[illegible]	[illegible]	[illegible]	[illegible]	[illegible]	[illegible]	[illegible]	[illegible]	[illegible]	[illegible]	[illegible]	[illegible]	[illegible]	[illegible]
III.	DIETETIC	[illegible]	[illegible]	[illegible]	[illegible]	[illegible]	[illegible]	[illegible]	[illegible]	[illegible]	[illegible]	[illegible]	[illegible]	[illegible]	[illegible]	[illegible]	[illegible]	[illegible]	[illegible]	[illegible]
IV.	CONSTITUTIONAL	[illegible]	[illegible]	[illegible]	[illegible]	[illegible]	[illegible]	[illegible]	[illegible]	[illegible]	[illegible]	[illegible]	[illegible]	[illegible]	[illegible]	[illegible]	[illegible]	[illegible]	[illegible]	[illegible]
V.	DEVELOPMENTAL	[illegible]	[illegible]	[illegible]	[illegible]	[illegible]	[illegible]	[illegible]	[illegible]	[illegible]	[illegible]	[illegible]	[illegible]	[illegible]	[illegible]	[illegible]	[illegible]	[illegible]	[illegible]	[illegible]
VI.	LOCAL	[illegible]	[illegible]	[illegible]	[illegible]	[illegible]	[illegible]	[illegible]	[illegible]	[illegible]	[illegible]	[illegible]	[illegible]	[illegible]	[illegible]	[illegible]	[illegible]	[illegible]	[illegible]	[illegible]
VII.	VIOLENCE	[illegible]	[illegible]	[illegible]	[illegible]	[illegible]	[illegible]	[illegible]	[illegible]	[illegible]	[illegible]	[illegible]	[illegible]	[illegible]	[illegible]	[illegible]	[illegible]	[illegible]	[illegible]	[illegible]
VIII.	ILL-DEFINED AND NOT SPECIFIED CAUSES	[illegible]	[illegible]	[illegible]	[illegible]	[illegible]	[illegible]	[illegible]	[illegible]	[illegible]	[illegible]	[illegible]	[illegible]	[illegible]	[illegible]	[illegible]	[illegible]	[illegible]	[illegible]	[illegible]
	(ORDERS.)																			
I.	1. Miasmatic Diseases	[illegible]	[illegible]	[illegible]	[illegible]	[illegible]	[illegible]	[illegible]	[illegible]	[illegible]	[illegible]	[illegible]	[illegible]	[illegible]	[illegible]	[illegible]	[illegible]	[illegible]	[illegible]	[illegible]
	2. Diarrhoeal	[illegible]	[illegible]	[illegible]	[illegible]	[illegible]	[illegible]	[illegible]	[illegible]	[illegible]	[illegible]	[illegible]	[illegible]	[illegible]	[illegible]	[illegible]	[illegible]	[illegible]	[illegible]	[illegible]
	3. Malarial	[illegible]	[illegible]	[illegible]	[illegible]	[illegible]	[illegible]	[illegible]	[illegible]	[illegible]	[illegible]	[illegible]	[illegible]	[illegible]	[illegible]	[illegible]	[illegible]	[illegible]	[illegible]	[illegible]
	4. Zoogenous	[illegible]	[illegible]	[illegible]	[illegible]	[illegible]	[illegible]	[illegible]	[illegible]	[illegible]	[illegible]	[illegible]	[illegible]	[illegible]	[illegible]	[illegible]	[illegible]	[illegible]	[illegible]	[illegible]
	5. Venereal	[illegible]	[illegible]	[illegible]	[illegible]	[illegible]	[illegible]	[illegible]	[illegible]	[illegible]	[illegible]	[illegible]	[illegible]	[illegible]	[illegible]	[illegible]	[illegible]	[illegible]	[illegible]	[illegible]
	6. Septic	[illegible]	[illegible]	[illegible]	[illegible]	[illegible]	[illegible]	[illegible]	[illegible]	[illegible]	[illegible]	[illegible]	[illegible]	[illegible]	[illegible]	[illegible]	[illegible]	[illegible]	[illegible]	[illegible]
II.	Parasitic	[illegible]	[illegible]	[illegible]	[illegible]	[illegible]	[illegible]	[illegible]	[illegible]	[illegible]	[illegible]	[illegible]	[illegible]	[illegible]	[illegible]	[illegible]	[illegible]	[illegible]	[illegible]	[illegible]
III.	Dietetic	[illegible]	[illegible]	[illegible]	[illegible]	[illegible]	[illegible]	[illegible]	[illegible]	[illegible]	[illegible]	[illegible]	[illegible]	[illegible]	[illegible]	[illegible]	[illegible]	[illegible]	[illegible]	[illegible]
IV.	Constitutional	[illegible]	[illegible]	[illegible]	[illegible]	[illegible]	[illegible]	[illegible]	[illegible]	[illegible]	[illegible]	[illegible]	[illegible]	[illegible]	[illegible]	[illegible]	[illegible]	[illegible]	[illegible]	[illegible]
V.	Developmental	[illegible]	[illegible]	[illegible]	[illegible]	[illegible]	[illegible]	[illegible]	[illegible]	[illegible]	[illegible]	[illegible]	[illegible]	[illegible]	[illegible]	[illegible]	[illegible]	[illegible]	[illegible]	[illegible]
VI.	1. Diseases of Nervous System	[illegible]	[illegible]	[illegible]	[illegible]	[illegible]	[illegible]	[illegible]	[illegible]	[illegible]	[illegible]	[illegible]	[illegible]	[illegible]	[illegible]	[illegible]	[illegible]	[illegible]	[illegible]	[illegible]
	2. „ Organs of Special Sense	[illegible]	[illegible]	[illegible]	[illegible]	[illegible]	[illegible]	[illegible]	[illegible]	[illegible]	[illegible]	[illegible]	[illegible]	[illegible]	[illegible]	[illegible]	[illegible]	[illegible]	[illegible]	[illegible]
	3. „ Circulatory System	[illegible]	[illegible]	[illegible]	[illegible]	[illegible]	[illegible]	[illegible]	[illegible]	[illegible]	[illegible]	[illegible]	[illegible]	[illegible]	[illegible]	[illegible]	[illegible]	[illegible]	[illegible]	[illegible]
	4. „ Respiratory System	[illegible]	[illegible]	[illegible]	[illegible]	[illegible]	[illegible]	[illegible]	[illegible]	[illegible]	[illegible]	[illegible]	[illegible]	[illegible]	[illegible]	[illegible]	[illegible]	[illegible]	[illegible]	[illegible]
	5. „ Digestive System	[illegible]	[illegible]	[illegible]	[illegible]	[illegible]	[illegible]	[illegible]	[illegible]	[illegible]	[illegible]	[illegible]	[illegible]	[illegible]	[illegible]	[illegible]	[illegible]	[illegible]	[illegible]	[illegible]
	6. „ Lymphatic System and Ductless Glands	[illegible]	[illegible]	[illegible]	[illegible]	[illegible]	[illegible]	[illegible]	[illegible]	[illegible]	[illegible]	[illegible]	[illegible]	[illegible]	[illegible]	[illegible]	[illegible]	[illegible]	[illegible]	[illegible]
	7. „ Urinary System	[illegible]	[illegible]	[illegible]	[illegible]	[illegible]	[illegible]	[illegible]	[illegible]	[illegible]	[illegible]	[illegible]	[illegible]	[illegible]	[illegible]	[illegible]	[illegible]	[illegible]	[illegible]	[illegible]
	8. „ Reproductive System:—																			
	(a) „ Organs of Generation	[illegible]	[illegible]	[illegible]	[illegible]	[illegible]	[illegible]	[illegible]	[illegible]	[illegible]	[illegible]	[illegible]	[illegible]	[illegible]	[illegible]	[illegible]	[illegible]	[illegible]	[illegible]	[illegible]
	(b) „ Parturition	[illegible]	[illegible]	[illegible]	[illegible]	[illegible]	[illegible]	[illegible]	[illegible]	[illegible]	[illegible]	[illegible]	[illegible]	[illegible]	[illegible]	[illegible]	[illegible]	[illegible]	[illegible]	[illegible]
	9. „ Locomotive System	[illegible]	[illegible]	[illegible]	[illegible]	[illegible]	[illegible]	[illegible]	[illegible]	[illegible]	[illegible]	[illegible]	[illegible]	[illegible]	[illegible]	[illegible]	[illegible]	[illegible]	[illegible]	[illegible]
	10. „ Integumentary System	[illegible]	[illegible]	[illegible]	[illegible]	[illegible]	[illegible]	[illegible]	[illegible]	[illegible]	[illegible]	[illegible]	[illegible]	[illegible]	[illegible]	[illegible]	[illegible]	[illegible]	[illegible]	[illegible]
VII.	1. Accident or Negligence	[illegible]	[illegible]	[illegible]	[illegible]	[illegible]	[illegible]	[illegible]	[illegible]	[illegible]	[illegible]	[illegible]	[illegible]	[illegible]	[illegible]	[illegible]	[illegible]	[illegible]	[illegible]	[illegible]
	2. Homicide	[illegible]	[illegible]	[illegible]	[illegible]	[illegible]	[illegible]	[illegible]	[illegible]	[illegible]	[illegible]	[illegible]	[illegible]	[illegible]	[illegible]	[illegible]	[illegible]	[illegible]	[illegible]	[illegible]
	3. Suicide	[illegible]	[illegible]	[illegible]	[illegible]	[illegible]	[illegible]	[illegible]	[illegible]	[illegible]	[illegible]	[illegible]	[illegible]	[illegible]	[illegible]	[illegible]	[illegible]	[illegible]	[illegible]	[illegible]
	4. Execution	[illegible]	[illegible]	[illegible]	[illegible]	[illegible]	[illegible]	[illegible]	[illegible]	[illegible]	[illegible]	[illegible]	[illegible]	[illegible]	[illegible]	[illegible]	[illegible]	[illegible]	[illegible]	[illegible]
VIII.	Ill-defined and not specified Causes	[illegible]	[illegible]	[illegible]	[illegible]	[illegible]	[illegible]	[illegible]	[illegible]	[illegible]	[illegible]	[illegible]	[illegible]	[illegible]	[illegible]	[illegible]	[illegible]	[illegible]	[illegible]	[illegible]

(Continued on page [illegible].)

IRELAND.—CAUSES of [illegible] at different Periods of Life in the Ten Years, 1881-90.—[illegible]

No.	CAUSES OF DEATH.	[illegible]
	[illegible]	[illegible]
I.	[illegible]	[illegible]
II.	Parasitic [illegible]	[illegible]
III.	Dietetic [illegible]	[illegible]
IV.	Constitutional [illegible]	[illegible]
V.	Developmental [illegible]	[illegible]
VI.	Local [illegible]	[illegible]
VII.	Violence [illegible]	[illegible]
VIII.	Ill-defined and not specified causes [illegible]	[illegible]
	[illegible]	[illegible]

IRELAND.—CAUSES of DEATHS at different Periods of Life in the Ten Years, 1881-90.—MALES.

Class.	CAUSES OF DEATH.	ALL AGES.	Under 1 year.	1	2	3	4	Total under 5 years.	5-	10-	15-	20-	25-	35-	45-	55-	65-	75-	85-	95 and upwards.
I.	GROUP 1.																			
	Small-pox: Vaccinated	[illegible]	[illegible]	[illegible]	[illegible]	[illegible]	[illegible]	[illegible]	[illegible]	[illegible]	[illegible]	[illegible]	[illegible]	[illegible]	[illegible]	[illegible]	[illegible]	[illegible]	[illegible]	[illegible]
	Small-pox: Unvaccinated	[illegible]	[illegible]	[illegible]	[illegible]	[illegible]	[illegible]	[illegible]	[illegible]	[illegible]	[illegible]	[illegible]	[illegible]	[illegible]	[illegible]	[illegible]	[illegible]	[illegible]	[illegible]	[illegible]
	Small-pox: No Statement	[illegible]	[illegible]	[illegible]	[illegible]	[illegible]	[illegible]	[illegible]	[illegible]	[illegible]	[illegible]	[illegible]	[illegible]	[illegible]	[illegible]	[illegible]	[illegible]	[illegible]	[illegible]	[illegible]
	Chicken-pox	[illegible]	[illegible]	[illegible]	[illegible]	[illegible]	[illegible]	[illegible]	[illegible]	[illegible]	[illegible]	[illegible]	[illegible]	[illegible]	[illegible]	[illegible]	[illegible]	[illegible]	[illegible]	[illegible]
	Measles	[illegible]	[illegible]	[illegible]	[illegible]	[illegible]	[illegible]	[illegible]	[illegible]	[illegible]	[illegible]	[illegible]	[illegible]	[illegible]	[illegible]	[illegible]	[illegible]	[illegible]	[illegible]	[illegible]
	Epidemic Rose Rash	[illegible]	[illegible]	[illegible]	[illegible]	[illegible]	[illegible]	[illegible]	[illegible]	[illegible]	[illegible]	[illegible]	[illegible]	[illegible]	[illegible]	[illegible]	[illegible]	[illegible]	[illegible]	[illegible]
	Scarlet Fever	[illegible]	[illegible]	[illegible]	[illegible]	[illegible]	[illegible]	[illegible]	[illegible]	[illegible]	[illegible]	[illegible]	[illegible]	[illegible]	[illegible]	[illegible]	[illegible]	[illegible]	[illegible]	[illegible]
	Typhus	[illegible]	[illegible]	[illegible]	[illegible]	[illegible]	[illegible]	[illegible]	[illegible]	[illegible]	[illegible]	[illegible]	[illegible]	[illegible]	[illegible]	[illegible]	[illegible]	[illegible]	[illegible]	[illegible]
	Relapsing Fever	[illegible]	[illegible]	[illegible]	[illegible]	[illegible]	[illegible]	[illegible]	[illegible]	[illegible]	[illegible]	[illegible]	[illegible]	[illegible]	[illegible]	[illegible]	[illegible]	[illegible]	[illegible]	[illegible]
	Influenza	[illegible]	[illegible]	[illegible]	[illegible]	[illegible]	[illegible]	[illegible]	[illegible]	[illegible]	[illegible]	[illegible]	[illegible]	[illegible]	[illegible]	[illegible]	[illegible]	[illegible]	[illegible]	[illegible]
	Whooping-cough	[illegible]	[illegible]	[illegible]	[illegible]	[illegible]	[illegible]	[illegible]	[illegible]	[illegible]	[illegible]	[illegible]	[illegible]	[illegible]	[illegible]	[illegible]	[illegible]	[illegible]	[illegible]	[illegible]
	Mumps	[illegible]	[illegible]	[illegible]	[illegible]	[illegible]	[illegible]	[illegible]	[illegible]	[illegible]	[illegible]	[illegible]	[illegible]	[illegible]	[illegible]	[illegible]	[illegible]	[illegible]	[illegible]	[illegible]
	Diphtheria	[illegible]	[illegible]	[illegible]	[illegible]	[illegible]	[illegible]	[illegible]	[illegible]	[illegible]	[illegible]	[illegible]	[illegible]	[illegible]	[illegible]	[illegible]	[illegible]	[illegible]	[illegible]	[illegible]
	[illegible] Fever	[illegible]	[illegible]	[illegible]	[illegible]	[illegible]	[illegible]	[illegible]	[illegible]	[illegible]	[illegible]	[illegible]	[illegible]	[illegible]	[illegible]	[illegible]	[illegible]	[illegible]	[illegible]	[illegible]
	Simple and Ill-defined Fever	[illegible]	[illegible]	[illegible]	[illegible]	[illegible]	[illegible]	[illegible]	[illegible]	[illegible]	[illegible]	[illegible]	[illegible]	[illegible]	[illegible]	[illegible]	[illegible]	[illegible]	[illegible]	[illegible]
	Enteric Fever	[illegible]	[illegible]	[illegible]	[illegible]	[illegible]	[illegible]	[illegible]	[illegible]	[illegible]	[illegible]	[illegible]	[illegible]	[illegible]	[illegible]	[illegible]	[illegible]	[illegible]	[illegible]	[illegible]
	Other Zymotic Diseases	[illegible]	[illegible]	[illegible]	[illegible]	[illegible]	[illegible]	[illegible]	[illegible]	[illegible]	[illegible]	[illegible]	[illegible]	[illegible]	[illegible]	[illegible]	[illegible]	[illegible]	[illegible]	[illegible]
	GROUP 2.																			
	Simple Cholera	[illegible]	[illegible]	[illegible]	[illegible]	[illegible]	[illegible]	[illegible]	[illegible]	[illegible]	[illegible]	[illegible]	[illegible]	[illegible]	[illegible]	[illegible]	[illegible]	[illegible]	[illegible]	[illegible]
	Diarrhoea, Dysentery	[illegible]	[illegible]	[illegible]	[illegible]	[illegible]	[illegible]	[illegible]	[illegible]	[illegible]	[illegible]	[illegible]	[illegible]	[illegible]	[illegible]	[illegible]	[illegible]	[illegible]	[illegible]	[illegible]
	GROUP 3.																			
	Remittent Fever	[illegible]	[illegible]	[illegible]	[illegible]	[illegible]	[illegible]	[illegible]	[illegible]	[illegible]	[illegible]	[illegible]	[illegible]	[illegible]	[illegible]	[illegible]	[illegible]	[illegible]	[illegible]	[illegible]
	Ague	[illegible]	[illegible]	[illegible]	[illegible]	[illegible]	[illegible]	[illegible]	[illegible]	[illegible]	[illegible]	[illegible]	[illegible]	[illegible]	[illegible]	[illegible]	[illegible]	[illegible]	[illegible]	[illegible]
	GROUP 4.																			
	Hydrophobia	[illegible]	[illegible]	[illegible]	[illegible]	[illegible]	[illegible]	[illegible]	[illegible]	[illegible]	[illegible]	[illegible]	[illegible]	[illegible]	[illegible]	[illegible]	[illegible]	[illegible]	[illegible]	[illegible]
	Glanders	[illegible]	[illegible]	[illegible]	[illegible]	[illegible]	[illegible]	[illegible]	[illegible]	[illegible]	[illegible]	[illegible]	[illegible]	[illegible]	[illegible]	[illegible]	[illegible]	[illegible]	[illegible]	[illegible]
	Splenic Fever	[illegible]	[illegible]	[illegible]	[illegible]	[illegible]	[illegible]	[illegible]	[illegible]	[illegible]	[illegible]	[illegible]	[illegible]	[illegible]	[illegible]	[illegible]	[illegible]	[illegible]	[illegible]	[illegible]
	Cowpox and other effects of Vaccination	[illegible]	[illegible]	[illegible]	[illegible]	[illegible]	[illegible]	[illegible]	[illegible]	[illegible]	[illegible]	[illegible]	[illegible]	[illegible]	[illegible]	[illegible]	[illegible]	[illegible]	[illegible]	[illegible]
	GROUP 5.																			
	Syphilis	[illegible]	[illegible]	[illegible]	[illegible]	[illegible]	[illegible]	[illegible]	[illegible]	[illegible]	[illegible]	[illegible]	[illegible]	[illegible]	[illegible]	[illegible]	[illegible]	[illegible]	[illegible]	[illegible]
	Gonorrhoea, Stricture of Urethra	[illegible]	[illegible]	[illegible]	[illegible]	[illegible]	[illegible]	[illegible]	[illegible]	[illegible]	[illegible]	[illegible]	[illegible]	[illegible]	[illegible]	[illegible]	[illegible]	[illegible]	[illegible]	[illegible]
	GROUP 6.																			
	Phagedaena	[illegible]	[illegible]	[illegible]	[illegible]	[illegible]	[illegible]	[illegible]	[illegible]	[illegible]	[illegible]	[illegible]	[illegible]	[illegible]	[illegible]	[illegible]	[illegible]	[illegible]	[illegible]	[illegible]
	Erysipelas	[illegible]	[illegible]	[illegible]	[illegible]	[illegible]	[illegible]	[illegible]	[illegible]	[illegible]	[illegible]	[illegible]	[illegible]	[illegible]	[illegible]	[illegible]	[illegible]	[illegible]	[illegible]	[illegible]
	Pyaemia, Septicaemia	[illegible]	[illegible]	[illegible]	[illegible]	[illegible]	[illegible]	[illegible]	[illegible]	[illegible]	[illegible]	[illegible]	[illegible]	[illegible]	[illegible]	[illegible]	[illegible]	[illegible]	[illegible]	[illegible]
	Puerperal Fever	[illegible]	[illegible]	[illegible]	[illegible]	[illegible]	[illegible]	[illegible]	[illegible]	[illegible]	[illegible]	[illegible]	[illegible]	[illegible]	[illegible]	[illegible]	[illegible]	[illegible]	[illegible]	[illegible]
II.	Thrush	[illegible]	[illegible]	[illegible]	[illegible]	[illegible]	[illegible]	[illegible]	[illegible]	[illegible]	[illegible]	[illegible]	[illegible]	[illegible]	[illegible]	[illegible]	[illegible]	[illegible]	[illegible]	[illegible]
	Other Diseases from Vegetable Parasites	[illegible]	[illegible]	[illegible]	[illegible]	[illegible]	[illegible]	[illegible]	[illegible]	[illegible]	[illegible]	[illegible]	[illegible]	[illegible]	[illegible]	[illegible]	[illegible]	[illegible]	[illegible]	[illegible]
	Hydatid Disease	[illegible]	[illegible]	[illegible]	[illegible]	[illegible]	[illegible]	[illegible]	[illegible]	[illegible]	[illegible]	[illegible]	[illegible]	[illegible]	[illegible]	[illegible]	[illegible]	[illegible]	[illegible]	[illegible]
	Other Diseases from Animal Parasites	[illegible]	[illegible]	[illegible]	[illegible]	[illegible]	[illegible]	[illegible]	[illegible]	[illegible]	[illegible]	[illegible]	[illegible]	[illegible]	[illegible]	[illegible]	[illegible]	[illegible]	[illegible]	[illegible]
III.	Starvation, Want of Breast Milk	[illegible]	[illegible]	[illegible]	[illegible]	[illegible]	[illegible]	[illegible]	[illegible]	[illegible]	[illegible]	[illegible]	[illegible]	[illegible]	[illegible]	[illegible]	[illegible]	[illegible]	[illegible]	[illegible]
	Scurvy	[illegible]	[illegible]	[illegible]	[illegible]	[illegible]	[illegible]	[illegible]	[illegible]	[illegible]	[illegible]	[illegible]	[illegible]	[illegible]	[illegible]	[illegible]	[illegible]	[illegible]	[illegible]	[illegible]
	Intemperance: Chronic Alcoholism	[illegible]	[illegible]	[illegible]	[illegible]	[illegible]	[illegible]	[illegible]	[illegible]	[illegible]	[illegible]	[illegible]	[illegible]	[illegible]	[illegible]	[illegible]	[illegible]	[illegible]	[illegible]	[illegible]
	Intemperance: Delirium Tremens	[illegible]	[illegible]	[illegible]	[illegible]	[illegible]	[illegible]	[illegible]	[illegible]	[illegible]	[illegible]	[illegible]	[illegible]	[illegible]	[illegible]	[illegible]	[illegible]	[illegible]	[illegible]	[illegible]
IV.	Rheumatic Fever, Rheumatism of Heart	[illegible]	[illegible]	[illegible]	[illegible]	[illegible]	[illegible]	[illegible]	[illegible]	[illegible]	[illegible]	[illegible]	[illegible]	[illegible]	[illegible]	[illegible]	[illegible]	[illegible]	[illegible]	[illegible]
	Rheumatism	[illegible]	[illegible]	[illegible]	[illegible]	[illegible]	[illegible]	[illegible]	[illegible]	[illegible]	[illegible]	[illegible]	[illegible]	[illegible]	[illegible]	[illegible]	[illegible]	[illegible]	[illegible]	[illegible]
	Gout	[illegible]	[illegible]	[illegible]	[illegible]	[illegible]	[illegible]	[illegible]	[illegible]	[illegible]	[illegible]	[illegible]	[illegible]	[illegible]	[illegible]	[illegible]	[illegible]	[illegible]	[illegible]	[illegible]
	Rickets	[illegible]	[illegible]	[illegible]	[illegible]	[illegible]	[illegible]	[illegible]	[illegible]	[illegible]	[illegible]	[illegible]	[illegible]	[illegible]	[illegible]	[illegible]	[illegible]	[illegible]	[illegible]	[illegible]
	Cancer	[illegible]	[illegible]	[illegible]	[illegible]	[illegible]	[illegible]	[illegible]	[illegible]	[illegible]	[illegible]	[illegible]	[illegible]	[illegible]	[illegible]	[illegible]	[illegible]	[illegible]	[illegible]	[illegible]

[Continued on page [illegible].]

IRELAND.—CAUSES of DEATH at different Periods of Life in the Ten Years, 1881–90.—FEMALES.

CAUSES OF DEATH.	All Ages.	Under 1 year.	1	2	3	4	Total under 5 years.	5–	10–	15–	20–	25–	35–	45–	55–	65–	75–	85–	95 and upwards.
	FEMALES.																		
		AGES AT DEATH.																	
CLASS I.																			
Small-pox { Vaccinated,	[illegible]	[illegible]	[illegible]	[illegible]	[illegible]	[illegible]	[illegible]	[illegible]	[illegible]	[illegible]	[illegible]	[illegible]	[illegible]	[illegible]	[illegible]	[illegible]	[illegible]	[illegible]	[illegible]
Small-pox { Unvaccinated,	[illegible]	[illegible]	[illegible]	[illegible]	[illegible]	[illegible]	[illegible]	[illegible]	[illegible]	[illegible]	[illegible]	[illegible]	[illegible]	[illegible]	[illegible]	[illegible]	[illegible]	[illegible]	[illegible]
Small-pox { Not stated,	[illegible]	[illegible]	[illegible]	[illegible]	[illegible]	[illegible]	[illegible]	[illegible]	[illegible]	[illegible]	[illegible]	[illegible]	[illegible]	[illegible]	[illegible]	[illegible]	[illegible]	[illegible]	[illegible]
Chicken-pox,	[illegible]	[illegible]	[illegible]	[illegible]	[illegible]	[illegible]	[illegible]	[illegible]	[illegible]	[illegible]	[illegible]	[illegible]	[illegible]	[illegible]	[illegible]	[illegible]	[illegible]	[illegible]	[illegible]
Measles,	[illegible]	[illegible]	[illegible]	[illegible]	[illegible]	[illegible]	[illegible]	[illegible]	[illegible]	[illegible]	[illegible]	[illegible]	[illegible]	[illegible]	[illegible]	[illegible]	[illegible]	[illegible]	[illegible]
Epidemic Rose Rash,	[illegible]	[illegible]	[illegible]	[illegible]	[illegible]	[illegible]	[illegible]	[illegible]	[illegible]	[illegible]	[illegible]	[illegible]	[illegible]	[illegible]	[illegible]	[illegible]	[illegible]	[illegible]	[illegible]
Scarlet Fever,	[illegible]	[illegible]	[illegible]	[illegible]	[illegible]	[illegible]	[illegible]	[illegible]	[illegible]	[illegible]	[illegible]	[illegible]	[illegible]	[illegible]	[illegible]	[illegible]	[illegible]	[illegible]	[illegible]
Typhus,	[illegible]	[illegible]	[illegible]	[illegible]	[illegible]	[illegible]	[illegible]	[illegible]	[illegible]	[illegible]	[illegible]	[illegible]	[illegible]	[illegible]	[illegible]	[illegible]	[illegible]	[illegible]	[illegible]
Relapsing Fever,	[illegible]	[illegible]	[illegible]	[illegible]	[illegible]	[illegible]	[illegible]	[illegible]	[illegible]	[illegible]	[illegible]	[illegible]	[illegible]	[illegible]	[illegible]	[illegible]	[illegible]	[illegible]	[illegible]
Influenza,	[illegible]	[illegible]	[illegible]	[illegible]	[illegible]	[illegible]	[illegible]	[illegible]	[illegible]	[illegible]	[illegible]	[illegible]	[illegible]	[illegible]	[illegible]	[illegible]	[illegible]	[illegible]	[illegible]
Whooping Cough,	[illegible]	[illegible]	[illegible]	[illegible]	[illegible]	[illegible]	[illegible]	[illegible]	[illegible]	[illegible]	[illegible]	[illegible]	[illegible]	[illegible]	[illegible]	[illegible]	[illegible]	[illegible]	[illegible]
Mumps,	[illegible]	[illegible]	[illegible]	[illegible]	[illegible]	[illegible]	[illegible]	[illegible]	[illegible]	[illegible]	[illegible]	[illegible]	[illegible]	[illegible]	[illegible]	[illegible]	[illegible]	[illegible]	[illegible]
Diphtheria,	[illegible]	[illegible]	[illegible]	[illegible]	[illegible]	[illegible]	[illegible]	[illegible]	[illegible]	[illegible]	[illegible]	[illegible]	[illegible]	[illegible]	[illegible]	[illegible]	[illegible]	[illegible]	[illegible]
[illegible]	[illegible]	[illegible]	[illegible]	[illegible]	[illegible]	[illegible]	[illegible]	[illegible]	[illegible]	[illegible]	[illegible]	[illegible]	[illegible]	[illegible]	[illegible]	[illegible]	[illegible]	[illegible]	[illegible]
Simple and Ill-defined Fever,	[illegible]	[illegible]	[illegible]	[illegible]	[illegible]	[illegible]	[illegible]	[illegible]	[illegible]	[illegible]	[illegible]	[illegible]	[illegible]	[illegible]	[illegible]	[illegible]	[illegible]	[illegible]	[illegible]
Enteric Fever,	[illegible]	[illegible]	[illegible]	[illegible]	[illegible]	[illegible]	[illegible]	[illegible]	[illegible]	[illegible]	[illegible]	[illegible]	[illegible]	[illegible]	[illegible]	[illegible]	[illegible]	[illegible]	[illegible]
Other Miasmatic Diseases,	[illegible]	[illegible]	[illegible]	[illegible]	[illegible]	[illegible]	[illegible]	[illegible]	[illegible]	[illegible]	[illegible]	[illegible]	[illegible]	[illegible]	[illegible]	[illegible]	[illegible]	[illegible]	[illegible]
Order 2.																			
Simple Cholera,	[illegible]	[illegible]	[illegible]	[illegible]	[illegible]	[illegible]	[illegible]	[illegible]	[illegible]	[illegible]	[illegible]	[illegible]	[illegible]	[illegible]	[illegible]	[illegible]	[illegible]	[illegible]	[illegible]
Diarrhoea, Dysentery,	[illegible]	[illegible]	[illegible]	[illegible]	[illegible]	[illegible]	[illegible]	[illegible]	[illegible]	[illegible]	[illegible]	[illegible]	[illegible]	[illegible]	[illegible]	[illegible]	[illegible]	[illegible]	[illegible]

IRELAND.—CAUSES of DEATHS at different Periods of Life in the Ten Years, 1881–90.—MALES.

Class.	Cause of Death.	All Ages.	Under 1 year.	1	2	3	4	Total under 5 years.	5–	10–	15–	20–	25–	35–	45–	55–	65–	75–	85–	95–
III.—contd.	Tabes Mesenterica,	[illegible]	[illegible]	[illegible]	[illegible]	[illegible]	[illegible]	[illegible]	[illegible]	[illegible]	[illegible]	[illegible]	[illegible]	[illegible]	[illegible]	[illegible]	[illegible]	[illegible]	[illegible]	[illegible]
	[illegible]	[illegible]	[illegible]	[illegible]	[illegible]	[illegible]	[illegible]	[illegible]	[illegible]	[illegible]	[illegible]	[illegible]	[illegible]	[illegible]	[illegible]	[illegible]	[illegible]	[illegible]	[illegible]	[illegible]
	Phthisis,	[illegible]	[illegible]	[illegible]	[illegible]	[illegible]	[illegible]	[illegible]	[illegible]	[illegible]	[illegible]	[illegible]	[illegible]	[illegible]	[illegible]	[illegible]	[illegible]	[illegible]	[illegible]	[illegible]
	[illegible]	[illegible]	[illegible]	[illegible]	[illegible]	[illegible]	[illegible]	[illegible]	[illegible]	[illegible]	[illegible]	[illegible]	[illegible]	[illegible]	[illegible]	[illegible]	[illegible]	[illegible]	[illegible]	[illegible]
	[illegible]	[illegible]	[illegible]	[illegible]	[illegible]	[illegible]	[illegible]	[illegible]	[illegible]	[illegible]	[illegible]	[illegible]	[illegible]	[illegible]	[illegible]	[illegible]	[illegible]	[illegible]	[illegible]	[illegible]
	[illegible]	[illegible]	[illegible]	[illegible]	[illegible]	[illegible]	[illegible]	[illegible]	[illegible]	[illegible]	[illegible]	[illegible]	[illegible]	[illegible]	[illegible]	[illegible]	[illegible]	[illegible]	[illegible]	[illegible]
	Diabetes Mellitus,	[illegible]	[illegible]	[illegible]	[illegible]	[illegible]	[illegible]	[illegible]	[illegible]	[illegible]	[illegible]	[illegible]	[illegible]	[illegible]	[illegible]	[illegible]	[illegible]	[illegible]	[illegible]	[illegible]
	Other Constitutional Diseases,	[illegible]	[illegible]	[illegible]	[illegible]	[illegible]	[illegible]	[illegible]	[illegible]	[illegible]	[illegible]	[illegible]	[illegible]	[illegible]	[illegible]	[illegible]	[illegible]	[illegible]	[illegible]	[illegible]
IV.	Premature Birth,	[illegible]	[illegible]	[illegible]	[illegible]	[illegible]	[illegible]	[illegible]	[illegible]	[illegible]	[illegible]	[illegible]	[illegible]	[illegible]	[illegible]	[illegible]	[illegible]	[illegible]	[illegible]	[illegible]
	Atelectasis,	[illegible]	[illegible]	[illegible]	[illegible]	[illegible]	[illegible]	[illegible]	[illegible]	[illegible]	[illegible]	[illegible]	[illegible]	[illegible]	[illegible]	[illegible]	[illegible]	[illegible]	[illegible]	[illegible]
	Cyanosis,	[illegible]	[illegible]	[illegible]	[illegible]	[illegible]	[illegible]	[illegible]	[illegible]	[illegible]	[illegible]	[illegible]	[illegible]	[illegible]	[illegible]	[illegible]	[illegible]	[illegible]	[illegible]	[illegible]
	Spina Bifida,	[illegible]	[illegible]	[illegible]	[illegible]	[illegible]	[illegible]	[illegible]	[illegible]	[illegible]	[illegible]	[illegible]	[illegible]	[illegible]	[illegible]	[illegible]	[illegible]	[illegible]	[illegible]	[illegible]
	Imperforate Anus,	[illegible]	[illegible]	[illegible]	[illegible]	[illegible]	[illegible]	[illegible]	[illegible]	[illegible]	[illegible]	[illegible]	[illegible]	[illegible]	[illegible]	[illegible]	[illegible]	[illegible]	[illegible]	[illegible]
	Cleft Palate,	[illegible]	[illegible]	[illegible]	[illegible]	[illegible]	[illegible]	[illegible]	[illegible]	[illegible]	[illegible]	[illegible]	[illegible]	[illegible]	[illegible]	[illegible]	[illegible]	[illegible]	[illegible]	[illegible]
	Other Congenital Defects,	[illegible]	[illegible]	[illegible]	[illegible]	[illegible]	[illegible]	[illegible]	[illegible]	[illegible]	[illegible]	[illegible]	[illegible]	[illegible]	[illegible]	[illegible]	[illegible]	[illegible]	[illegible]	[illegible]
	Old Age,	[illegible]	[illegible]	[illegible]	[illegible]	[illegible]	[illegible]	[illegible]	[illegible]	[illegible]	[illegible]	[illegible]	[illegible]	[illegible]	[illegible]	[illegible]	[illegible]	[illegible]	[illegible]	[illegible]
	ORDER 1.																			
V.	[illegible]	[illegible]	[illegible]	[illegible]	[illegible]	[illegible]	[illegible]	[illegible]	[illegible]	[illegible]	[illegible]	[illegible]	[illegible]	[illegible]	[illegible]	[illegible]	[illegible]	[illegible]	[illegible]	[illegible]
	Apoplexy,	[illegible]	[illegible]	[illegible]	[illegible]	[illegible]	[illegible]	[illegible]	[illegible]	[illegible]	[illegible]	[illegible]	[illegible]	[illegible]	[illegible]	[illegible]	[illegible]	[illegible]	[illegible]	[illegible]
	Softening of Brain,	[illegible]	[illegible]	[illegible]	[illegible]	[illegible]	[illegible]	[illegible]	[illegible]	[illegible]	[illegible]	[illegible]	[illegible]	[illegible]	[illegible]	[illegible]	[illegible]	[illegible]	[illegible]	[illegible]
	[illegible]	[illegible]	[illegible]	[illegible]	[illegible]	[illegible]	[illegible]	[illegible]	[illegible]	[illegible]	[illegible]	[illegible]	[illegible]	[illegible]	[illegible]	[illegible]	[illegible]	[illegible]	[illegible]	[illegible]
	[illegible]	[illegible]	[illegible]	[illegible]	[illegible]	[illegible]	[illegible]	[illegible]	[illegible]	[illegible]	[illegible]	[illegible]	[illegible]	[illegible]	[illegible]	[illegible]	[illegible]	[illegible]	[illegible]	[illegible]
	[illegible]	[illegible]	[illegible]	[illegible]	[illegible]	[illegible]	[illegible]	[illegible]	[illegible]	[illegible]	[illegible]	[illegible]	[illegible]	[illegible]	[illegible]	[illegible]	[illegible]	[illegible]	[illegible]	[illegible]
	Chorea,	[illegible]	[illegible]	[illegible]	[illegible]	[illegible]	[illegible]	[illegible]	[illegible]	[illegible]	[illegible]	[illegible]	[illegible]	[illegible]	[illegible]	[illegible]	[illegible]	[illegible]	[illegible]	[illegible]
	Epilepsy,	[illegible]	[illegible]	[illegible]	[illegible]	[illegible]	[illegible]	[illegible]	[illegible]	[illegible]	[illegible]	[illegible]	[illegible]	[illegible]	[illegible]	[illegible]	[illegible]	[illegible]	[illegible]	[illegible]
	Convulsions,	[illegible]	[illegible]	[illegible]	[illegible]	[illegible]	[illegible]	[illegible]	[illegible]	[illegible]	[illegible]	[illegible]	[illegible]	[illegible]	[illegible]	[illegible]	[illegible]	[illegible]	[illegible]	[illegible]
	Laryngismus Stridulus,	[illegible]	[illegible]	[illegible]	[illegible]	[illegible]	[illegible]	[illegible]	[illegible]	[illegible]	[illegible]	[illegible]	[illegible]	[illegible]	[illegible]	[illegible]	[illegible]	[illegible]	[illegible]	[illegible]
	Idiopathic Tetanus,	[illegible]	[illegible]	[illegible]	[illegible]	[illegible]	[illegible]	[illegible]	[illegible]	[illegible]	[illegible]	[illegible]	[illegible]	[illegible]	[illegible]	[illegible]	[illegible]	[illegible]	[illegible]	[illegible]
	[illegible]	[illegible]	[illegible]	[illegible]	[illegible]	[illegible]	[illegible]	[illegible]	[illegible]	[illegible]	[illegible]	[illegible]	[illegible]	[illegible]	[illegible]	[illegible]	[illegible]	[illegible]	[illegible]	[illegible]
	Other Diseases of Nervous System,	[illegible]	[illegible]	[illegible]	[illegible]	[illegible]	[illegible]	[illegible]	[illegible]	[illegible]	[illegible]	[illegible]	[illegible]	[illegible]	[illegible]	[illegible]	[illegible]	[illegible]	[illegible]	[illegible]
	ORDER 2.																			
	Otitis, Otorrhoea,	[illegible]	[illegible]	[illegible]	[illegible]	[illegible]	[illegible]	[illegible]	[illegible]	[illegible]	[illegible]	[illegible]	[illegible]	[illegible]	[illegible]	[illegible]	[illegible]	[illegible]	[illegible]	[illegible]
	Epistaxis, and Dis. of Nose,	[illegible]	[illegible]	[illegible]	[illegible]	[illegible]	[illegible]	[illegible]	[illegible]	[illegible]	[illegible]	[illegible]	[illegible]	[illegible]	[illegible]	[illegible]	[illegible]	[illegible]	[illegible]	[illegible]
	Ophthalmia and Dis. of Eye,	[illegible]	[illegible]	[illegible]	[illegible]	[illegible]	[illegible]	[illegible]	[illegible]	[illegible]	[illegible]	[illegible]	[illegible]	[illegible]	[illegible]	[illegible]	[illegible]	[illegible]	[illegible]	[illegible]
	ORDER 3.																			
	[illegible]	[illegible]	[illegible]	[illegible]	[illegible]	[illegible]	[illegible]	[illegible]	[illegible]	[illegible]	[illegible]	[illegible]	[illegible]	[illegible]	[illegible]	[illegible]	[illegible]	[illegible]	[illegible]	[illegible]
	[illegible]	[illegible]	[illegible]	[illegible]	[illegible]	[illegible]	[illegible]	[illegible]	[illegible]	[illegible]	[illegible]	[illegible]	[illegible]	[illegible]	[illegible]	[illegible]	[illegible]	[illegible]	[illegible]	[illegible]
	Hypertrophy of Heart,	[illegible]	[illegible]	[illegible]	[illegible]	[illegible]	[illegible]	[illegible]	[illegible]	[illegible]	[illegible]	[illegible]	[illegible]	[illegible]	[illegible]	[illegible]	[illegible]	[illegible]	[illegible]	[illegible]
	Angina Pectoris,	[illegible]	[illegible]	[illegible]	[illegible]	[illegible]	[illegible]	[illegible]	[illegible]	[illegible]	[illegible]	[illegible]	[illegible]	[illegible]	[illegible]	[illegible]	[illegible]	[illegible]	[illegible]	[illegible]
	Syncope,	[illegible]	[illegible]	[illegible]	[illegible]	[illegible]	[illegible]	[illegible]	[illegible]	[illegible]	[illegible]	[illegible]	[illegible]	[illegible]	[illegible]	[illegible]	[illegible]	[illegible]	[illegible]	[illegible]
	Aneurism,	[illegible]	[illegible]	[illegible]	[illegible]	[illegible]	[illegible]	[illegible]	[illegible]	[illegible]	[illegible]	[illegible]	[illegible]	[illegible]	[illegible]	[illegible]	[illegible]	[illegible]	[illegible]	[illegible]
	Senile Gangrene,	[illegible]	[illegible]	[illegible]	[illegible]	[illegible]	[illegible]	[illegible]	[illegible]	[illegible]	[illegible]	[illegible]	[illegible]	[illegible]	[illegible]	[illegible]	[illegible]	[illegible]	[illegible]	[illegible]
	Embolism, Thrombosis,	[illegible]	[illegible]	[illegible]	[illegible]	[illegible]	[illegible]	[illegible]	[illegible]	[illegible]	[illegible]	[illegible]	[illegible]	[illegible]	[illegible]	[illegible]	[illegible]	[illegible]	[illegible]	[illegible]
	Phlebitis,	[illegible]	[illegible]	[illegible]	[illegible]	[illegible]	[illegible]	[illegible]	[illegible]	[illegible]	[illegible]	[illegible]	[illegible]	[illegible]	[illegible]	[illegible]	[illegible]	[illegible]	[illegible]	[illegible]
	Varicose Veins,	[illegible]	[illegible]	[illegible]	[illegible]	[illegible]	[illegible]	[illegible]	[illegible]	[illegible]	[illegible]	[illegible]	[illegible]	[illegible]	[illegible]	[illegible]	[illegible]	[illegible]	[illegible]	[illegible]
	Other Diseases of Circulatory System,	[illegible]	[illegible]	[illegible]	[illegible]	[illegible]	[illegible]	[illegible]	[illegible]	[illegible]	[illegible]	[illegible]	[illegible]	[illegible]	[illegible]	[illegible]	[illegible]	[illegible]	[illegible]	[illegible]

IRELAND.—CAUSES of DEATH at different Periods of Life in the Ten Years 1881-90.—FEMALES—*cont.*

IRELAND.—CAUSES of DEATH at different Periods of Life in the Ten Years 1881-90—MALES—con.

Class	Causes of Death	All Ages	Under 1 year	1	2	3	4	Total under 5 years	5-	10-	15-	20-	25-	35-	45-	55-	65-	75-	85-	95
	ORDER 3.—continued.																			
	Bronchitis,	[illegible]	[illegible]	[illegible]	[illegible]	[illegible]	[illegible]	[illegible]	[illegible]	[illegible]	[illegible]	[illegible]	[illegible]	[illegible]	[illegible]	[illegible]	[illegible]	[illegible]	[illegible]	[illegible]
	Pneumonia,	[illegible]	[illegible]	[illegible]	[illegible]	[illegible]	[illegible]	[illegible]	[illegible]	[illegible]	[illegible]	[illegible]	[illegible]	[illegible]	[illegible]	[illegible]	[illegible]	[illegible]	[illegible]	[illegible]
	Pleurisy,	[illegible]	[illegible]	[illegible]	[illegible]	[illegible]	[illegible]	[illegible]	[illegible]	[illegible]	[illegible]	[illegible]	[illegible]	[illegible]	[illegible]	[illegible]	[illegible]	[illegible]	[illegible]	[illegible]
	Other Diseases of Respiratory System,	[illegible]	[illegible]	[illegible]	[illegible]	[illegible]	[illegible]	[illegible]	[illegible]	[illegible]	[illegible]	[illegible]	[illegible]	[illegible]	[illegible]	[illegible]	[illegible]	[illegible]	[illegible]	[illegible]
	ORDER 4.																			
	Stomatitis,	[illegible]	[illegible]	[illegible]	[illegible]	[illegible]	[illegible]	[illegible]	[illegible]	[illegible]	[illegible]	[illegible]	[illegible]	[illegible]	[illegible]	[illegible]	[illegible]	[illegible]	[illegible]	[illegible]
	Dentition,	[illegible]	[illegible]	[illegible]	[illegible]	[illegible]	[illegible]	[illegible]	[illegible]	[illegible]	[illegible]	[illegible]	[illegible]	[illegible]	[illegible]	[illegible]	[illegible]	[illegible]	[illegible]	[illegible]
	Sore-throat, Quinsy,	[illegible]	[illegible]	[illegible]	[illegible]	[illegible]	[illegible]	[illegible]	[illegible]	[illegible]	[illegible]	[illegible]	[illegible]	[illegible]	[illegible]	[illegible]	[illegible]	[illegible]	[illegible]	[illegible]
	Dyspepsia,	[illegible]	[illegible]	[illegible]	[illegible]	[illegible]	[illegible]	[illegible]	[illegible]	[illegible]	[illegible]	[illegible]	[illegible]	[illegible]	[illegible]	[illegible]	[illegible]	[illegible]	[illegible]	[illegible]
	[illegible],	[illegible]	[illegible]	[illegible]	[illegible]	[illegible]	[illegible]	[illegible]	[illegible]	[illegible]	[illegible]	[illegible]	[illegible]	[illegible]	[illegible]	[illegible]	[illegible]	[illegible]	[illegible]	[illegible]
	Melaena,	[illegible]	[illegible]	[illegible]	[illegible]	[illegible]	[illegible]	[illegible]	[illegible]	[illegible]	[illegible]	[illegible]	[illegible]	[illegible]	[illegible]	[illegible]	[illegible]	[illegible]	[illegible]	[illegible]
	Diseases of Stomach,	[illegible]	[illegible]	[illegible]	[illegible]	[illegible]	[illegible]	[illegible]	[illegible]	[illegible]	[illegible]	[illegible]	[illegible]	[illegible]	[illegible]	[illegible]	[illegible]	[illegible]	[illegible]	[illegible]
	Enteritis,	[illegible]	[illegible]	[illegible]	[illegible]	[illegible]	[illegible]	[illegible]	[illegible]	[illegible]	[illegible]	[illegible]	[illegible]	[illegible]	[illegible]	[illegible]	[illegible]	[illegible]	[illegible]	[illegible]
	[illegible] of Intestines,	[illegible]	[illegible]	[illegible]	[illegible]	[illegible]	[illegible]	[illegible]	[illegible]	[illegible]	[illegible]	[illegible]	[illegible]	[illegible]	[illegible]	[illegible]	[illegible]	[illegible]	[illegible]	[illegible]
	[illegible] Obstruction of Intestines,	[illegible]	[illegible]	[illegible]	[illegible]	[illegible]	[illegible]	[illegible]	[illegible]	[illegible]	[illegible]	[illegible]	[illegible]	[illegible]	[illegible]	[illegible]	[illegible]	[illegible]	[illegible]	[illegible]
	Stricture or Strangulation of Intestines,	[illegible]	[illegible]	[illegible]	[illegible]	[illegible]	[illegible]	[illegible]	[illegible]	[illegible]	[illegible]	[illegible]	[illegible]	[illegible]	[illegible]	[illegible]	[illegible]	[illegible]	[illegible]	[illegible]
	Intussusception of Intestines,	[illegible]	[illegible]	[illegible]	[illegible]	[illegible]	[illegible]	[illegible]	[illegible]	[illegible]	[illegible]	[illegible]	[illegible]	[illegible]	[illegible]	[illegible]	[illegible]	[illegible]	[illegible]	[illegible]
	Hernia,	[illegible]	[illegible]	[illegible]	[illegible]	[illegible]	[illegible]	[illegible]	[illegible]	[illegible]	[illegible]	[illegible]	[illegible]	[illegible]	[illegible]	[illegible]	[illegible]	[illegible]	[illegible]	[illegible]
	Fistula,	[illegible]	[illegible]	[illegible]	[illegible]	[illegible]	[illegible]	[illegible]	[illegible]	[illegible]	[illegible]	[illegible]	[illegible]	[illegible]	[illegible]	[illegible]	[illegible]	[illegible]	[illegible]	[illegible]
	Peritonitis,	[illegible]	[illegible]	[illegible]	[illegible]	[illegible]	[illegible]	[illegible]	[illegible]	[illegible]	[illegible]	[illegible]	[illegible]	[illegible]	[illegible]	[illegible]	[illegible]	[illegible]	[illegible]	[illegible]
	Ascites,	[illegible]	[illegible]	[illegible]	[illegible]	[illegible]	[illegible]	[illegible]	[illegible]	[illegible]	[illegible]	[illegible]	[illegible]	[illegible]	[illegible]	[illegible]	[illegible]	[illegible]	[illegible]	[illegible]
	Gallstones,	[illegible]	[illegible]	[illegible]	[illegible]	[illegible]	[illegible]	[illegible]	[illegible]	[illegible]	[illegible]	[illegible]	[illegible]	[illegible]	[illegible]	[illegible]	[illegible]	[illegible]	[illegible]	[illegible]
	Cirrhosis of Liver,	[illegible]	[illegible]	[illegible]	[illegible]	[illegible]	[illegible]	[illegible]	[illegible]	[illegible]	[illegible]	[illegible]	[illegible]	[illegible]	[illegible]	[illegible]	[illegible]	[illegible]	[illegible]	[illegible]
	Other Diseases of Liver,	[illegible]	[illegible]	[illegible]	[illegible]	[illegible]	[illegible]	[illegible]	[illegible]	[illegible]	[illegible]	[illegible]	[illegible]	[illegible]	[illegible]	[illegible]	[illegible]	[illegible]	[illegible]	[illegible]
	Other Diseases of Digestive System,	[illegible]	[illegible]	[illegible]	[illegible]	[illegible]	[illegible]	[illegible]	[illegible]	[illegible]	[illegible]	[illegible]	[illegible]	[illegible]	[illegible]	[illegible]	[illegible]	[illegible]	[illegible]	[illegible]
	ORDER 5.																			
	Dis. of Lymphatic System,	[illegible]	[illegible]	[illegible]	[illegible]	[illegible]	[illegible]	[illegible]	[illegible]	[illegible]	[illegible]	[illegible]	[illegible]	[illegible]	[illegible]	[illegible]	[illegible]	[illegible]	[illegible]	[illegible]
	Diseases of Spleen,	[illegible]	[illegible]	[illegible]	[illegible]	[illegible]	[illegible]	[illegible]	[illegible]	[illegible]	[illegible]	[illegible]	[illegible]	[illegible]	[illegible]	[illegible]	[illegible]	[illegible]	[illegible]	[illegible]
	Bronchocele,	[illegible]	[illegible]	[illegible]	[illegible]	[illegible]	[illegible]	[illegible]	[illegible]	[illegible]	[illegible]	[illegible]	[illegible]	[illegible]	[illegible]	[illegible]	[illegible]	[illegible]	[illegible]	[illegible]
	Addison's Disease,	[illegible]	[illegible]	[illegible]	[illegible]	[illegible]	[illegible]	[illegible]	[illegible]	[illegible]	[illegible]	[illegible]	[illegible]	[illegible]	[illegible]	[illegible]	[illegible]	[illegible]	[illegible]	[illegible]
	ORDER 6.																			
	Acute Nephritis,	[illegible]	[illegible]	[illegible]	[illegible]	[illegible]	[illegible]	[illegible]	[illegible]	[illegible]	[illegible]	[illegible]	[illegible]	[illegible]	[illegible]	[illegible]	[illegible]	[illegible]	[illegible]	[illegible]
	Bright's Disease,	[illegible]	[illegible]	[illegible]	[illegible]	[illegible]	[illegible]	[illegible]	[illegible]	[illegible]	[illegible]	[illegible]	[illegible]	[illegible]	[illegible]	[illegible]	[illegible]	[illegible]	[illegible]	[illegible]
	Uraemia,	[illegible]	[illegible]	[illegible]	[illegible]	[illegible]	[illegible]	[illegible]	[illegible]	[illegible]	[illegible]	[illegible]	[illegible]	[illegible]	[illegible]	[illegible]	[illegible]	[illegible]	[illegible]	[illegible]
	Suppression of Urine,	[illegible]	[illegible]	[illegible]	[illegible]	[illegible]	[illegible]	[illegible]	[illegible]	[illegible]	[illegible]	[illegible]	[illegible]	[illegible]	[illegible]	[illegible]	[illegible]	[illegible]	[illegible]	[illegible]
	Calculus,	[illegible]	[illegible]	[illegible]	[illegible]	[illegible]	[illegible]	[illegible]	[illegible]	[illegible]	[illegible]	[illegible]	[illegible]	[illegible]	[illegible]	[illegible]	[illegible]	[illegible]	[illegible]	[illegible]
	Haematuria,	[illegible]	[illegible]	[illegible]	[illegible]	[illegible]	[illegible]	[illegible]	[illegible]	[illegible]	[illegible]	[illegible]	[illegible]	[illegible]	[illegible]	[illegible]	[illegible]	[illegible]	[illegible]	[illegible]
	Diseases of Bladder and of Prostate,	[illegible]	[illegible]	[illegible]	[illegible]	[illegible]	[illegible]	[illegible]	[illegible]	[illegible]	[illegible]	[illegible]	[illegible]	[illegible]	[illegible]	[illegible]	[illegible]	[illegible]	[illegible]	[illegible]
	Other Diseases of Urinary [illegible]	[illegible]	[illegible]	[illegible]	[illegible]	[illegible]	[illegible]	[illegible]	[illegible]	[illegible]	[illegible]	[illegible]	[illegible]	[illegible]	[illegible]	[illegible]	[illegible]	[illegible]	[illegible]	[illegible]

IRELAND.—CAUSES of Death at different Periods of Life in the Ten Years 1881-90—FEMALES—con.

No.	CAUSES OF DEATH.	FEMALES.
[illegible]	[illegible]	[illegible]

IRELAND.—CAUSES of DEATH at different Periods of Life in the Ten Years 1881-90.—MALES—con.

Class	CAUSES OF DEATH.	MALES. All Ages	Ages at Death: Under 1 year	1	2	3	4	Total under 5 years	5-	10-	15-	20-	25-	35-	45-	55-	65-	75-	85-	95 and upwards
VI.—con.	ORDER 7 (2).																			
	Abortion, Miscarriage,	.	.	.	.	.	.	.	.	.	.	.	.	.	.	.	.	.	.	.
	Puerperal Mania,	.	.	.	.	.	.	.	.	.	.	.	.	.	.	.	.	.	.	.
	Puerperal Convulsions,	.	.	.	.	.	.	.	.	.	.	.	.	.	.	.	.	.	.	.
	Placenta praevia, Flooding,	.	.	.	.	.	.	.	.	.	.	.	.	.	.	.	.	.	.	.
	Phlegmasia Dolens,	.	.	.	.	.	.	.	.	.	.	.	.	.	.	.	.	.	.	.
	Other Accidents of Childbirth,	.	.	.	.	.	.	.	.	.	.	.	.	.	.	.	.	.	.	.
	ORDER 8.																			
	Caries, Necrosis,	[illegible]	.	[illegible]	[illegible]	[illegible]	[illegible]	[illegible]	[illegible]	[illegible]	[illegible]	[illegible]	[illegible]	[illegible]	[illegible]	[illegible]	[illegible]	[illegible]	.	[illegible]
	Arthritis, Ostitis, Periostitis,	[illegible]	[illegible]	[illegible]	[illegible]	[illegible]	[illegible]	[illegible]	[illegible]	[illegible]	[illegible]	[illegible]	[illegible]	[illegible]	[illegible]	[illegible]	[illegible]	[illegible]	.	.
	Other Diseases of Organs of Locomotion,	[illegible]	[illegible]	[illegible]	[illegible]	[illegible]	[illegible]	[illegible]	[illegible]	[illegible]	[illegible]	[illegible]	[illegible]	[illegible]	[illegible]	[illegible]	[illegible]	[illegible]	.	.
	ORDER 9.																			
	Carbuncle,	[illegible]	.	[illegible]	[illegible]	[illegible]	.	[illegible]	.	.	[illegible]	[illegible]	[illegible]	[illegible]	[illegible]	[illegible]	[illegible]	[illegible]	[illegible]	.
	Phlegmon, Cellulitis,	[illegible]	[illegible]	[illegible]	[illegible]	[illegible]	[illegible]	[illegible]	[illegible]	[illegible]	[illegible]	[illegible]	[illegible]	[illegible]	[illegible]	[illegible]	[illegible]	[illegible]	.	.
	Lupus,	[illegible]	.	.	.	.	.	.	.	.	[illegible]	[illegible]	[illegible]	[illegible]	[illegible]	[illegible]	[illegible]	[illegible]	[illegible]	.
	Ulcer, Bedsore,	[illegible]	[illegible]	[illegible]	[illegible]	[illegible]	[illegible]	[illegible]	[illegible]	[illegible]	[illegible]	[illegible]	[illegible]	[illegible]	[illegible]	[illegible]	[illegible]	[illegible]	[illegible]	.
	Eczema,	[illegible]	[illegible]	[illegible]	[illegible]	[illegible]	[illegible]	[illegible]	[illegible]	.	.	[illegible]	[illegible]	[illegible]	.	[illegible]	[illegible]	[illegible]	[illegible]	.
	Pemphigus,	[illegible]	[illegible]	[illegible]	[illegible]	[illegible]	[illegible]	[illegible]	.	[illegible]	.	[illegible]	[illegible]	[illegible]	.	[illegible]	[illegible]	[illegible]	.	.
	Other Diseases of Integumentary System,	[illegible]	[illegible]	[illegible]	[illegible]	[illegible]	.	[illegible]	[illegible]	[illegible]	[illegible]	[illegible]	[illegible]	[illegible]	[illegible]	[illegible]	[illegible]	[illegible]	[illegible]	.
VII.	ORDER 1.																			
	Accident or negligence:																			
	Fractures, Contusions,	[illegible]	[illegible]	[illegible]	[illegible]	[illegible]	[illegible]	[illegible]	[illegible]	[illegible]	[illegible]	[illegible]	[illegible]	[illegible]	[illegible]	[illegible]	[illegible]	[illegible]	[illegible]	[illegible]
	Gunshot Wounds,	177	.	.	[illegible]	[illegible]	.	[illegible]	[illegible]	[illegible]	[illegible]	[illegible]	[illegible]	[illegible]	[illegible]	[illegible]	[illegible]	.	.	.
	Cut, Stab,	[illegible]	.	[illegible]	[illegible]	[illegible]	[illegible]	[illegible]	[illegible]	[illegible]	[illegible]	[illegible]	[illegible]	[illegible]	[illegible]	[illegible]	[illegible]	[illegible]	[illegible]	.
	Burn, Scald,	[illegible]	[illegible]	[illegible]	[illegible]	[illegible]	[illegible]	[illegible]	[illegible]	[illegible]	[illegible]	[illegible]	[illegible]	[illegible]	[illegible]	[illegible]	[illegible]	[illegible]	[illegible]	[illegible]
	Poison,	[illegible]	[illegible]	[illegible]	[illegible]	[illegible]	[illegible]	[illegible]	[illegible]	[illegible]	[illegible]	[illegible]	[illegible]	[illegible]	[illegible]	[illegible]	[illegible]	[illegible]	.	.
	Drowning,	[illegible]	[illegible]	[illegible]	[illegible]	[illegible]	[illegible]	[illegible]	[illegible]	[illegible]	[illegible]	[illegible]	[illegible]	[illegible]	[illegible]	[illegible]	[illegible]	[illegible]	[illegible]	.
	Suffocation,	[illegible]	[illegible]	[illegible]	[illegible]	[illegible]	[illegible]	[illegible]	[illegible]	[illegible]	[illegible]	[illegible]	[illegible]	[illegible]	[illegible]	[illegible]	[illegible]	[illegible]	[illegible]	.
	Otherwise,	[illegible]	[illegible]	[illegible]	[illegible]	[illegible]	[illegible]	[illegible]	[illegible]	[illegible]	[illegible]	[illegible]	[illegible]	[illegible]	[illegible]	[illegible]	[illegible]	[illegible]	[illegible]	.
	ORDER 2.																			
	Murder, Manslaughter,	[illegible]	[illegible]	[illegible]	[illegible]	[illegible]	.	[illegible]	[illegible]	[illegible]	[illegible]	[illegible]	[illegible]	[illegible]	[illegible]	[illegible]	[illegible]	[illegible]	[illegible]	.
	ORDER 3.																			
	Suicide:																			
	Gunshot Wounds,	[illegible]	.	.	.	.	.	.	.	.	.	[illegible]	[illegible]	[illegible]	[illegible]	[illegible]	[illegible]	[illegible]	.	.
	Cut, Stab,	[illegible]	.	.	.	.	.	.	.	.	.	[illegible]	[illegible]	[illegible]	[illegible]	[illegible]	[illegible]	[illegible]	[illegible]	.
	Poison,	[illegible]	.	.	.	.	.	.	.	.	.	.	[illegible]	[illegible]	[illegible]	[illegible]	[illegible]	[illegible]	.	.
	Drowning,	[illegible]	.	.	.	.	.	.	.	.	.	[illegible]	[illegible]	[illegible]	[illegible]	[illegible]	[illegible]	[illegible]	.	.
	Hanging,	[illegible]	.	.	.	.	.	.	.	.	.	[illegible]	[illegible]	[illegible]	[illegible]	[illegible]	[illegible]	[illegible]	[illegible]	.
	Otherwise,	[illegible]	.	.	.	.	.	.	.	.	.	[illegible]	[illegible]	[illegible]	[illegible]	[illegible]	[illegible]	[illegible]	.	.
	ORDER 4.																			
	Hanging (Homicidal),	[illegible]	.	.	.	.	.	.	.	.	.	.	[illegible]	[illegible]	[illegible]	[illegible]	[illegible]	[illegible]	.	.
VIII.	Dropsy,	[illegible]	[illegible]	[illegible]	[illegible]	[illegible]	[illegible]	[illegible]	[illegible]	[illegible]	[illegible]	[illegible]	[illegible]	[illegible]	[illegible]	[illegible]	[illegible]	[illegible]	[illegible]	[illegible]
	Debility, Atrophy, Inanition,	[illegible]	[illegible]	[illegible]	[illegible]	[illegible]	[illegible]	[illegible]	[illegible]	[illegible]	[illegible]	[illegible]	[illegible]	[illegible]	[illegible]	[illegible]	[illegible]	[illegible]	[illegible]	[illegible]
	Mortification,	[illegible]	[illegible]	[illegible]	[illegible]	[illegible]	[illegible]	[illegible]	[illegible]	[illegible]	[illegible]	[illegible]	[illegible]	[illegible]	[illegible]	[illegible]	[illegible]	[illegible]	[illegible]	[illegible]
	Tumour,	[illegible]	[illegible]	[illegible]	[illegible]	[illegible]	[illegible]	[illegible]	[illegible]	[illegible]	[illegible]	[illegible]	[illegible]	[illegible]	[illegible]	[illegible]	[illegible]	[illegible]	[illegible]	[illegible]
	Abscess,	[illegible]	[illegible]	[illegible]	[illegible]	[illegible]	[illegible]	[illegible]	[illegible]	[illegible]	[illegible]	[illegible]	[illegible]	[illegible]	[illegible]	[illegible]	[illegible]	[illegible]	[illegible]	[illegible]
	Haemorrhage,	[illegible]	[illegible]	.	[illegible]	[illegible]	[illegible]	[illegible]	[illegible]	[illegible]	[illegible]	[illegible]	[illegible]	[illegible]	[illegible]	[illegible]	[illegible]	[illegible]	[illegible]	[illegible]
	Sudden (cause unascertained),	[illegible]	[illegible]	[illegible]	[illegible]	[illegible]	[illegible]	[illegible]	[illegible]	[illegible]	[illegible]	[illegible]	[illegible]	[illegible]	[illegible]	[illegible]	[illegible]	[illegible]	[illegible]	.
	Other ill-defined and not specified causes,	[illegible]	[illegible]	[illegible]	[illegible]	[illegible]	[illegible]	[illegible]	[illegible]	[illegible]	[illegible]	[illegible]	[illegible]	[illegible]	[illegible]	[illegible]	[illegible]	[illegible]	[illegible]	[illegible]

IRELAND—CAUSES of DEATH at different Periods of Life in the Ten Years, 1881-90—FEMALES—*con.*

Class	CAUSES OF DEATH	All Ages	Under 1 year	1	2	3	4	Under 5 years	5-	10-	15-	20-	25-	35-	45-	55-	65-	75-	85-	95 and upwards
	ORDER 8 (*f*).																			
VI.—*con.*	Abortion, Miscarriage,	[illegible]	[illegible]	[illegible]	[illegible]	[illegible]	[illegible]	[illegible]	[illegible]	[illegible]	[illegible]	[illegible]	[illegible]	[illegible]	[illegible]	[illegible]	[illegible]	[illegible]	[illegible]	[illegible]
	Puerperal Mania,	[illegible]	[illegible]	[illegible]	[illegible]	[illegible]	[illegible]	[illegible]	[illegible]	[illegible]	[illegible]	[illegible]	[illegible]	[illegible]	[illegible]	[illegible]	[illegible]	[illegible]	[illegible]	[illegible]
	Puerperal Convulsions,	[illegible]	[illegible]	[illegible]	[illegible]	[illegible]	[illegible]	[illegible]	[illegible]	[illegible]	[illegible]	[illegible]	[illegible]	[illegible]	[illegible]	[illegible]	[illegible]	[illegible]	[illegible]	[illegible]
	Puerperal fever, Pyaemia,	[illegible]	[illegible]	[illegible]	[illegible]	[illegible]	[illegible]	[illegible]	[illegible]	[illegible]	[illegible]	[illegible]	[illegible]	[illegible]	[illegible]	[illegible]	[illegible]	[illegible]	[illegible]	[illegible]
	Phlegmasia Dolens,	[illegible]	[illegible]	[illegible]	[illegible]	[illegible]	[illegible]	[illegible]	[illegible]	[illegible]	[illegible]	[illegible]	[illegible]	[illegible]	[illegible]	[illegible]	[illegible]	[illegible]	[illegible]	[illegible]
	Other Accidents of Childbirth,	[illegible]	[illegible]	[illegible]	[illegible]	[illegible]	[illegible]	[illegible]	[illegible]	[illegible]	[illegible]	[illegible]	[illegible]	[illegible]	[illegible]	[illegible]	[illegible]	[illegible]	[illegible]	[illegible]
	ORDER 9.																			
	Caries, Necrosis,	[illegible]	[illegible]	[illegible]	[illegible]	[illegible]	[illegible]	[illegible]	[illegible]	[illegible]	[illegible]	[illegible]	[illegible]	[illegible]	[illegible]	[illegible]	[illegible]	[illegible]	[illegible]	[illegible]
	Arthritis, Ostitis, Periostitis,	[illegible]	[illegible]	[illegible]	[illegible]	[illegible]	[illegible]	[illegible]	[illegible]	[illegible]	[illegible]	[illegible]	[illegible]	[illegible]	[illegible]	[illegible]	[illegible]	[illegible]	[illegible]	[illegible]
	Other Diseases of Organs of Locomotion,	[illegible]	[illegible]	[illegible]	[illegible]	[illegible]	[illegible]	[illegible]	[illegible]	[illegible]	[illegible]	[illegible]	[illegible]	[illegible]	[illegible]	[illegible]	[illegible]	[illegible]	[illegible]	[illegible]
	ORDER 10.																			
	Carbuncle,	[illegible]	[illegible]	[illegible]	[illegible]	[illegible]	[illegible]	[illegible]	[illegible]	[illegible]	[illegible]	[illegible]	[illegible]	[illegible]	[illegible]	[illegible]	[illegible]	[illegible]	[illegible]	[illegible]
	Phlegmon, Cellulitis,	[illegible]	[illegible]	[illegible]	[illegible]	[illegible]	[illegible]	[illegible]	[illegible]	[illegible]	[illegible]	[illegible]	[illegible]	[illegible]	[illegible]	[illegible]	[illegible]	[illegible]	[illegible]	[illegible]
	Lupus,	[illegible]	[illegible]	[illegible]	[illegible]	[illegible]	[illegible]	[illegible]	[illegible]	[illegible]	[illegible]	[illegible]	[illegible]	[illegible]	[illegible]	[illegible]	[illegible]	[illegible]	[illegible]	[illegible]
	Ulcer, Bedsore,	[illegible]	[illegible]	[illegible]	[illegible]	[illegible]	[illegible]	[illegible]	[illegible]	[illegible]	[illegible]	[illegible]	[illegible]	[illegible]	[illegible]	[illegible]	[illegible]	[illegible]	[illegible]	[illegible]
	Eczema,	[illegible]	[illegible]	[illegible]	[illegible]	[illegible]	[illegible]	[illegible]	[illegible]	[illegible]	[illegible]	[illegible]	[illegible]	[illegible]	[illegible]	[illegible]	[illegible]	[illegible]	[illegible]	[illegible]
	Pemphigus,	[illegible]	[illegible]	[illegible]	[illegible]	[illegible]	[illegible]	[illegible]	[illegible]	[illegible]	[illegible]	[illegible]	[illegible]	[illegible]	[illegible]	[illegible]	[illegible]	[illegible]	[illegible]	[illegible]
	Other Diseases of Integumentary System,	[illegible]	[illegible]	[illegible]	[illegible]	[illegible]	[illegible]	[illegible]	[illegible]	[illegible]	[illegible]	[illegible]	[illegible]	[illegible]	[illegible]	[illegible]	[illegible]	[illegible]	[illegible]	[illegible]
VII.	ORDER 1.																			
	Accident or Negligence:—																			
	Fractures, Contusions,	[illegible]	[illegible]	[illegible]	[illegible]	[illegible]	[illegible]	[illegible]	[illegible]	[illegible]	[illegible]	[illegible]	[illegible]	[illegible]	[illegible]	[illegible]	[illegible]	[illegible]	[illegible]	[illegible]
	Gunshot Wounds,	[illegible]	[illegible]	[illegible]	[illegible]	[illegible]	[illegible]	[illegible]	[illegible]	[illegible]	[illegible]	[illegible]	[illegible]	[illegible]	[illegible]	[illegible]	[illegible]	[illegible]	[illegible]	[illegible]
	Cut, Stab,	[illegible]	[illegible]	[illegible]	[illegible]	[illegible]	[illegible]	[illegible]	[illegible]	[illegible]	[illegible]	[illegible]	[illegible]	[illegible]	[illegible]	[illegible]	[illegible]	[illegible]	[illegible]	[illegible]
	Burn, Scald,	[illegible]	[illegible]	[illegible]	[illegible]	[illegible]	[illegible]	[illegible]	[illegible]	[illegible]	[illegible]	[illegible]	[illegible]	[illegible]	[illegible]	[illegible]	[illegible]	[illegible]	[illegible]	[illegible]
	Poison,	[illegible]	[illegible]	[illegible]	[illegible]	[illegible]	[illegible]	[illegible]	[illegible]	[illegible]	[illegible]	[illegible]	[illegible]	[illegible]	[illegible]	[illegible]	[illegible]	[illegible]	[illegible]	[illegible]
	Drowning,	[illegible]	[illegible]	[illegible]	[illegible]	[illegible]	[illegible]	[illegible]	[illegible]	[illegible]	[illegible]	[illegible]	[illegible]	[illegible]	[illegible]	[illegible]	[illegible]	[illegible]	[illegible]	[illegible]
	Suffocation,	[illegible]	[illegible]	[illegible]	[illegible]	[illegible]	[illegible]	[illegible]	[illegible]	[illegible]	[illegible]	[illegible]	[illegible]	[illegible]	[illegible]	[illegible]	[illegible]	[illegible]	[illegible]	[illegible]
	Otherwise,	[illegible]	[illegible]	[illegible]	[illegible]	[illegible]	[illegible]	[illegible]	[illegible]	[illegible]	[illegible]	[illegible]	[illegible]	[illegible]	[illegible]	[illegible]	[illegible]	[illegible]	[illegible]	[illegible]
	ORDER 2.																			
	Murder, Manslaughter,	[illegible]	[illegible]	[illegible]	[illegible]	[illegible]	[illegible]	[illegible]	[illegible]	[illegible]	[illegible]	[illegible]	[illegible]	[illegible]	[illegible]	[illegible]	[illegible]	[illegible]	[illegible]	[illegible]
	ORDER 3.																			
	Suicide:—																			
	Gunshot Wounds,	[illegible]	[illegible]	[illegible]	[illegible]	[illegible]	[illegible]	[illegible]	[illegible]	[illegible]	[illegible]	[illegible]	[illegible]	[illegible]	[illegible]	[illegible]	[illegible]	[illegible]	[illegible]	[illegible]
	Cut, Stab,	[illegible]	[illegible]	[illegible]	[illegible]	[illegible]	[illegible]	[illegible]	[illegible]	[illegible]	[illegible]	[illegible]	[illegible]	[illegible]	[illegible]	[illegible]	[illegible]	[illegible]	[illegible]	[illegible]
	Poison,	[illegible]	[illegible]	[illegible]	[illegible]	[illegible]	[illegible]	[illegible]	[illegible]	[illegible]	[illegible]	[illegible]	[illegible]	[illegible]	[illegible]	[illegible]	[illegible]	[illegible]	[illegible]	[illegible]
	Drowning,	[illegible]	[illegible]	[illegible]	[illegible]	[illegible]	[illegible]	[illegible]	[illegible]	[illegible]	[illegible]	[illegible]	[illegible]	[illegible]	[illegible]	[illegible]	[illegible]	[illegible]	[illegible]	[illegible]
	Hanging,	[illegible]	[illegible]	[illegible]	[illegible]	[illegible]	[illegible]	[illegible]	[illegible]	[illegible]	[illegible]	[illegible]	[illegible]	[illegible]	[illegible]	[illegible]	[illegible]	[illegible]	[illegible]	[illegible]
	Otherwise,	[illegible]	[illegible]	[illegible]	[illegible]	[illegible]	[illegible]	[illegible]	[illegible]	[illegible]	[illegible]	[illegible]	[illegible]	[illegible]	[illegible]	[illegible]	[illegible]	[illegible]	[illegible]	[illegible]
	ORDER 4.																			
	Hanging (Execution),	.	.	.	.	.	.	.	.	.	.	.	.	.	.	.	.	.	.	.
VIII.	Dropsy,	[illegible]	[illegible]	[illegible]	[illegible]	[illegible]	[illegible]	[illegible]	[illegible]	[illegible]	[illegible]	[illegible]	[illegible]	[illegible]	[illegible]	[illegible]	[illegible]	[illegible]	[illegible]	[illegible]
	Debility, Atrophy, Inanition,	[illegible]	[illegible]	[illegible]	[illegible]	[illegible]	[illegible]	[illegible]	[illegible]	[illegible]	[illegible]	[illegible]	[illegible]	[illegible]	[illegible]	[illegible]	[illegible]	[illegible]	[illegible]	[illegible]
	Mortification,	[illegible]	[illegible]	[illegible]	[illegible]	[illegible]	[illegible]	[illegible]	[illegible]	[illegible]	[illegible]	[illegible]	[illegible]	[illegible]	[illegible]	[illegible]	[illegible]	[illegible]	[illegible]	[illegible]
	Tumour,	[illegible]	[illegible]	[illegible]	[illegible]	[illegible]	[illegible]	[illegible]	[illegible]	[illegible]	[illegible]	[illegible]	[illegible]	[illegible]	[illegible]	[illegible]	[illegible]	[illegible]	[illegible]	[illegible]
	Abscess,	[illegible]	[illegible]	[illegible]	[illegible]	[illegible]	[illegible]	[illegible]	[illegible]	[illegible]	[illegible]	[illegible]	[illegible]	[illegible]	[illegible]	[illegible]	[illegible]	[illegible]	[illegible]	[illegible]
	Haemorrhage,	[illegible]	[illegible]	[illegible]	[illegible]	[illegible]	[illegible]	[illegible]	[illegible]	[illegible]	[illegible]	[illegible]	[illegible]	[illegible]	[illegible]	[illegible]	[illegible]	[illegible]	[illegible]	[illegible]
	Sudden (cause unascertained),	[illegible]	[illegible]	[illegible]	[illegible]	[illegible]	[illegible]	[illegible]	[illegible]	[illegible]	[illegible]	[illegible]	[illegible]	[illegible]	[illegible]	[illegible]	[illegible]	[illegible]	[illegible]	[illegible]
	Other ill-defined and unspecified causes,	[illegible]	[illegible]	[illegible]	[illegible]	[illegible]	[illegible]	[illegible]	[illegible]	[illegible]	[illegible]	[illegible]	[illegible]	[illegible]	[illegible]	[illegible]	[illegible]	[illegible]	[illegible]	[illegible]

TOTAL NUMBER OF DEATHS.—NUMBER of PERSONS who died (1), in WORKHOUSES and GENERAL and OWN HOMES, &c.; NUMBER of DEATHS from the PRINCIPAL CAUSES and REGISTRARS' DISTRICTS in IRELAND

SUPERINTENDENT REGISTRARS' DISTRICTS, OR

Superintendent Registrars' Districts or Poor Law Unions	Mean Population	Average Annual Death-rate	Total Number of Deaths	In Union Workhouses	In Public Lunatic Asylums	In Hospitals, &c.	At their own Homes, &c.	Small-pox	Measles	Scarlatina	Typhus	Whooping-cough	Diphtheria	Simple continued and ill-defined Fever	Enteric Fever	Cholera	Diarrhoea and Dysentery	Puerperal Fever	Other Septic Diseases
IRELAND	[illegible]	[illegible]	[illegible]	[illegible]	[illegible]	[illegible]	[illegible]	[illegible]	[illegible]	[illegible]	[illegible]	[illegible]	[illegible]	[illegible]	[illegible]	[illegible]	[illegible]	[illegible]	[illegible]
Abbeyleix	[illegible]	[illegible]	[illegible]	[illegible]	[illegible]	[illegible]	[illegible]	[illegible]	[illegible]	[illegible]	[illegible]	[illegible]	[illegible]	[illegible]	[illegible]	[illegible]	[illegible]	[illegible]	[illegible]
Antrim	[illegible]	[illegible]	[illegible]	[illegible]	[illegible]	[illegible]	[illegible]	[illegible]	[illegible]	[illegible]	[illegible]	[illegible]	[illegible]	[illegible]	[illegible]	[illegible]	[illegible]	[illegible]	[illegible]
Ardee	[illegible]	[illegible]	[illegible]	[illegible]	[illegible]	[illegible]	[illegible]	[illegible]	[illegible]	[illegible]	[illegible]	[illegible]	[illegible]	[illegible]	[illegible]	[illegible]	[illegible]	[illegible]	[illegible]
Armagh	[illegible]	[illegible]	[illegible]	[illegible]	[illegible]	[illegible]	[illegible]	[illegible]	[illegible]	[illegible]	[illegible]	[illegible]	[illegible]	[illegible]	[illegible]	[illegible]	[illegible]	[illegible]	[illegible]
Athlone	[illegible]	[illegible]	[illegible]	[illegible]	[illegible]	[illegible]	[illegible]	[illegible]	[illegible]	[illegible]	[illegible]	[illegible]	[illegible]	[illegible]	[illegible]	[illegible]	[illegible]	[illegible]	[illegible]
Athy	[illegible]	[illegible]	[illegible]	[illegible]	[illegible]	[illegible]	[illegible]	[illegible]	[illegible]	[illegible]	[illegible]	[illegible]	[illegible]	[illegible]	[illegible]	[illegible]	[illegible]	[illegible]	[illegible]
Bailieborough	[illegible]	[illegible]	[illegible]	[illegible]	[illegible]	[illegible]	[illegible]	[illegible]	[illegible]	[illegible]	[illegible]	[illegible]	[illegible]	[illegible]	[illegible]	[illegible]	[illegible]	[illegible]	[illegible]
Ballina	[illegible]	[illegible]	[illegible]	[illegible]	[illegible]	[illegible]	[illegible]	[illegible]	[illegible]	[illegible]	[illegible]	[illegible]	[illegible]	[illegible]	[illegible]	[illegible]	[illegible]	[illegible]	[illegible]
Ballinasloe	[illegible]	[illegible]	[illegible]	[illegible]	[illegible]	[illegible]	[illegible]	[illegible]	[illegible]	[illegible]	[illegible]	[illegible]	[illegible]	[illegible]	[illegible]	[illegible]	[illegible]	[illegible]	[illegible]
Ballinrobe	[illegible]	[illegible]	[illegible]	[illegible]	[illegible]	[illegible]	[illegible]	[illegible]	[illegible]	[illegible]	[illegible]	[illegible]	[illegible]	[illegible]	[illegible]	[illegible]	[illegible]	[illegible]	[illegible]
Ballycastle	[illegible]	[illegible]	[illegible]	[illegible]	[illegible]	[illegible]	[illegible]	[illegible]	[illegible]	[illegible]	[illegible]	[illegible]	[illegible]	[illegible]	[illegible]	[illegible]	[illegible]	[illegible]	[illegible]
Ballymahon	[illegible]	[illegible]	[illegible]	[illegible]	[illegible]	[illegible]	[illegible]	[illegible]	[illegible]	[illegible]	[illegible]	[illegible]	[illegible]	[illegible]	[illegible]	[illegible]	[illegible]	[illegible]	[illegible]
Ballymena	[illegible]	[illegible]	[illegible]	[illegible]	[illegible]	[illegible]	[illegible]	[illegible]	[illegible]	[illegible]	[illegible]	[illegible]	[illegible]	[illegible]	[illegible]	[illegible]	[illegible]	[illegible]	[illegible]
Ballymoney	[illegible]	[illegible]	[illegible]	[illegible]	[illegible]	[illegible]	[illegible]	[illegible]	[illegible]	[illegible]	[illegible]	[illegible]	[illegible]	[illegible]	[illegible]	[illegible]	[illegible]	[illegible]	[illegible]
Ballyshannon	[illegible]	[illegible]	[illegible]	[illegible]	[illegible]	[illegible]	[illegible]	[illegible]	[illegible]	[illegible]	[illegible]	[illegible]	[illegible]	[illegible]	[illegible]	[illegible]	[illegible]	[illegible]	[illegible]
Ballyvaughan	[illegible]	[illegible]	[illegible]	[illegible]	[illegible]	[illegible]	[illegible]	[illegible]	[illegible]	[illegible]	[illegible]	[illegible]	[illegible]	[illegible]	[illegible]	[illegible]	[illegible]	[illegible]	[illegible]
Balrothery	[illegible]	[illegible]	[illegible]	[illegible]	[illegible]	[illegible]	[illegible]	[illegible]	[illegible]	[illegible]	[illegible]	[illegible]	[illegible]	[illegible]	[illegible]	[illegible]	[illegible]	[illegible]	[illegible]
Baltinglass	[illegible]	[illegible]	[illegible]	[illegible]	[illegible]	[illegible]	[illegible]	[illegible]	[illegible]	[illegible]	[illegible]	[illegible]	[illegible]	[illegible]	[illegible]	[illegible]	[illegible]	[illegible]	[illegible]
Banbridge	[illegible]	[illegible]	[illegible]	[illegible]	[illegible]	[illegible]	[illegible]	[illegible]	[illegible]	[illegible]	[illegible]	[illegible]	[illegible]	[illegible]	[illegible]	[illegible]	[illegible]	[illegible]	[illegible]
Bandon	[illegible]	[illegible]	[illegible]	[illegible]	[illegible]	[illegible]	[illegible]	[illegible]	[illegible]	[illegible]	[illegible]	[illegible]	[illegible]	[illegible]	[illegible]	[illegible]	[illegible]	[illegible]	[illegible]
Bantry	[illegible]	[illegible]	[illegible]	[illegible]	[illegible]	[illegible]	[illegible]	[illegible]	[illegible]	[illegible]	[illegible]	[illegible]	[illegible]	[illegible]	[illegible]	[illegible]	[illegible]	[illegible]	[illegible]
Bawnboy	[illegible]	[illegible]	[illegible]	[illegible]	[illegible]	[illegible]	[illegible]	[illegible]	[illegible]	[illegible]	[illegible]	[illegible]	[illegible]	[illegible]	[illegible]	[illegible]	[illegible]	[illegible]	[illegible]
Belfast	[illegible]	[illegible]	[illegible]	[illegible]	[illegible]	[illegible]	[illegible]	[illegible]	[illegible]	[illegible]	[illegible]	[illegible]	[illegible]	[illegible]	[illegible]	[illegible]	[illegible]	[illegible]	[illegible]
Belmullet	[illegible]	[illegible]	[illegible]	[illegible]	[illegible]	[illegible]	[illegible]	[illegible]	[illegible]	[illegible]	[illegible]	[illegible]	[illegible]	[illegible]	[illegible]	[illegible]	[illegible]	[illegible]	[illegible]
Borrisokane	[illegible]	[illegible]	[illegible]	[illegible]	[illegible]	[illegible]	[illegible]	[illegible]	[illegible]	[illegible]	[illegible]	[illegible]	[illegible]	[illegible]	[illegible]	[illegible]	[illegible]	[illegible]	[illegible]
Boyle	[illegible]	[illegible]	[illegible]	[illegible]	[illegible]	[illegible]	[illegible]	[illegible]	[illegible]	[illegible]	[illegible]	[illegible]	[illegible]	[illegible]	[illegible]	[illegible]	[illegible]	[illegible]	[illegible]
Cahersiveen	[illegible]	[illegible]	[illegible]	[illegible]	[illegible]	[illegible]	[illegible]	[illegible]	[illegible]	[illegible]	[illegible]	[illegible]	[illegible]	[illegible]	[illegible]	[illegible]	[illegible]	[illegible]	[illegible]
Callan	[illegible]	[illegible]	[illegible]	[illegible]	[illegible]	[illegible]	[illegible]	[illegible]	[illegible]	[illegible]	[illegible]	[illegible]	[illegible]	[illegible]	[illegible]	[illegible]	[illegible]	[illegible]	[illegible]
Carlow	[illegible]	[illegible]	[illegible]	[illegible]	[illegible]	[illegible]	[illegible]	[illegible]	[illegible]	[illegible]	[illegible]	[illegible]	[illegible]	[illegible]	[illegible]	[illegible]	[illegible]	[illegible]	[illegible]
Carrickmacross	[illegible]	[illegible]	[illegible]	[illegible]	[illegible]	[illegible]	[illegible]	[illegible]	[illegible]	[illegible]	[illegible]	[illegible]	[illegible]	[illegible]	[illegible]	[illegible]	[illegible]	[illegible]	[illegible]
Carrick-on-Shannon	[illegible]	[illegible]	[illegible]	[illegible]	[illegible]	[illegible]	[illegible]	[illegible]	[illegible]	[illegible]	[illegible]	[illegible]	[illegible]	[illegible]	[illegible]	[illegible]	[illegible]	[illegible]	[illegible]
Carrick-on-Suir	[illegible]	[illegible]	[illegible]	[illegible]	[illegible]	[illegible]	[illegible]	[illegible]	[illegible]	[illegible]	[illegible]	[illegible]	[illegible]	[illegible]	[illegible]	[illegible]	[illegible]	[illegible]	[illegible]
Cashel	[illegible]	[illegible]	[illegible]	[illegible]	[illegible]	[illegible]	[illegible]	[illegible]	[illegible]	[illegible]	[illegible]	[illegible]	[illegible]	[illegible]	[illegible]	[illegible]	[illegible]	[illegible]	[illegible]
Castlebar	[illegible]	[illegible]	[illegible]	[illegible]	[illegible]	[illegible]	[illegible]	[illegible]	[illegible]	[illegible]	[illegible]	[illegible]	[illegible]	[illegible]	[illegible]	[illegible]	[illegible]	[illegible]	[illegible]
Castleblayney	[illegible]	[illegible]	[illegible]	[illegible]	[illegible]	[illegible]	[illegible]	[illegible]	[illegible]	[illegible]	[illegible]	[illegible]	[illegible]	[illegible]	[illegible]	[illegible]	[illegible]	[illegible]	[illegible]
Castlecomer	[illegible]	[illegible]	[illegible]	[illegible]	[illegible]	[illegible]	[illegible]	[illegible]	[illegible]	[illegible]	[illegible]	[illegible]	[illegible]	[illegible]	[illegible]	[illegible]	[illegible]	[illegible]	[illegible]
Castlederg	[illegible]	[illegible]	[illegible]	[illegible]	[illegible]	[illegible]	[illegible]	[illegible]	[illegible]	[illegible]	[illegible]	[illegible]	[illegible]	[illegible]	[illegible]	[illegible]	[illegible]	[illegible]	[illegible]
Castlereagh	[illegible]	[illegible]	[illegible]	[illegible]	[illegible]	[illegible]	[illegible]	[illegible]	[illegible]	[illegible]	[illegible]	[illegible]	[illegible]	[illegible]	[illegible]	[illegible]	[illegible]	[illegible]	[illegible]
Castletown	[illegible]	[illegible]	[illegible]	[illegible]	[illegible]	[illegible]	[illegible]	[illegible]	[illegible]	[illegible]	[illegible]	[illegible]	[illegible]	[illegible]	[illegible]	[illegible]	[illegible]	[illegible]	[illegible]
Cavan	[illegible]	[illegible]	[illegible]	[illegible]	[illegible]	[illegible]	[illegible]	[illegible]	[illegible]	[illegible]	[illegible]	[illegible]	[illegible]	[illegible]	[illegible]	[illegible]	[illegible]	[illegible]	[illegible]
Celbridge	[illegible]	[illegible]	[illegible]	[illegible]	[illegible]	[illegible]	[illegible]	[illegible]	[illegible]	[illegible]	[illegible]	[illegible]	[illegible]	[illegible]	[illegible]	[illegible]	[illegible]	[illegible]	[illegible]
[illegible]	[illegible]	[illegible]	[illegible]	[illegible]	[illegible]	[illegible]	[illegible]	[illegible]	[illegible]	[illegible]	[illegible]	[illegible]	[illegible]	[illegible]	[illegible]	[illegible]	[illegible]	[illegible]	[illegible]
[illegible]	[illegible]	[illegible]	[illegible]	[illegible]	[illegible]	[illegible]	[illegible]	[illegible]	[illegible]	[illegible]	[illegible]	[illegible]	[illegible]	[illegible]	[illegible]	[illegible]	[illegible]	[illegible]	[illegible]
[illegible]	[illegible]	[illegible]	[illegible]	[illegible]	[illegible]	[illegible]	[illegible]	[illegible]	[illegible]	[illegible]	[illegible]	[illegible]	[illegible]	[illegible]	[illegible]	[illegible]	[illegible]	[illegible]	[illegible]
[illegible]	[illegible]	[illegible]	[illegible]	[illegible]	[illegible]	[illegible]	[illegible]	[illegible]	[illegible]	[illegible]	[illegible]	[illegible]	[illegible]	[illegible]	[illegible]	[illegible]	[illegible]	[illegible]	[illegible]
[illegible]	[illegible]	[illegible]	[illegible]	[illegible]	[illegible]	[illegible]	[illegible]	[illegible]	[illegible]	[illegible]	[illegible]	[illegible]	[illegible]	[illegible]	[illegible]	[illegible]	[illegible]	[illegible]	[illegible]
[illegible]	[illegible]	[illegible]	[illegible]	[illegible]	[illegible]	[illegible]	[illegible]	[illegible]	[illegible]	[illegible]	[illegible]	[illegible]	[illegible]	[illegible]	[illegible]	[illegible]	[illegible]	[illegible]	[illegible]

Special Hospitals; (2), in Public Lunatic Asylums; (3), in Workhouses; and (4), at their Number of Inquests in the Provinces, Counties, and Superintendents during the Ten Years 1881–90.

Poor Law Unions arranged Alphabetically.

Deaths. Constitutional Diseases: [illegible]	[illegible]	[illegible]	[illegible]	[illegible]	Local Diseases: Diseases of [illegible]	[illegible]	[illegible]	[illegible]	[illegible]	[illegible]	Other Local Diseases	Violence: [illegible]	[illegible]	[illegible]	[illegible]	All other Causes	[illegible]	[illegible] Districts or Poor Law Unions
[illegible]	[illegible]	[illegible]	[illegible]	[illegible]	[illegible]	[illegible]	[illegible]	[illegible]	[illegible]	[illegible]	[illegible]	[illegible]	[illegible]	[illegible]	[illegible]	[illegible]	[illegible]	Ireland.
[illegible]	[illegible]	[illegible]	[illegible]	[illegible]	[illegible]	[illegible]	[illegible]	[illegible]	[illegible]	[illegible]	[illegible]	[illegible]	[illegible]	[illegible]	[illegible]	[illegible]	[illegible]	[illegible]
[illegible]	[illegible]	[illegible]	[illegible]	[illegible]	[illegible]	[illegible]	[illegible]	[illegible]	[illegible]	[illegible]	[illegible]	[illegible]	[illegible]	[illegible]	[illegible]	[illegible]	[illegible]	[illegible]
[illegible]	[illegible]	[illegible]	[illegible]	[illegible]	[illegible]	[illegible]	[illegible]	[illegible]	[illegible]	[illegible]	[illegible]	[illegible]	[illegible]	[illegible]	[illegible]	[illegible]	[illegible]	[illegible]
[illegible]	[illegible]	[illegible]	[illegible]	[illegible]	[illegible]	[illegible]	[illegible]	[illegible]	[illegible]	[illegible]	[illegible]	[illegible]	[illegible]	[illegible]	[illegible]	[illegible]	[illegible]	[illegible]
[illegible]	[illegible]	[illegible]	[illegible]	[illegible]	[illegible]	[illegible]	[illegible]	[illegible]	[illegible]	[illegible]	[illegible]	[illegible]	[illegible]	[illegible]	[illegible]	[illegible]	[illegible]	[illegible]
[illegible]	[illegible]	[illegible]	[illegible]	[illegible]	[illegible]	[illegible]	[illegible]	[illegible]	[illegible]	[illegible]	[illegible]	[illegible]	[illegible]	[illegible]	[illegible]	[illegible]	[illegible]	[illegible]
[illegible]	[illegible]	[illegible]	[illegible]	[illegible]	[illegible]	[illegible]	[illegible]	[illegible]	[illegible]	[illegible]	[illegible]	[illegible]	[illegible]	[illegible]	[illegible]	[illegible]	[illegible]	[illegible]
[illegible]	[illegible]	[illegible]	[illegible]	[illegible]	[illegible]	[illegible]	[illegible]	[illegible]	[illegible]	[illegible]	[illegible]	[illegible]	[illegible]	[illegible]	[illegible]	[illegible]	[illegible]	[illegible]
[illegible]	[illegible]	[illegible]	[illegible]	[illegible]	[illegible]	[illegible]	[illegible]	[illegible]	[illegible]	[illegible]	[illegible]	[illegible]	[illegible]	[illegible]	[illegible]	[illegible]	[illegible]	[illegible]
[illegible]	[illegible]	[illegible]	[illegible]	[illegible]	[illegible]	[illegible]	[illegible]	[illegible]	[illegible]	[illegible]	[illegible]	[illegible]	[illegible]	[illegible]	[illegible]	[illegible]	[illegible]	[illegible]
[illegible]	[illegible]	[illegible]	[illegible]	[illegible]	[illegible]	[illegible]	[illegible]	[illegible]	[illegible]	[illegible]	[illegible]	[illegible]	[illegible]	[illegible]	[illegible]	[illegible]	[illegible]	[illegible]
[illegible]	[illegible]	[illegible]	[illegible]	[illegible]	[illegible]	[illegible]	[illegible]	[illegible]	[illegible]	[illegible]	[illegible]	[illegible]	[illegible]	[illegible]	[illegible]	[illegible]	[illegible]	[illegible]
[illegible]	[illegible]	[illegible]	[illegible]	[illegible]	[illegible]	[illegible]	[illegible]	[illegible]	[illegible]	[illegible]	[illegible]	[illegible]	[illegible]	[illegible]	[illegible]	[illegible]	[illegible]	[illegible]
[illegible]	[illegible]	[illegible]	[illegible]	[illegible]	[illegible]	[illegible]	[illegible]	[illegible]	[illegible]	[illegible]	[illegible]	[illegible]	[illegible]	[illegible]	[illegible]	[illegible]	[illegible]	[illegible]
[illegible]	[illegible]	[illegible]	[illegible]	[illegible]	[illegible]	[illegible]	[illegible]	[illegible]	[illegible]	[illegible]	[illegible]	[illegible]	[illegible]	[illegible]	[illegible]	[illegible]	[illegible]	[illegible]
[illegible]	[illegible]	[illegible]	[illegible]	[illegible]	[illegible]	[illegible]	[illegible]	[illegible]	[illegible]	[illegible]	[illegible]	[illegible]	[illegible]	[illegible]	[illegible]	[illegible]	[illegible]	[illegible]
[illegible]	[illegible]	[illegible]	[illegible]	[illegible]	[illegible]	[illegible]	[illegible]	[illegible]	[illegible]	[illegible]	[illegible]	[illegible]	[illegible]	[illegible]	[illegible]	[illegible]	[illegible]	[illegible]
[illegible]	[illegible]	[illegible]	[illegible]	[illegible]	[illegible]	[illegible]	[illegible]	[illegible]	[illegible]	[illegible]	[illegible]	[illegible]	[illegible]	[illegible]	[illegible]	[illegible]	[illegible]	[illegible]
[illegible]	[illegible]	[illegible]	[illegible]	[illegible]	[illegible]	[illegible]	[illegible]	[illegible]	[illegible]	[illegible]	[illegible]	[illegible]	[illegible]	[illegible]	[illegible]	[illegible]	[illegible]	[illegible]
[illegible]	[illegible]	[illegible]	[illegible]	[illegible]	[illegible]	[illegible]	[illegible]	[illegible]	[illegible]	[illegible]	[illegible]	[illegible]	[illegible]	[illegible]	[illegible]	[illegible]	[illegible]	[illegible]
[illegible]	[illegible]	[illegible]	[illegible]	[illegible]	[illegible]	[illegible]	[illegible]	[illegible]	[illegible]	[illegible]	[illegible]	[illegible]	[illegible]	[illegible]	[illegible]	[illegible]	[illegible]	[illegible]
[illegible]	[illegible]	[illegible]	[illegible]	[illegible]	[illegible]	[illegible]	[illegible]	[illegible]	[illegible]	[illegible]	[illegible]	[illegible]	[illegible]	[illegible]	[illegible]	[illegible]	[illegible]	[illegible]
[illegible]	[illegible]	[illegible]	[illegible]	[illegible]	[illegible]	[illegible]	[illegible]	[illegible]	[illegible]	[illegible]	[illegible]	[illegible]	[illegible]	[illegible]	[illegible]	[illegible]	[illegible]	[illegible]
[illegible]	[illegible]	[illegible]	[illegible]	[illegible]	[illegible]	[illegible]	[illegible]	[illegible]	[illegible]	[illegible]	[illegible]	[illegible]	[illegible]	[illegible]	[illegible]	[illegible]	[illegible]	[illegible]
[illegible]	[illegible]	[illegible]	[illegible]	[illegible]	[illegible]	[illegible]	[illegible]	[illegible]	[illegible]	[illegible]	[illegible]	[illegible]	[illegible]	[illegible]	[illegible]	[illegible]	[illegible]	[illegible]
[illegible]	[illegible]	[illegible]	[illegible]	[illegible]	[illegible]	[illegible]	[illegible]	[illegible]	[illegible]	[illegible]	[illegible]	[illegible]	[illegible]	[illegible]	[illegible]	[illegible]	[illegible]	[illegible]
[illegible]	[illegible]	[illegible]	[illegible]	[illegible]	[illegible]	[illegible]	[illegible]	[illegible]	[illegible]	[illegible]	[illegible]	[illegible]	[illegible]	[illegible]	[illegible]	[illegible]	[illegible]	[illegible]
[illegible]	[illegible]	[illegible]	[illegible]	[illegible]	[illegible]	[illegible]	[illegible]	[illegible]	[illegible]	[illegible]	[illegible]	[illegible]	[illegible]	[illegible]	[illegible]	[illegible]	[illegible]	[illegible]
[illegible]	[illegible]	[illegible]	[illegible]	[illegible]	[illegible]	[illegible]	[illegible]	[illegible]	[illegible]	[illegible]	[illegible]	[illegible]	[illegible]	[illegible]	[illegible]	[illegible]	[illegible]	[illegible]
[illegible]	[illegible]	[illegible]	[illegible]	[illegible]	[illegible]	[illegible]	[illegible]	[illegible]	[illegible]	[illegible]	[illegible]	[illegible]	[illegible]	[illegible]	[illegible]	[illegible]	[illegible]	[illegible]
[illegible]	[illegible]	[illegible]	[illegible]	[illegible]	[illegible]	[illegible]	[illegible]	[illegible]	[illegible]	[illegible]	[illegible]	[illegible]	[illegible]	[illegible]	[illegible]	[illegible]	[illegible]	[illegible]
[illegible]	[illegible]	[illegible]	[illegible]	[illegible]	[illegible]	[illegible]	[illegible]	[illegible]	[illegible]	[illegible]	[illegible]	[illegible]	[illegible]	[illegible]	[illegible]	[illegible]	[illegible]	[illegible]
[illegible]	[illegible]	[illegible]	[illegible]	[illegible]	[illegible]	[illegible]	[illegible]	[illegible]	[illegible]	[illegible]	[illegible]	[illegible]	[illegible]	[illegible]	[illegible]	[illegible]	[illegible]	[illegible]
[illegible]	[illegible]	[illegible]	[illegible]	[illegible]	[illegible]	[illegible]	[illegible]	[illegible]	[illegible]	[illegible]	[illegible]	[illegible]	[illegible]	[illegible]	[illegible]	[illegible]	[illegible]	[illegible]
[illegible]	[illegible]	[illegible]	[illegible]	[illegible]	[illegible]	[illegible]	[illegible]	[illegible]	[illegible]	[illegible]	[illegible]	[illegible]	[illegible]	[illegible]	[illegible]	[illegible]	[illegible]	[illegible]
[illegible]	[illegible]	[illegible]	[illegible]	[illegible]	[illegible]	[illegible]	[illegible]	[illegible]	[illegible]	[illegible]	[illegible]	[illegible]	[illegible]	[illegible]	[illegible]	[illegible]	[illegible]	[illegible]
[illegible]	[illegible]	[illegible]	[illegible]	[illegible]	[illegible]	[illegible]	[illegible]	[illegible]	[illegible]	[illegible]	[illegible]	[illegible]	[illegible]	[illegible]	[illegible]	[illegible]	[illegible]	[illegible]
[illegible]	[illegible]	[illegible]	[illegible]	[illegible]	[illegible]	[illegible]	[illegible]	[illegible]	[illegible]	[illegible]	[illegible]	[illegible]	[illegible]	[illegible]	[illegible]	[illegible]	[illegible]	[illegible]
[illegible]	[illegible]	[illegible]	[illegible]	[illegible]	[illegible]	[illegible]	[illegible]	[illegible]	[illegible]	[illegible]	[illegible]	[illegible]	[illegible]	[illegible]	[illegible]	[illegible]	[illegible]	[illegible]
[illegible]	[illegible]	[illegible]	[illegible]	[illegible]	[illegible]	[illegible]	[illegible]	[illegible]	[illegible]	[illegible]	[illegible]	[illegible]	[illegible]	[illegible]	[illegible]	[illegible]	[illegible]	[illegible]
[illegible]	[illegible]	[illegible]	[illegible]	[illegible]	[illegible]	[illegible]	[illegible]	[illegible]	[illegible]	[illegible]	[illegible]	[illegible]	[illegible]	[illegible]	[illegible]	[illegible]	[illegible]	[illegible]
[illegible]	[illegible]	[illegible]	[illegible]	[illegible]	[illegible]	[illegible]	[illegible]	[illegible]	[illegible]	[illegible]	[illegible]	[illegible]	[illegible]	[illegible]	[illegible]	[illegible]	[illegible]	[illegible]
[illegible]	[illegible]	[illegible]	[illegible]	[illegible]	[illegible]	[illegible]	[illegible]	[illegible]	[illegible]	[illegible]	[illegible]	[illegible]	[illegible]	[illegible]	[illegible]	[illegible]	[illegible]	[illegible]
[illegible]	[illegible]	[illegible]	[illegible]	[illegible]	[illegible]	[illegible]	[illegible]	[illegible]	[illegible]	[illegible]	[illegible]	[illegible]	[illegible]	[illegible]	[illegible]	[illegible]	[illegible]	[illegible]
[illegible]	[illegible]	[illegible]	[illegible]	[illegible]	[illegible]	[illegible]	[illegible]	[illegible]	[illegible]	[illegible]	[illegible]	[illegible]	[illegible]	[illegible]	[illegible]	[illegible]	[illegible]	[illegible]
[illegible]	[illegible]	[illegible]	[illegible]	[illegible]	[illegible]	[illegible]	[illegible]	[illegible]	[illegible]	[illegible]	[illegible]	[illegible]	[illegible]	[illegible]	[illegible]	[illegible]	[illegible]	[illegible]
[illegible]	[illegible]	[illegible]	[illegible]	[illegible]	[illegible]	[illegible]	[illegible]	[illegible]	[illegible]	[illegible]	[illegible]	[illegible]	[illegible]	[illegible]	[illegible]	[illegible]	[illegible]	[illegible]

TOTAL NUMBER OF DEATHS.—NUMBER of PERSONS who died (1), in INFIRMARIES and GENERAL, and OWN HOMES, &c.; NUMBER of DEATHS from the PRINCIPAL CAUSES; and REGISTRARS' DISTRICTS in IRELAND during

SUPERINTENDENT REGISTRARS' DISTRICTS, or

TOTAL NUMBER OF DEATHS.—NUMBER of PERSONS who died (1), in INFIRMARIES and GENERAL and [illegible] OWN HOMES, &c.; NUMBER of DEATHS from the PRINCIPAL CAUSES; and [illegible] REGISTRARS' DISTRICTS in IRELAND during [illegible]

SUPERINTENDENT REGISTRARS' DISTRICTS, OR [illegible]

Superintendent Registrars' Districts, or Poor Law Unions	Population, [illegible]	[illegible]	Total Number of Deaths	In Workhouses and [illegible]	In Public Lunatic Asylums	In [illegible]	At their own Homes, &c.	Small-pox	Measles	Scarlatina	Typhus	Whooping-cough	Diarrhoea	[illegible]	[illegible]	[illegible]	[illegible]	Puerperal Fever	[illegible]
[illegible]	[illegible]	[illegible]	[illegible]	[illegible]	[illegible]	[illegible]	[illegible]	[illegible]	[illegible]	[illegible]	[illegible]	[illegible]	[illegible]	[illegible]	[illegible]	[illegible]	[illegible]	[illegible]	[illegible]

TOTAL NUMBER OF DEATHS.—NUMBER of PERSONS who died (1), in INFIRMARIES and GENERAL and OWN HOMES, &c.; NUMBER of DEATHS from the PRINCIPAL CAUSES; and REGISTRARS' DISTRICTS in IRELAND during

SUPERINTENDENT REGISTRARS' DISTRICTS, OR

SUPERINTENDENT REGISTRARS' DISTRICTS OR POOR LAW UNIONS.	Population, 1891	Annual Death-rate	Total Number of Deaths	NUMBER OF PERSONS WHO DIED: In Infirmaries and General and Special Hospitals	In Public Lunatic Asylums	In Workhouses	At own homes, &c.	CAUSES OF — Smallpox	Measles	Scarlatina	Typhus	Whooping-cough	Diphtheria	Simple continued Fever	Enteric Fever	Simple Cholera	Diarrhoea and Dysentery	Puerperal Fever	[illegible]
Shillelagh,	[illegible]	[illegible]	[illegible]	.	.	[illegible]	[illegible]	.	[illegible]	[illegible]	[illegible]	[illegible]	[illegible]	[illegible]	[illegible]	[illegible]	[illegible]	[illegible]	[illegible]
Skibbereen,	[illegible]	[illegible]	[illegible]	.	.	[illegible]	[illegible]	.	[illegible]	[illegible]	[illegible]	[illegible]	[illegible]	[illegible]	[illegible]	[illegible]	[illegible]	[illegible]	[illegible]
Skull,	[illegible]	[illegible]	[illegible]	.	.	[illegible]	[illegible]	.	[illegible]	[illegible]	[illegible]	[illegible]	[illegible]	[illegible]	[illegible]	[illegible]	[illegible]	[illegible]	[illegible]
Sligo,	[illegible]	[illegible]	[illegible]	[illegible]	[illegible]	[illegible]	[illegible]	.	[illegible]	[illegible]	[illegible]	[illegible]	[illegible]	[illegible]	[illegible]	[illegible]	[illegible]	[illegible]	[illegible]
Strabane,*	[illegible]	[illegible]	[illegible]	[illegible]	.	[illegible]	[illegible]	.	[illegible]	[illegible]	[illegible]	[illegible]	[illegible]	[illegible]	[illegible]	[illegible]	[illegible]	[illegible]	[illegible]
Stranorlar,	[illegible]	[illegible]	[illegible]	.	.	[illegible]	[illegible]	.	[illegible]	[illegible]	[illegible]	[illegible]	[illegible]	[illegible]	[illegible]	[illegible]	[illegible]	[illegible]	[illegible]
Strokestown,	[illegible]	[illegible]	[illegible]	.	.	[illegible]	[illegible]	.	[illegible]	[illegible]	[illegible]	[illegible]	[illegible]	[illegible]	[illegible]	[illegible]	[illegible]	[illegible]	[illegible]
Swineford,	[illegible]	[illegible]	[illegible]	-	.	[illegible]	[illegible]	.	[illegible]	[illegible]	[illegible]	[illegible]	[illegible]	[illegible]	[illegible]	[illegible]	[illegible]	[illegible]	[illegible]
Thomastown,	[illegible]	[illegible]	[illegible]	-	.	[illegible]	[illegible]	.	[illegible]	[illegible]	[illegible]	[illegible]	[illegible]	[illegible]	[illegible]	[illegible]	[illegible]	[illegible]	[illegible]
Thurles,	[illegible]	[illegible]	[illegible]	[illegible]	.	[illegible]	[illegible]	.	[illegible]	[illegible]	[illegible]	[illegible]	[illegible]	[illegible]	[illegible]	[illegible]	[illegible]	[illegible]	[illegible]
Tipperary,	[illegible]	[illegible]	[illegible]	[illegible]	.	[illegible]	[illegible]	.	[illegible]	[illegible]	[illegible]	[illegible]	[illegible]	[illegible]	[illegible]	[illegible]	[illegible]	[illegible]	[illegible]
Tobercurry,	[illegible]	[illegible]	[illegible]	.	.	[illegible]	[illegible]	.	[illegible]	[illegible]	[illegible]	[illegible]	[illegible]	[illegible]	[illegible]	[illegible]	[illegible]	[illegible]	[illegible]
Tralee,	[illegible]	[illegible]	[illegible]	[illegible]	.	[illegible]	[illegible]	.	[illegible]	[illegible]	[illegible]	[illegible]	[illegible]	[illegible]	[illegible]	[illegible]	[illegible]	[illegible]	[illegible]
Trim,	[illegible]	[illegible]	[illegible]	.	.	[illegible]	[illegible]	.	[illegible]	[illegible]	[illegible]	[illegible]	[illegible]	[illegible]	[illegible]	[illegible]	[illegible]	[illegible]	[illegible]
Tuam,	[illegible]	[illegible]	[illegible]	.	.	[illegible]	[illegible]	.	[illegible]	[illegible]	[illegible]	[illegible]	[illegible]	[illegible]	[illegible]	[illegible]	[illegible]	[illegible]	[illegible]
Tulla,	[illegible]	[illegible]	[illegible]	.	.	[illegible]	[illegible]	.	[illegible]	[illegible]	[illegible]	[illegible]	[illegible]	[illegible]	[illegible]	[illegible]	[illegible]	[illegible]	[illegible]
Tullamore,	[illegible]	[illegible]	[illegible]	[illegible]	.	[illegible]	[illegible]	[illegible]	[illegible]	[illegible]	[illegible]	[illegible]	[illegible]	[illegible]	[illegible]	[illegible]	[illegible]	[illegible]	[illegible]
[illegible]*	[illegible]	[illegible]	[illegible]	.	.	[illegible]	[illegible]	.	[illegible]	[illegible]	[illegible]	[illegible]	[illegible]	[illegible]	[illegible]	[illegible]	[illegible]	[illegible]	[illegible]
Waterford,	[illegible]	[illegible]	[illegible]	[illegible]	[illegible]	[illegible]	[illegible]	[illegible]	[illegible]	[illegible]	[illegible]	[illegible]	[illegible]	[illegible]	[illegible]	[illegible]	[illegible]	[illegible]	[illegible]
Westport,*	[illegible]	[illegible]	[illegible]	.	.	[illegible]	[illegible]	.	[illegible]	[illegible]	[illegible]	[illegible]	[illegible]	[illegible]	[illegible]	[illegible]	[illegible]	[illegible]	[illegible]
Wexford,	[illegible]	[illegible]	[illegible]	[illegible]	.	[illegible]	[illegible]	.	[illegible]	[illegible]	[illegible]	[illegible]	[illegible]	[illegible]	[illegible]	[illegible]	[illegible]	[illegible]	[illegible]
Youghal,	[illegible]	[illegible]	[illegible]	-	.	[illegible]	[illegible]	.	[illegible]	[illegible]	[illegible]	[illegible]	[illegible]	[illegible]	[illegible]	[illegible]	[illegible]	[illegible]	[illegible]

Special Hospitals; (2), in Public Lunatic Asylums; (3), in Workhouses; and (4), at their ... Number of Inquests in the Provinces, Counties, and Superintendent ... the Ten Years 1881-90—*continued*.

Poor Law Unions arranged Alphabetically.

[illegible]	[illegible]	[illegible]	[illegible]	[illegible]	[illegible]	[illegible]	[illegible]	[illegible]	[illegible]	[illegible]	[illegible]	[illegible]	[illegible]	[illegible]	[illegible]	[illegible]	[illegible]	Superintendent Registrars' Districts and Poor Law Unions.
[illegible]	[illegible]	[illegible]	[illegible]	[illegible]	[illegible]	[illegible]	[illegible]	[illegible]	[illegible]	[illegible]	[illegible]	[illegible]	[illegible]	[illegible]	[illegible]	[illegible]	[illegible]	[illegible]
[illegible]	[illegible]	[illegible]	[illegible]	[illegible]	[illegible]	[illegible]	[illegible]	[illegible]	[illegible]	[illegible]	[illegible]	[illegible]	[illegible]	[illegible]	[illegible]	[illegible]	[illegible]	[illegible]
[illegible]	[illegible]	[illegible]	[illegible]	[illegible]	[illegible]	[illegible]	[illegible]	[illegible]	[illegible]	[illegible]	[illegible]	[illegible]	[illegible]	[illegible]	[illegible]	[illegible]	[illegible]	Skull.
[illegible]	[illegible]	[illegible]	[illegible]	[illegible]	[illegible]	[illegible]	[illegible]	[illegible]	[illegible]	[illegible]	[illegible]	[illegible]	[illegible]	[illegible]	[illegible]	[illegible]	[illegible]	Sligo.
[illegible]	[illegible]	[illegible]	[illegible]	[illegible]	[illegible]	[illegible]	[illegible]	[illegible]	[illegible]	[illegible]	[illegible]	[illegible]	[illegible]	[illegible]	[illegible]	[illegible]	[illegible]	Strabane.*
[illegible]	[illegible]	[illegible]	[illegible]	[illegible]	[illegible]	[illegible]	[illegible]	[illegible]	[illegible]	[illegible]	[illegible]	[illegible]	[illegible]	[illegible]	[illegible]	[illegible]	[illegible]	[illegible]
[illegible]	[illegible]	[illegible]	[illegible]	[illegible]	[illegible]	[illegible]	[illegible]	[illegible]	[illegible]	[illegible]	[illegible]	[illegible]	[illegible]	[illegible]	[illegible]	[illegible]	[illegible]	[illegible]
[illegible]	[illegible]	[illegible]	[illegible]	[illegible]	[illegible]	[illegible]	[illegible]	[illegible]	[illegible]	[illegible]	[illegible]	[illegible]	[illegible]	[illegible]	[illegible]	[illegible]	[illegible]	[illegible]
[illegible]	[illegible]	[illegible]	[illegible]	[illegible]	[illegible]	[illegible]	[illegible]	[illegible]	[illegible]	[illegible]	[illegible]	[illegible]	[illegible]	[illegible]	[illegible]	[illegible]	[illegible]	[illegible]
[illegible]	[illegible]	[illegible]	[illegible]	[illegible]	[illegible]	[illegible]	[illegible]	[illegible]	[illegible]	[illegible]	[illegible]	[illegible]	[illegible]	[illegible]	[illegible]	[illegible]	[illegible]	[illegible]
[illegible]	[illegible]	[illegible]	[illegible]	[illegible]	[illegible]	[illegible]	[illegible]	[illegible]	[illegible]	[illegible]	[illegible]	[illegible]	[illegible]	[illegible]	[illegible]	[illegible]	[illegible]	[illegible]
[illegible]	[illegible]	[illegible]	[illegible]	[illegible]	[illegible]	[illegible]	[illegible]	[illegible]	[illegible]	[illegible]	[illegible]	[illegible]	[illegible]	[illegible]	[illegible]	[illegible]	[illegible]	[illegible]
[illegible]	[illegible]	[illegible]	[illegible]	[illegible]	[illegible]	[illegible]	[illegible]	[illegible]	[illegible]	[illegible]	[illegible]	[illegible]	[illegible]	[illegible]	[illegible]	[illegible]	[illegible]	Tralee.
[illegible]	[illegible]	[illegible]	[illegible]	[illegible]	[illegible]	[illegible]	[illegible]	[illegible]	[illegible]	[illegible]	[illegible]	[illegible]	[illegible]	[illegible]	[illegible]	[illegible]	[illegible]	Trim.
[illegible]	[illegible]	[illegible]	[illegible]	[illegible]	[illegible]	[illegible]	[illegible]	[illegible]	[illegible]	[illegible]	[illegible]	[illegible]	[illegible]	[illegible]	[illegible]	[illegible]	[illegible]	Tuam.
[illegible]	[illegible]	[illegible]	[illegible]	[illegible]	[illegible]	[illegible]	[illegible]	[illegible]	[illegible]	[illegible]	[illegible]	[illegible]	[illegible]	[illegible]	[illegible]	[illegible]	[illegible]	Tulla.
[illegible]	[illegible]	[illegible]	[illegible]	[illegible]	[illegible]	[illegible]	[illegible]	[illegible]	[illegible]	[illegible]	[illegible]	[illegible]	[illegible]	[illegible]	[illegible]	[illegible]	[illegible]	Tullamore.
[illegible]	[illegible]	[illegible]	[illegible]	[illegible]	[illegible]	[illegible]	[illegible]	[illegible]	[illegible]	[illegible]	[illegible]	[illegible]	[illegible]	[illegible]	[illegible]	[illegible]	[illegible]	[illegible]*
[illegible]	[illegible]	[illegible]	[illegible]	[illegible]	[illegible]	[illegible]	[illegible]	[illegible]	[illegible]	[illegible]	[illegible]	[illegible]	[illegible]	[illegible]	[illegible]	[illegible]	[illegible]	Waterford.
[illegible]	[illegible]	[illegible]	[illegible]	[illegible]	[illegible]	[illegible]	[illegible]	[illegible]	[illegible]	[illegible]	[illegible]	[illegible]	[illegible]	[illegible]	[illegible]	[illegible]	[illegible]	Westport.*
[illegible]	[illegible]	[illegible]	[illegible]	[illegible]	[illegible]	[illegible]	[illegible]	[illegible]	[illegible]	[illegible]	[illegible]	[illegible]	[illegible]	[illegible]	[illegible]	[illegible]	[illegible]	Wexford.
[illegible]	[illegible]	[illegible]	[illegible]	[illegible]	[illegible]	[illegible]	[illegible]	[illegible]	[illegible]	[illegible]	[illegible]	[illegible]	[illegible]	[illegible]	[illegible]	[illegible]	[illegible]	Youghal.

* See note [illegible]

INDEX TO SUPERINTENDENT REGISTRARS' DISTRICTS.

[The following Index furnishes a reference to the *Number* or *Numbers* of each Superintendent Registrar's District in the Abstract of Marriages, Births, and Deaths, pages 69–74, in which the numbers run consecutively from 1 to 163.]

www.ingramcontent.com/pod-product-compliance
Lightning Source LLC
Chambersburg PA
CBHW030548270326
41927CB00008B/1566
9783741199837